Quilling Patterns for Beginners

The Modern Guide with Step-by-Step Instructions and Color Pictures to Realize Your First Projects and Amaze Your Loved Ones on a Budget

Diana Turner

TABLE OF CONTENTS

INTRODUCTION	6
THE MOOD FOR QUILLING	11
Learn Quilling Fast	12
Wonderful Gift	13
Useful Art Technique	14
Quilling Painting	15
Especially for Art and Craft Lovers	17
Types of Quilling Patterns	17
Getting The Perfect Quilling Paper.	23
Advantages & Disadvantages Of Getting The Precut-Strip.	24
THE INEXPENSIVE TOOLS AND MATERIALS NEEDED	27
Quilling Paper Strips	28
Quilling Needle	28
Fevicol or Fevistick	29
Tweezers	30
Scissors	30
Circle Sized Ruler	31
BASIC QUILLING SHAPES	33
Start with basic shapes	33
Move beyond the shapes	34
Open and Closed Coils	35
Teardrop	37
Marquis	41

Tulip	43
Slug	43
Square or Diamond	44
Square Variations	45
Rectangle	47
Rectangle Variations	48
Semi-Circle	49
Triangle	50
Triangle Variation	51
Arrow	52
Arrowhead	53
Heart	54
Pentagon and Star	55
Holly Leaf	57

EASY 2D PROJECTS FOR BEGINNERS — 61

Greeting Cards	61
Quilled Letters	67
Birthday Card	70
Simple Flowers	72
Simple Heart	74
Butterfly	75
Rose	79

EASY 3D PROJECTS FOR BEGINNERS — 82

Jewelry Box	83
Earrings	86
Wall Frames	100

Christmas Time	100
Snowflake	107
Christmas Tree	118
Snowman	123
Christmas Lights	127

TIPS AND TRICKS 136

Using a Background Platform that is Colored	136
Use Paper Strip (Shredder)	137
Use The Needle Before The Comb	138
Learn To Roll Two Strips Together	139
Get a Quilling Sponge	140
Rolling Using a Slotted Tool	140
Rolling Using a Needle Tool, Toothpick, or Any Other Alternative	142
Rolling Using a Border Buddy or Any of Its Alternatives	143
Gluing Coils Together	145
Gluing Coils on a Medium	146
Inserting Small Coils into Big Coils	146

CONCLUSION 149

INTRODUCTION

Paper quilling is a favored creating pastime; however, not new at all, this craftsmanship has existed since the disclosure of paper and, like numerous types of art, Paper quilling can follow its inception back many years too, in any event, the fifteenth century.

Paper quilling is a favored creating pastime; however, not new at all, this craftsmanship has existed since the disclosure of paper and, like numerous types of art. Although the quilting pattern is simple to do, you may find there are lots of angles involved, so you will need to learn and practice both your paper arrangement and your quilting abilities.

Specialists are all over the place and many of them have created a big network online where quilling patterns and models become available on the net, along with detailed explanations and techniques. What's nice about paper quilling is that you can devote as little or much time as you like on it. You can be a creative person and make your own patterns and models if you want to. It isn't difficult to do using tools such as paper quilling guides and online quilling patterns. Just pick a quilling tool of your choice pick the paper and enjoy the relaxing fun.

The beginning of this craftsmanship isn't known, yet a few people accept that quilling began in China after the paper's innovation when a plume was utilized to roll the paper's portions. The quilters' initial set didn't have these ongoing accommodations of precise machine-cut paper strips, opened quilling devices, circle layouts, and other twisting/molding materials.

Notwithstanding, others accepted that the specialty had its inception from/during the Renaissance when French and Italian nuns and priests utilized quilling to enrich book spreads and strict things with an end goal to set aside cash. The most ordinarily utilized was portions of paper managed from the edges of books. They would move pieces of these overlaid paper strips to make the quilled shapes. Quilling frequently imitated the first two outrageous itemized ironwork adornments: the Ivory and Wrought Iron, which was utilized as metal ornamentation in home style. When the paper quilling was overlaid, it was difficult to separate it from metal, settling a reasonable decision for worship houses that is battling.

While the starting point or quilling is fairly unknown, history discloses that quilling got popular in Europe in the late eighteenth and the mid-nineteenth centuries. Notwithstanding weaving, it was viewed as an "appropriate hobby" for the ladies of the privileged. It was educated in all-inclusive schools rehearsed by delicate women of recreation (a lady who is free and not utilized to work) since it was one of only a handful barely any things women could do that was the idea not to be mind-entrusting for them on their delicate mien.

Afterward, the impact of quilling began spreading from Europe to American provinces, where its prominence continued developing and was exceptionally preferred by the American homesteaders as a brightening strategy. Nonetheless, the training appears to blur by the nineteenth century because there are a significant number of chronicled instances of paper quilling during this time; quilling appeared nearly to be craftsmanship that has been overlooked. Even though there were sharp crafters and quilters around the globe who proceeded with this work of art, keeping it from being obsolete, still relatively few individuals thought about the presence of paper quilling.

Paper quilling appears to have had a resurgence in ubiquity through the previous twenty years and has been raised to a fine art. The arrangement of numerous neighborhood quilling gatherings and specialty clubs rediscovered the inventive presented paper quilling exercises and exercises that incorporate quilling things. The artistry has gone through numerous changes and contrasts during that time, utilizing present-day procedures, styles, and instruments.

As of now, quilling is seeing recharging in fame with individuals who practice the craft of quilling on each mainland and social status. Quilling is not, at this point, confined to the advantaged; however, these are everybody fine art. Also, the magnificence of the artistry is continually expanding because of the ease of the quilling materials. It is utilized to finish wedding solicitations cards, birth declarations cards, welcoming cards, and save and show photos. Quilling expressions can be seen in artistry displays in Europe and the United States and is an art that is polished all through the world.

Of all the forms of craft-making that involves paper, quilling is undeniably among the most intricate ones. Also known as paper filigree, this features colorful paper strips that are rolled, shaped, arranged and glued to create a multidimensional artwork. You might have seen such in cards, invitations and wall decors. It is becoming more popular recently, but this art form is not new. In fact, it has been around since the Renaissance.

THE MOOD FOR QUILLING

To practice quilling, you need to be relaxed, serene, and cheerful to express your creativity to the fullest. It can be done by listening to good music while watching your favorite movie or together with a loved one.

The most important ingredient is your imagination.

As with other types of handicrafts, quilling offers the opportunity to uncover creative potential. Using this technique, you can create unusual and original paintings that give you a real aesthetic pleasure. A successful first creative work will surely stimulate the continuation of masterpieces of our production.

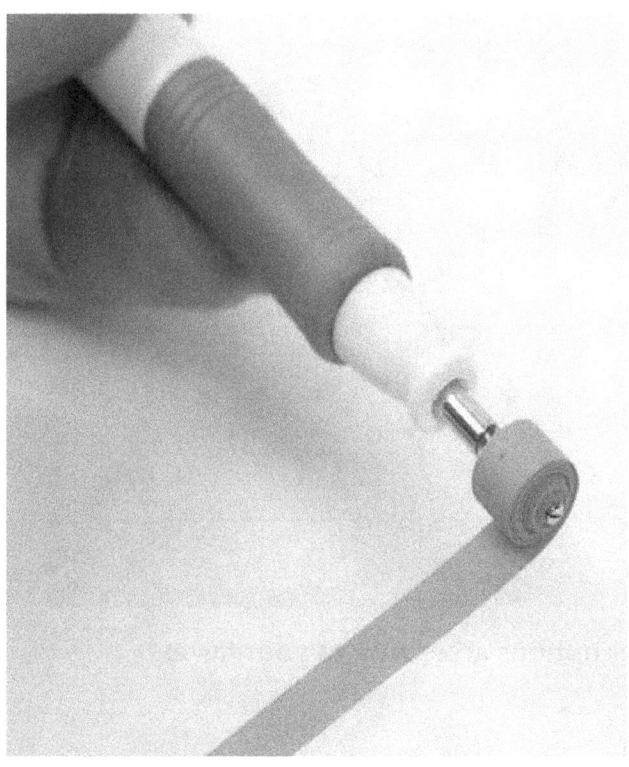

Learn Quilling Fast

You can pick other options according to your taste:

You can register for a handicraft group in which experts will help you master the technique.

You can purchase a self-study book that contains basic schemes, rules, and recommendations.

You can use video tutorials on the Internet.

In any case, it is worth starting with a simple one. These can be single flowers, simple drawings. Over time, you can try something more complicated and increase the number of items with all new forms. Additional to paper, you can also use various decorative elements such as pearls, glitter, etc. It creates amazing quilling pictures in a frame that can decorate any room. It is especially true for the holiday when the necessary atmosphere is created with original things that correspond to its theme.

Wonderful Gift

It is so nice to receive a gift made with the soul and your own hands in the modern trading world. You can make relatives, friends, and work colleagues happy in a very original way. The intriguing process of creating quilling pictures will delight the maker himself, and the recipient of the gift will appreciate the result of hard work. A shapely volume element in a frame fits perfectly into any interior and will delight you with its aesthetic beauty for a long time.

What is needed for this skill is the technique of manual crafting. No complicated quilling schemes. Quilling originated in the 14th century and is now experiencing a new birth.

Many are drawn to the fact that such beauty can be made from paper strips with your own hands.

Useful Art Technique

Many artists, designers, and illustrators who know how to do quilling have adopted this technique. The secret of success is the use of bright colors and unusual patterns in work.

The size of the structure is also important due to the careful assembly. To have learned how to make quilling, you can make very nice things from twisted paper strips. You can choose one of the traditional shapes, but this usually doesn't limit the artist's imagination.

Quilling Painting

Step-by-step instructions can help a beginner to master the technique. However, complex work requires a lot of skill. The big plus is that these beautiful handicrafts do not require high cash costs.

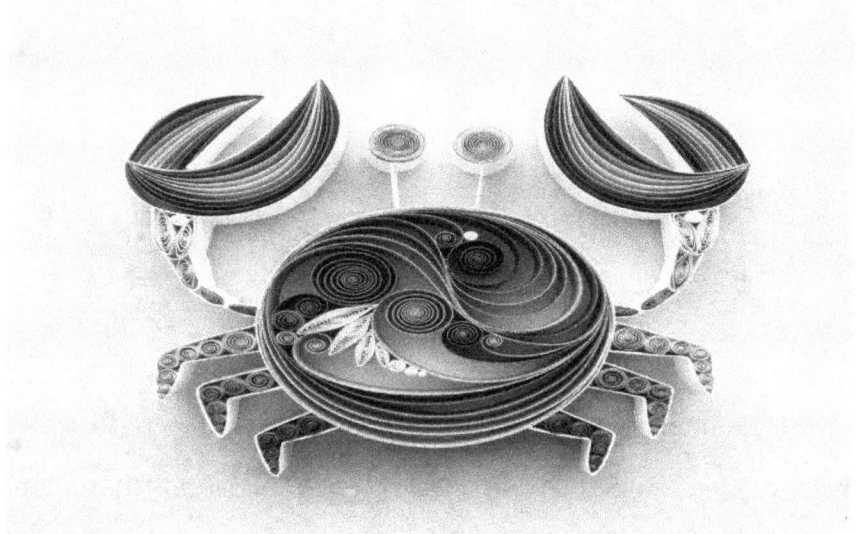

There are currently many different quilling tools available in specialty stores that can make work easier, but the purchase is not mandatory. Everything that is needed can be found at home or made independently of improvised materials.

You need scissors with sharp tips that should be sanded well as well as an inch and a ruler. It is best to use cardboard in various color schemes as the basis for structural strength.

Prefabricated stencils with circles with different diameters help a lot. For lazy people who still want to learn paper rolls and save time, there are ready-made quilling kits containing everything needed to work.

Especially for Art and Craft Lovers

The art of swelling or volumetric twisting of paper has appealed to many art and handicraft fans. There are several interest groups, circles in which everyone, regardless of gender or age, can engage in this type of work. The demand for this craft is based on its advantages, namely the availability, the low material costs, the simple manufacture, and the result's astonishing beauty.

Types of Quilling Patterns

There are notably a variety of quilling patterns that, as a quilter, you should get yourself acquainted with within no distant time, but you have to take it easy on yourself.

The Classic Quilling: This is the most advised quilling style for beginners. It is easy to learn and apply. It involves creating both tight and loosed coils (with the help of a quilling board) that are round or circular through the use of the slotted quilling tool material.

A quill board

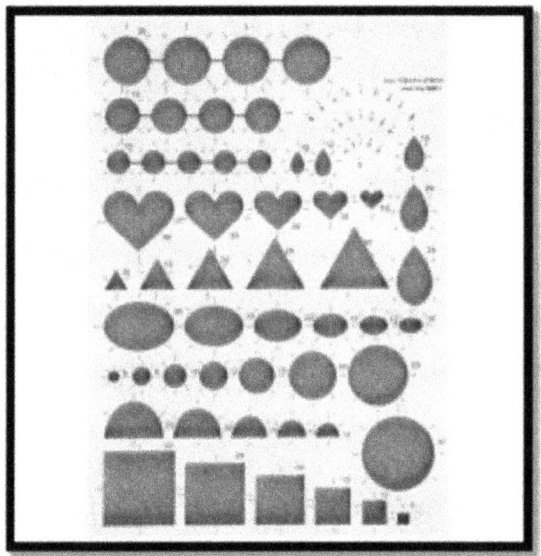

The 3-D Quilling Pattern: This quilling style largely entails creating a tight paper coil that is more than one strip, and you adjust the shape using the quilling mold. This quill pattern could require you to produce coils that are as much as possible, dependent upon the design the quilter has in mind.

The Loop Based Quilling Pattern: This quilling technique is accomplished with the aid of a quilling comb, which contains multiple needles. It is the creation of a paper loop around the quilling comb needles in different styles and shapes. This pattern cannot be achieved alone with just the use of a slotted tool because of the loop creation and, as such, requires you to get more tools.

The Quillography: This quilling pattern is commonly practiced by professionals in the art of paper quilling. It involves the creation of complex designs and shapes from paper.

- Paper Weight.

It is a very vital consideration to put in place before choosing a particular paper. It means that it has to do with the available thickness of the paper as it goes a long way to affect your finished project/work's outer appearance.

For a better understanding of what this means, here is a breakdown of what the text weight paper strip and the writing weight paper strip is all about;

- Text Weight & Writing Quilling Paper Type.

The Paper text weight paper type of quilling paper has been proven to be the best type of art paper. It is much heavier than a standard writing weight paper and lasts longer in durability than a standard writing paper. One other thing about the writing weight paper strip is that it can easily get torn using it to work.

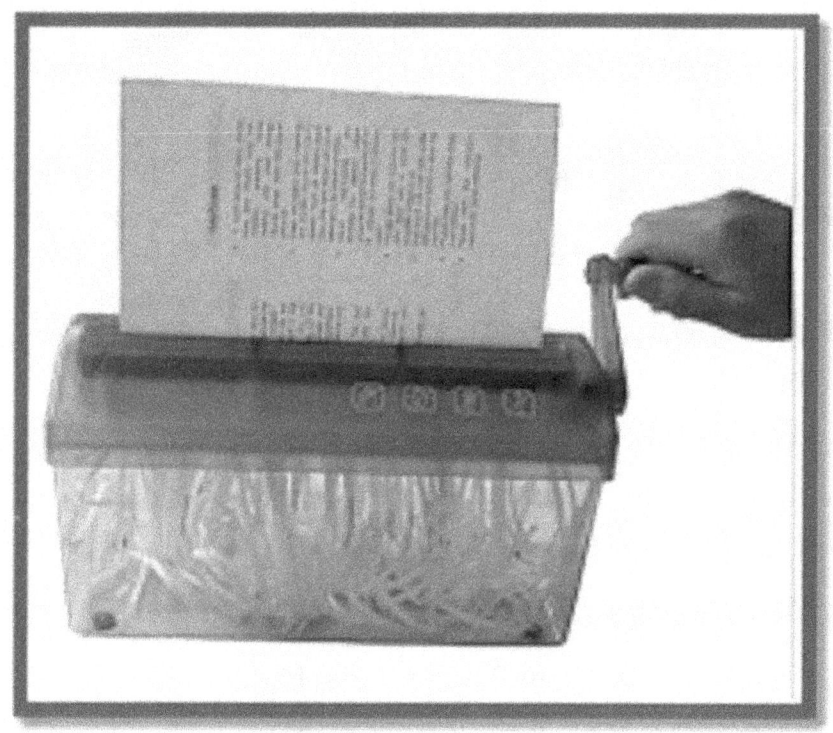

However, this does not mean that the writing paper sheet is not sufficient enough for the job of paper quilling. To be more sincere. Text weight paper type is great for many high-tech projects/tasks. The standard A4 paper type (writing type) can fit into any design and project you may wish to embark upon.

- Vat-Dyed Paper Type.

One of the best descriptions for the Vat-dyed paper is that the paper is often time colored, but sometimes you may wish to get some colorless paper and color it. So you should

usually choose paper that is easy to color.

The vat-dyed paper from the research is the easiest paper to find in local supermarkets, cut, and easy to get worked on (in terms of quilling).

- Classified Papers Type.

Classified papers are also known as specialty papers. They come in diverse, beautiful forms and textures. They are, however, quite difficult to work with as they can't be easily cut. Except maybe you have the mechanical paper strips cutter. But for a beginner, this shouldn't be your priority choice of paper as there are still many papers out there that you can still engage yourself with.

- Sourcing For The Right Paper Length.

It is something every beginner should/must watch out for. Some papers are longer than some, and you might feel cheated when you don't check or measure as appropriate before paying for it. The standard writing office papers measure about 11 inches in length by 8.5 inches in breadth. If you happen to get your hands laid on papers that are longer in both length and breadth, you are obviously at an advantage because it can give you more paper strips after cutting.

However, if you find it uncomfortable using a lengthy paper, kindly use your quilling scissors to trim the parts you don't want out. The trimmed out part can still be used in subsequent projects. So you see, you are now at an advantage, and this will save you some money in the long run.

Getting The Perfect Quilling Paper.

If you are a first-timer in this craft, there is every possibility that you might, at a point or another, make a wrong choice as to the right kind of paper material to use for a specific kind of job. However, it is also applicable even to those who seem to be professionals in this craft. So don't get yourself all worried because of that. It's only a stage that you will soon graduate from.

Some persons tend to purchase papers in open markets, online mall, or supermarkets (as I said earlier, this could come in varying color dependent on the taste of the quilter) and do the strip cutting by themselves with either scissors or the handy paper shredder and others just go ahead and get the already-made ones (called precut paper strips).

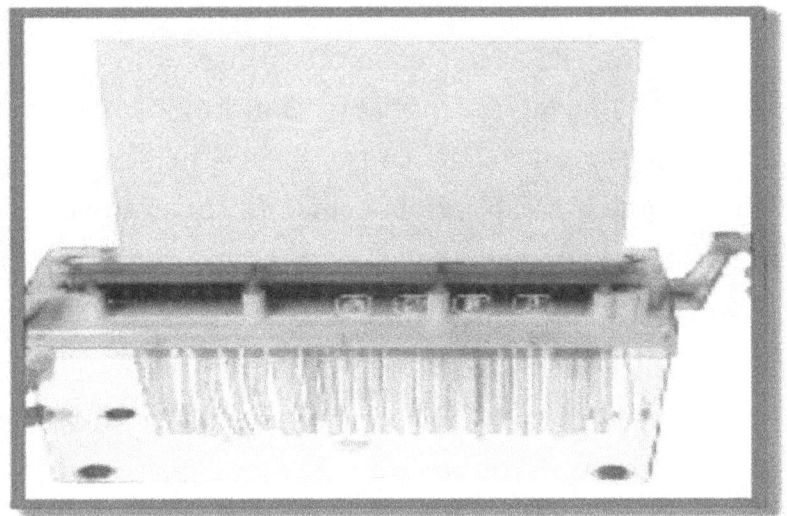

Advantages & Disadvantages Of Getting The Precut-Strip.

I will just go straight forward to the point;

Advantages

- It is easy to locate and stuff your material store with.
- It saves time.
- It reduces undue stress, just to mention but a few.

Disadvantages

- If you look for yourself in a situation where you can't get those precut paper strips, you get stranded.

- If you find it difficult to get the type, color of the material you predetermined, you get worried and might even get upset.

- You might see or find a good raw uncut hand-dyed paper but can't make do with it, simply because you cannot cut strip yourself.

- What if you are in the center of a job, and suddenly the precut paper strips you bought got finished in the middle of the project? What would you do? Abandon the project? Get rid of it? Or get more? What if you couldn't lay your hands on the exact type anymore?

-

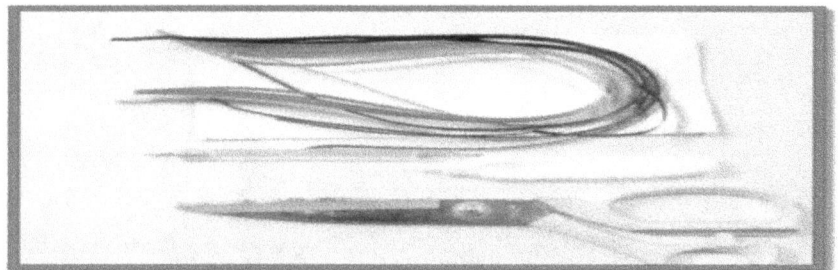

It is just to mention and let you know or see the reasons why you MUST learn how to cut these papers into strips yourself. Don't get worried if you don't know how-to; you will learn gradually. Just put your mind to it!

THE INEXPENSIVE TOOLS AND MATERIALS NEEDED

Quilling is a minimal effort to create that you'll love to make your next side interest once you attempt. The ideal approach to begin in quilling is to discover motivation. Study quilt manifestations that you appreciate and use as a springboard to make your own wonderful and interesting plans; before long, individuals will respect your specialty and utilize it to motivate their quilling ventures.

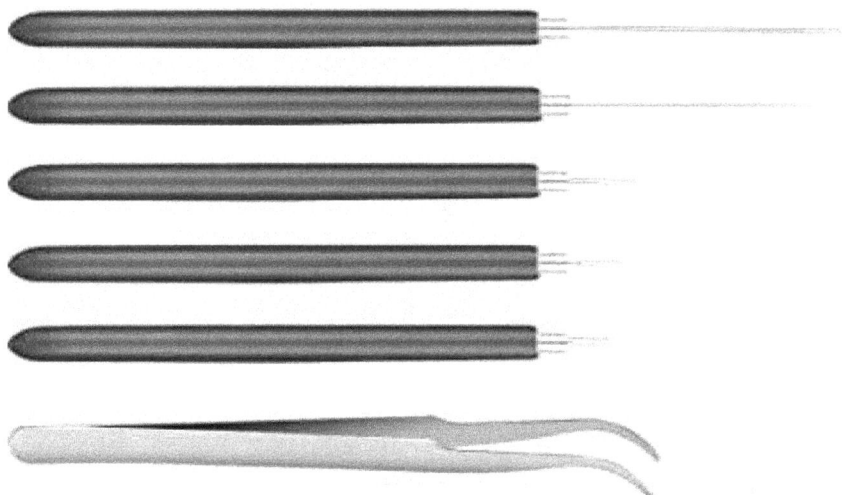

To achieve dazzling and excellent plans, all you require are some fundamental instruments effectively open. The short rundown of necessities incorporates segments of lightweight paper, stick, and a device to roll the paper. One prerequisite that is not accessible for procurement but rather will likewise be required is a considerable measure of persistence. Anyway, like different expressions, new gear for quilling is presented each day, so you could likewise put resources into legitimate quilling instruments pack to make your employment that a lot simpler.

Quilling Paper Strips

There is no quilling without papers, except for some crafters who don't focus on the quality. Also, that is awful because of the better the paper, the more lovely the undertaking. Get quilling paper in the scope of tones planned exceptionally with standard widths 1/8 inches, text paperweight, and wraps up.

Many experienced quilters favor cutting their strips. However, in any case, you can purchase many packs of precut paper and simply begin quilling!

Quilling Needle

It is a device with a handle of agreeable hold that has a needle toward one side. It is valuable for applying the paste to the finishes of your paper strips with the needle instrument. You turn the paper strip around the point and into a little, prevalent loop without a wrinkle.

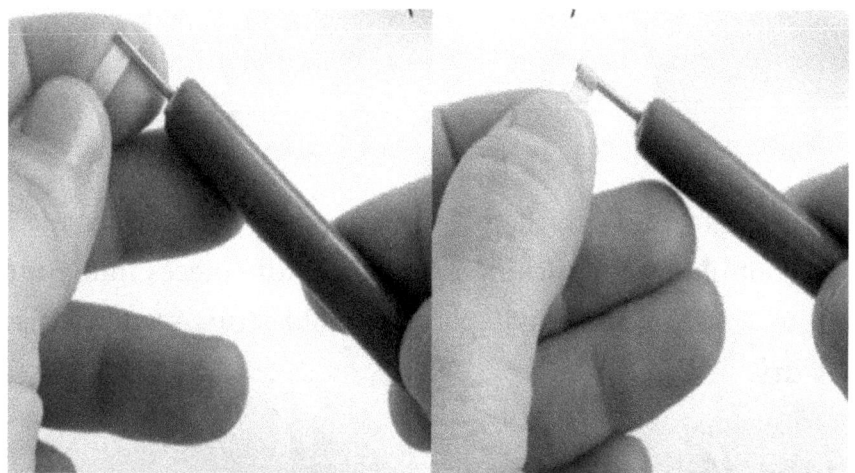

The needle apparatus is somewhat difficult to become accustomed to; however, the prize will be a loop with a magnificent round focus.

Fevicol or Fevistick

Fevicol is a dustproof substance. However, contemplates show that it isn't waterproof. Fevicol compound is known to give a shiny cover to your specialty work, and it likewise blesses your work with quality and brilliant coloration to the strips utilized.

The covering should be done more than once to keep it dynamic on the quilling work venture. That a serious issue with fevicol.

Tweezers

They are exceptionally helpful, and you'll require calculated ones continually for sticking or picking little pieces into your loop to work in restricted spaces or hold strips set up while they dry.

Scissors

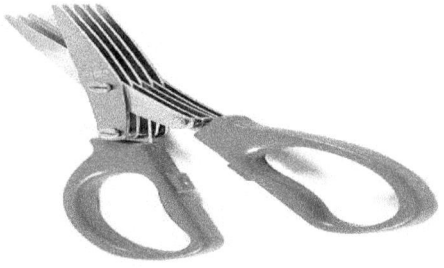

The typical scissors are regularly utilized close by the bordering scissors, even though there might be times when you have to clip some paper, so it's expected to make a brilliant cut.

Bordering scissors is suggested for making paper blossoms; you can likewise utilize the typical scissors, and anyway, the five sharp edges found in bordering scissors shape little strips that work superbly for fancy blooms.

Circle Sized Ruler

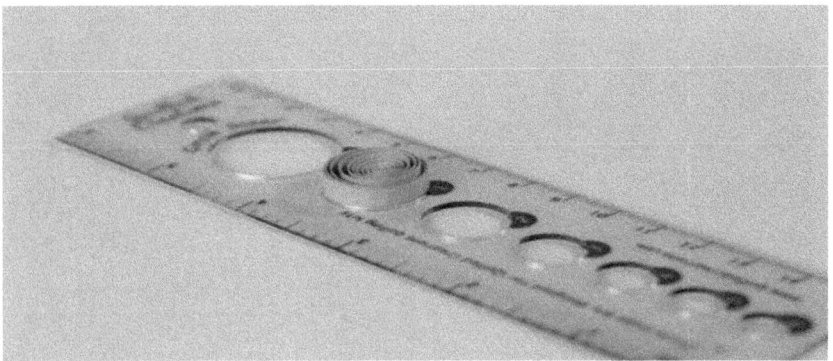

This quilling instrument is more similar to a ruler with many measured gaps in its center sides. Spot your folded paper curl into the gaps and get an accurate estimation with a union.

BASIC QUILLING SHAPES

Start with basic shapes

Start with the essential shape, similar to the roundabout paper curl. Expand upon this fundamental structure as you ace the capacity notwithstanding make a spread of shapes like the paisley, tear, marquis, tulip, or slug. You can crush, squeeze, and manage the moving paper loop's degree until you get the quilled shape your inclination.

Here are some helpful rules for developing the key moved paper loop:

Addition portion of paper into the space of your device, and with your thumb and index finger on both sides of the paper strip, keep it up with even strain even as you switch apparatus in reverse or advances.

At the point when you accomplish the finish of your paper strip, take it off the gadget. Ensure you don't wind it too firmly; else, you could find it a piece dangerous to take it off the apparatus.

On the off chance that you simply ought to make a free curl shape, you may permit the paper loop to reach out before getting rid of it from the gadget, yet if you need a tighter loop, don't permit it to intensify before you take it off.

Move beyond the shapes

- Whenever you have made the energizing shapes, cross heretofore and play around with them. You may:
- Use them to embellish a welcome card
- Make alluring, carefully assembled studs
- Create outlined fine art to include a scramble of shading and imagination to your dividers
- Create 3-dimensional figures and miniatures
- The openings are perpetual!

Building up a bloom is one of the most straightforward quilling activities that will let you get the elements' grip. Simply watch this means:

Make two flimsy portions of shaded quilling paper to make the focal point of the bloom. Cut a lot more extensive strip - double the more slender strips' width - for the bloom petals.

Utilizing a quilling needle or toothpick, make a nice move of the more slender strip. The paste end part of the more slender curled strip.

Incorporate paste to other slender strip and move it around the main roll. Paste the end of some portion of the strip to make a firmly moving center for the blossom.

Presently make cuts all close by the more extensive strip half of the path down its expansiveness. Add the paste to one finish of this strip and move it over the firmly moved blossom center we made inside the initial step.

Paste the finish of the greater strip. When the paste is evaporated pleasantly, utilize your thumb and palms to overlay the petals outward. It genuinely is it - your blossom is readied!

What You Need:

- Quilling device opened
- Quilling paste in a needle-tip bottle
- Scissors
- Tweezers

The heap of quilling paper strips — for starter, I endorse ¼-inch wide (it's not hard to handle and control); when you've aced the basic shapes, you may lean toward more modest strips. Cut the strips eight and a half inches long for this instructional exercise.

Open and Closed Coils

Basic circles are the reason for the most different shapes you'll make.

Stage 1: Insert paper into the instrument

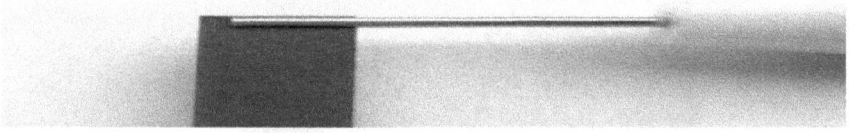

Supplement a touch of quilling paper into the space of your quilling contraption; endeavor to orchestrate the paper's boundary with the margin of the opening as immaculately as could be expected under the circumstances. An opened apparatus will normally leave a little wrinkle in the focal point of your loop. On the off chance that it can like the crease to be more obvious, permit the paper to hang marginally over the edge.

Stage 2: Start Rollin'

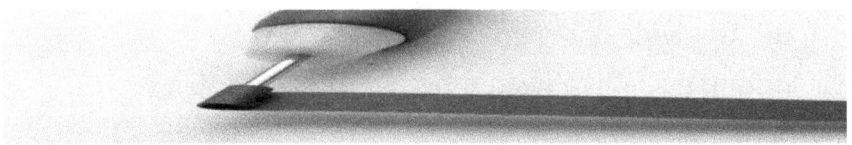

Roll the apparatus with your predominant hand towards your body or away from it (whichever feels commonly extraordinary) while holding the strip inflexible with your other hand.

Stage 3: Glue It

For a shut-loop: When you're nearly done snaking, place a touch of paste close to the furthest limit of the strip and move to finish. You don't need it to grow after you eliminate it from the apparatus.

For an open twist: Finish the circle by disposing it from the gadget and license it to expand. When it has broadened, incorporate a bit of glue and press the strip down circumspectly to ensure about.

Teardrop

Step 1: Make an open loop, and afterward place it between the thumb and index finger of your non-prevailing hand. Mastermind within curls equitably or any way you'd like.

~ 37 ~

Step 2: With your overall hand, press the paper where you need the feature to be to make a tear shape.

Teardrop Variations

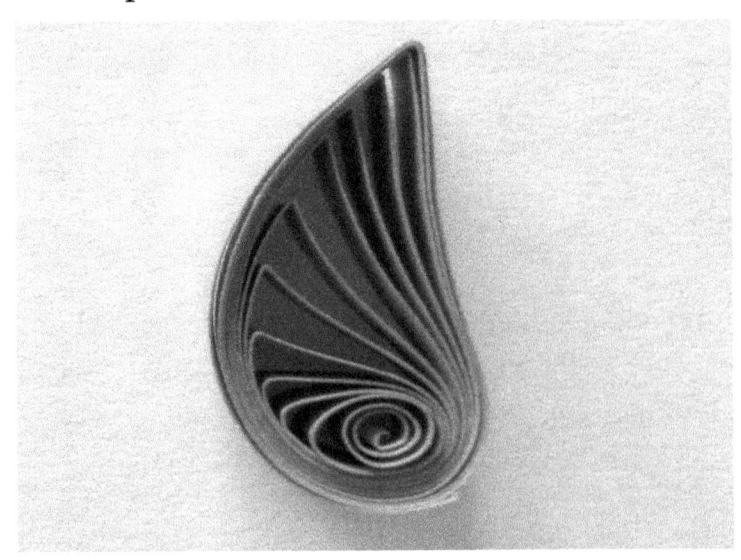

Essential shapes can be controlled to make considerably more shapes. The tear is an amazing case of this.

By fairly twisting the tear around your thumb as you shape it, you can make a subtle move in structure without compromising the center twists. You can overlay the tear over your quilling device or another round and empty article to distort this effect.

For a more evident bent shape all through, press the shape around your quilling apparatus. From here, you can, without much of a stretch, make a paisley shape.

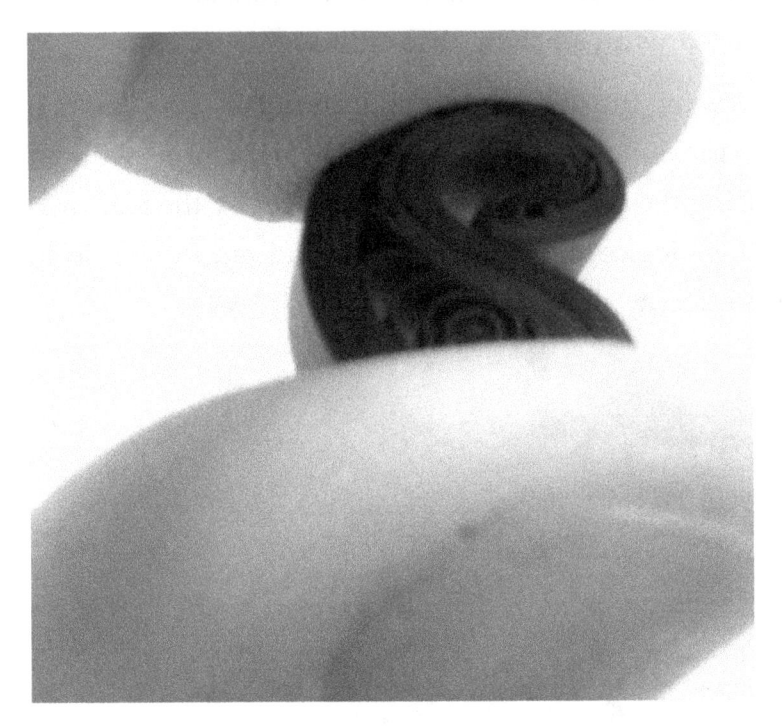

You can twist the shape from the highlight of the base by moving it between your fingers.

Countless shapes!

Marquis

Step1: Make a tear shape, and afterward squeeze the furthest edge also.

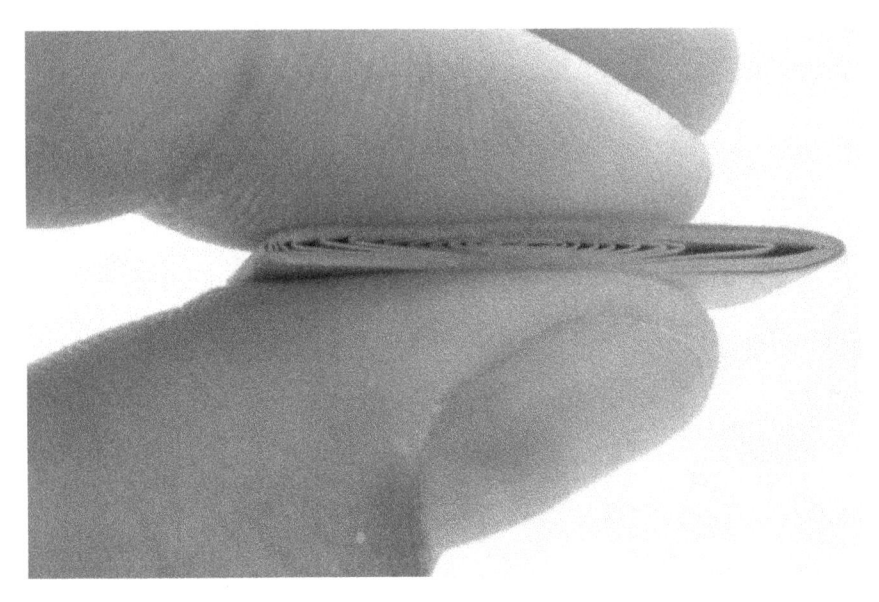

Step 2: The last shape will be controlled by the amount you squeeze or press the loop together and where you place its middle.

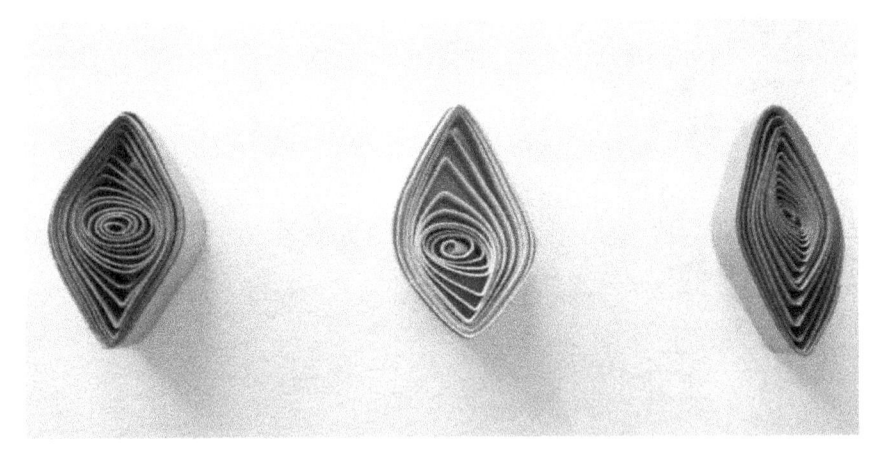

Play around with various positions and strain to make loads of marquis variants.

Tulip

First, make a marquis shape. At that point, turn the shape on its side and squeeze a middle top with your fingers.

Slug

Start with a marquis, and afterward fold one end over the tip of your finger or a quilling apparatus.

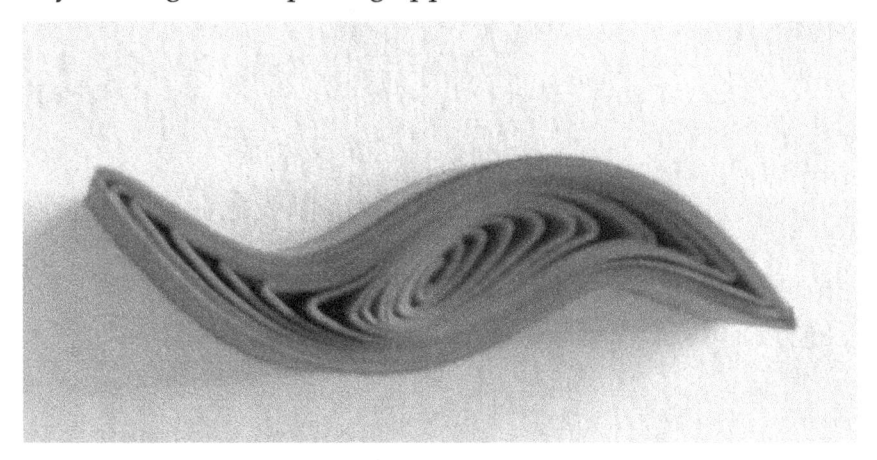

Do likewise to the opposite end yet the other way. Searches beautiful for a slug doesn't it!

Square or Diamond

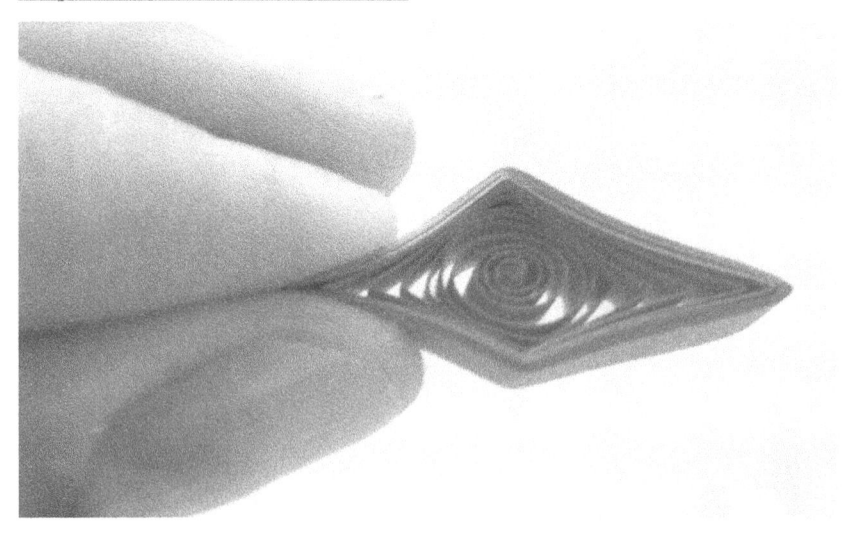

Make a marquis shape. At that point, pivot it 90 degrees and squeeze the two sides once more. It will make a precious stone shape.

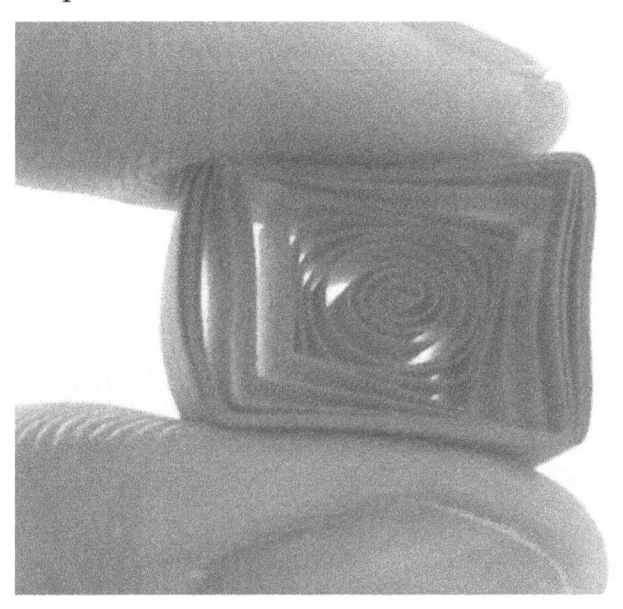

If you need to proceed to make a square, tenderly open up the shape between your fingers.

Square Variations

By messing with each corner, you decide to squeeze while making your square and you can get different outcomes.

~ 45 ~

Above left: By applying strain to the external corners, you can make a square with an adjusted focus.

Above focus: This was made by totally squeezing the open curl together on one side, at that point opening it up and squeezing simply the corners on the contrary side.

Above right: This got its exceptional focus by totally pushing down the loop on the two turns.

One more minor departure from the square: You can make these by applying strain to the external structure with your fingers or the stem of your quilling device.

Rectangle

If you can create a square, you can create a rectangle shape. What is important is in the sum you turn the marquis shape before pressing additional focuses.

Pivot it just somewhat (rather than 90 degrees) before crushing and later open the shape to reveal the ideal square shape.

Rectangle Variations

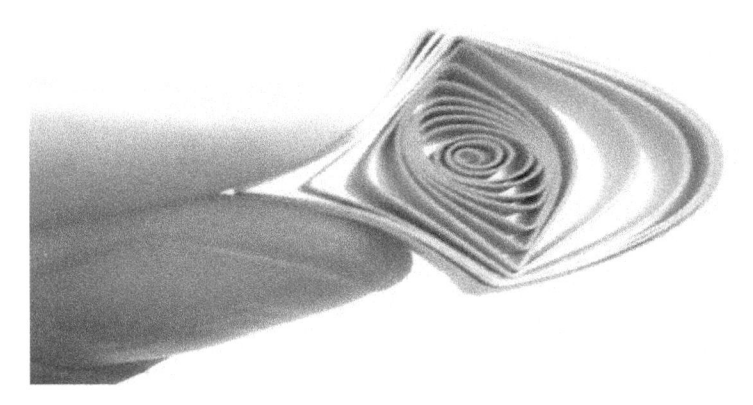

Then again, you can make a quadrilateral shape by making your four corners at lopsided stretches.

This shape is especially significant when making quilled paper mosaics, and you need to consume in an uneven space.

~ 48 ~

Semi-Circle

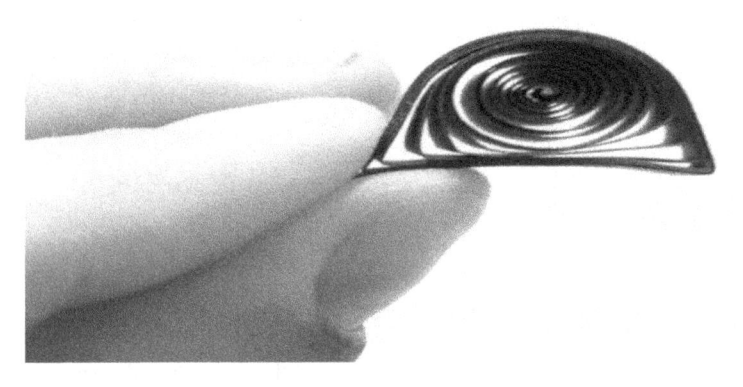

Start with an open twist, and after that, press two corners while leaving the paper above them round. Moreover, you can do this by crushing an open circle onto a difficult surface like a table and gliding your fingers down the sides carefully. Endeavor the two systems to see which suits you best.

Bending the shape's straight edge will permit you to transform a semi-hover into even more a sickle moon shape.

Triangle

Make a tear shape and squeeze two extra points utilizing either your fingers or the tabletop technique.

Attempting both to perceive what works best for you.

Triangle Variation

To make a shape that takes after a shark blade, press on different sides of your triangle and leave the third side level.

Arrow

Make a tear; at that point, pull the middle down towards the base and hold it set up with your fingers.

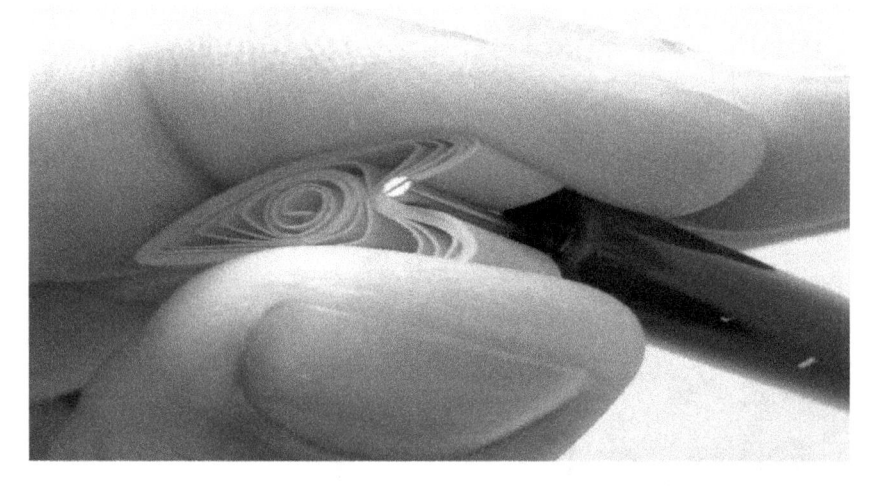

Utilizing the long side of the opened needle, push down profoundly into the base.

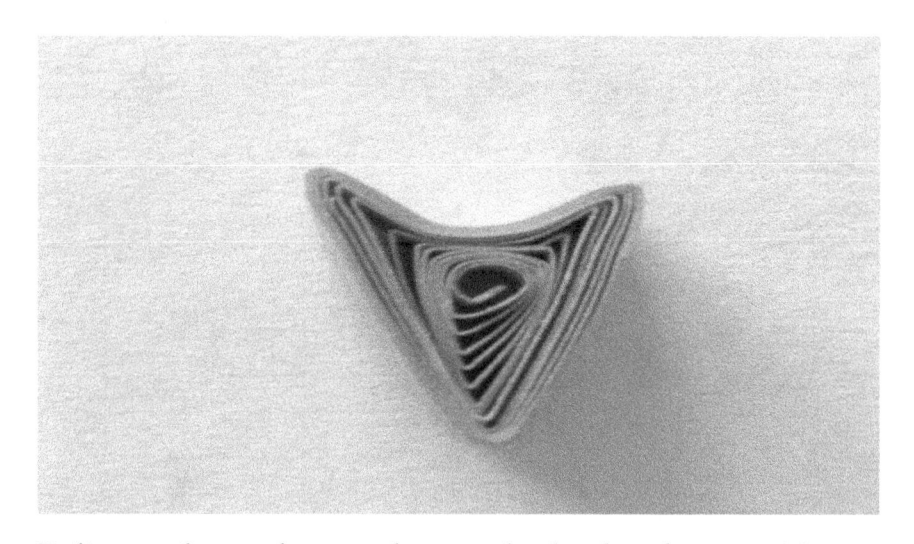

Delivery the gadget and smooth the bend out with your fingers to shape.

Arrowhead

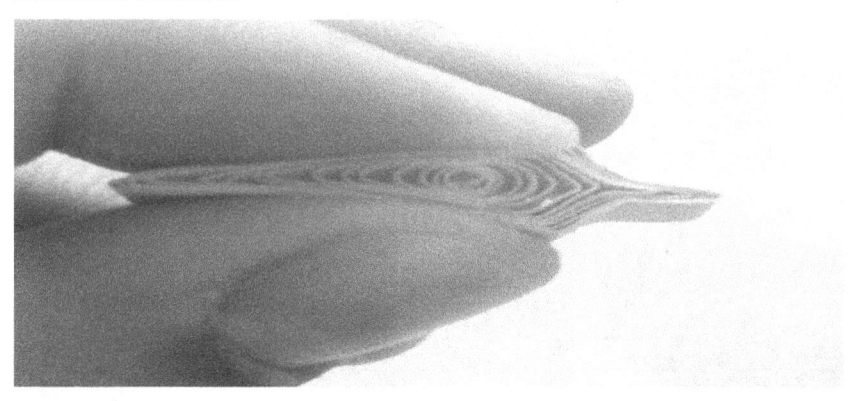

Beginning with a tear shape, hold the sharped end in the non-transcendent hand and press the base end into a tight point.

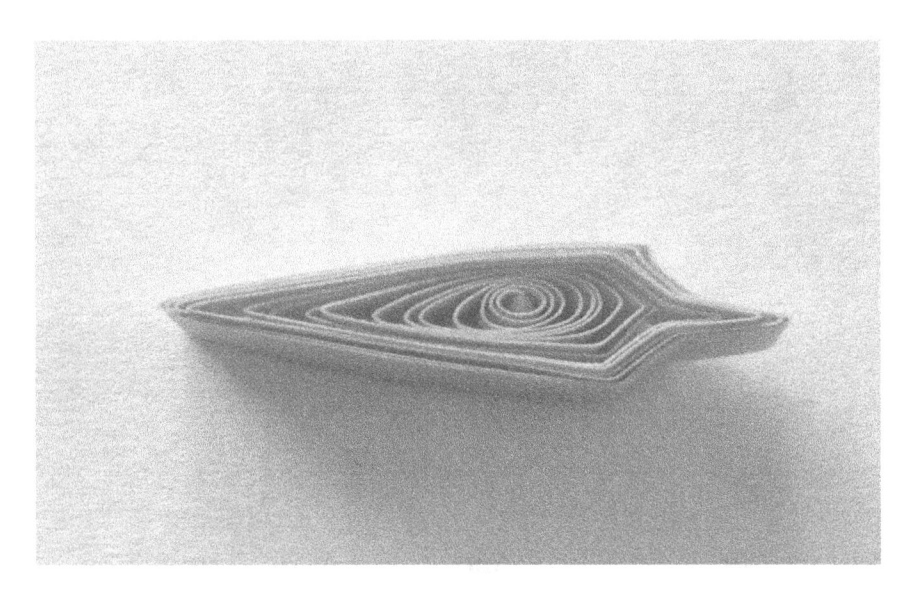

Without surrendering, sliding your fingers down to meet the fingers of your opposite hand to make the site focuses.

Heart

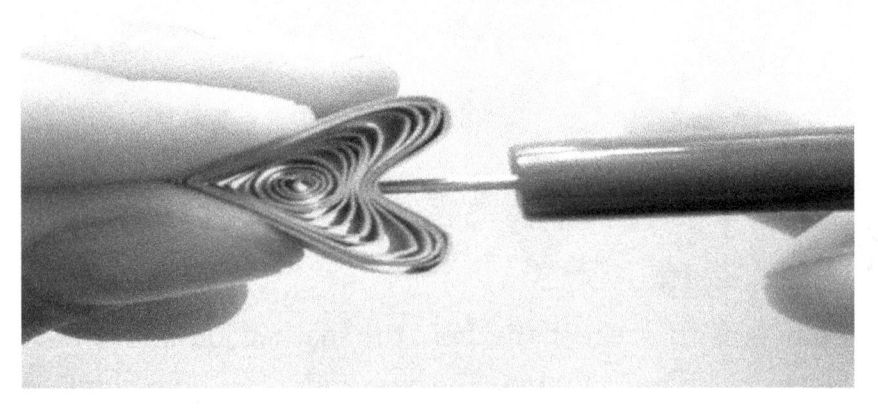

By and by, start with a tear. Push in the base of the shape by utilizing your quilling device to make a little space.

Delivery the apparatus and cautiously press in each side of the heart to finish the middle wrinkle.

Pentagon and Star

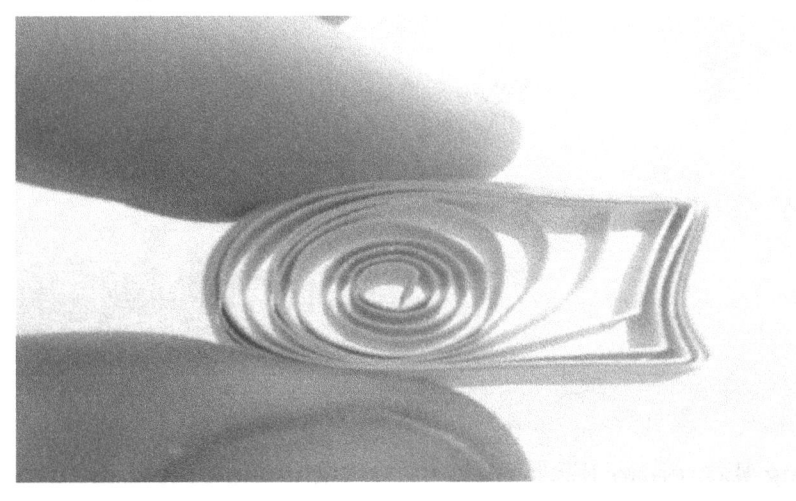

To make a pentagon, first, make a stretched semi-hover as appeared previously.

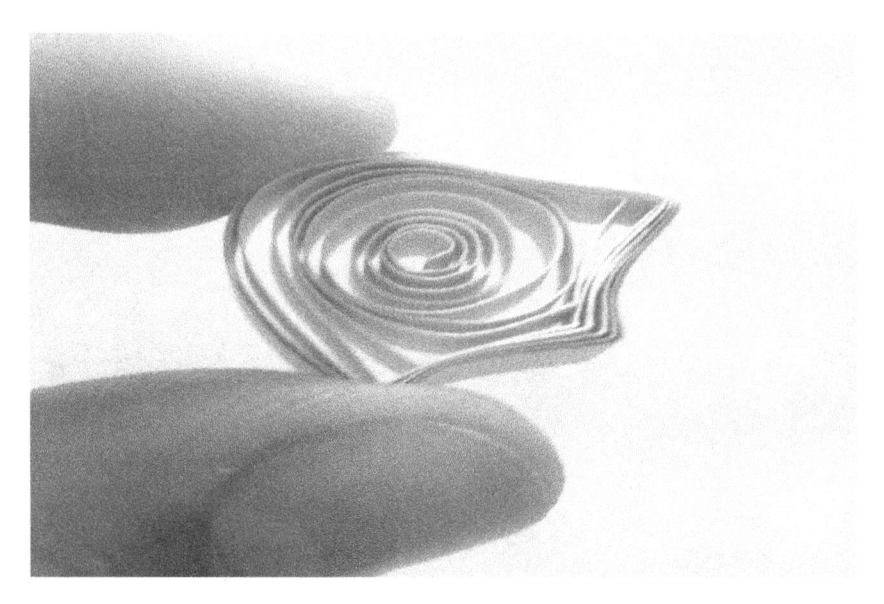

Squeeze the focal point of the level side utilizing a similar strategy you utilized when making the tulip shape; this is the pinnacle of your pentagon.

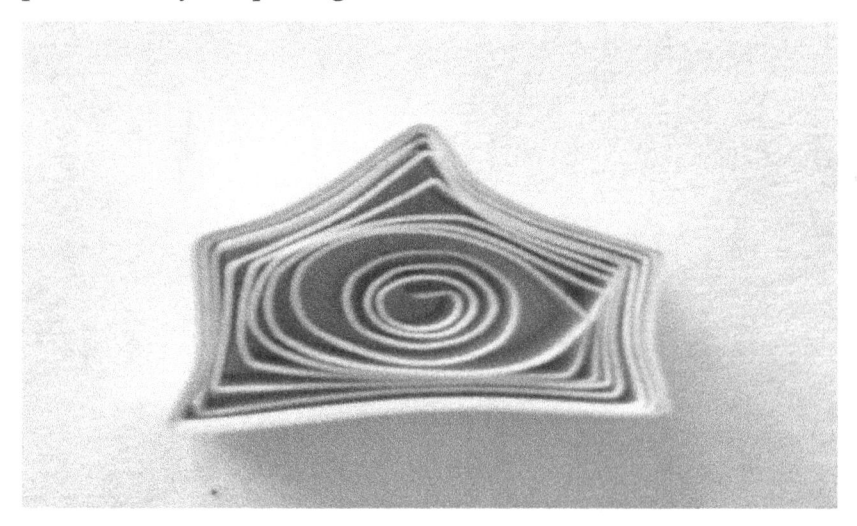

Keeping the top in the center, make right the base with two equal presses on either side.

To change the pentagon into a star, press in on each level surface with your fingers or a quilling gadget and further refine each point into tops.

Holly Leaf

This shape is by a wide margin the hardest to make. For the good of sanity, you'll need to become happy with making the entirety of different shapes before endeavoring this one!

Start by making a marquis. Supplement a ton of tweezers into the shape and hold pretty much 33% of inside twists.

Keeping the hold with your tweezers turns the marquis differing and presses a little point on either side of each zenith.

Moreover, you could make the holly leaf by first creation a square, including a feature at each end and subsequently shaping all the focuses into tops. I find the tweezers system less complex. Anyway, endeavor the two distinct approaches to see, which gives you better results.

EASY 2D PROJECTS FOR BEGINNERS

Greeting Cards

Step 1: Normally, for some kind of quilling patterns, you will need to do some sketching, and to do this, you will need a pencil and paper (canvas) if you have one. It's best to sketch on a firm piece of cardboard paper or a paper with a desirable thickness level.

Your sketch could be anything, a house, a flower, a bicycle or car bird, tree, or anything that comes to your mind.

Step 2: The most fundamental shapes in quilling originate from making circles or curls and squeezing them into wanted shapes.

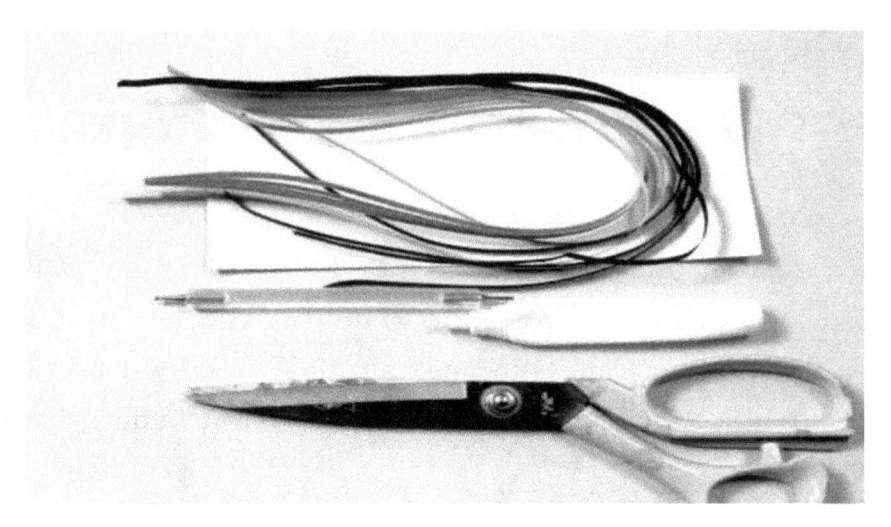

If your ideal blossom sketch needs a leaf-like teardrop shape, simply squeeze one side of the loop, and you will be amazed that you can shape any style of yourself by squeezing pleating and sticking cycles. Be allowed to explore! Having done the previously mentioned ventures above, follow the subsequent stages constantly to finish up.

Step 3: Put a small amount of gum/glue to your shapes at their various points of interfacing with the end edge part of the strip(s) as well at joinery points. Always prepare your shapes over your sketches and apply a little pressure while waiting for the glue to harden.

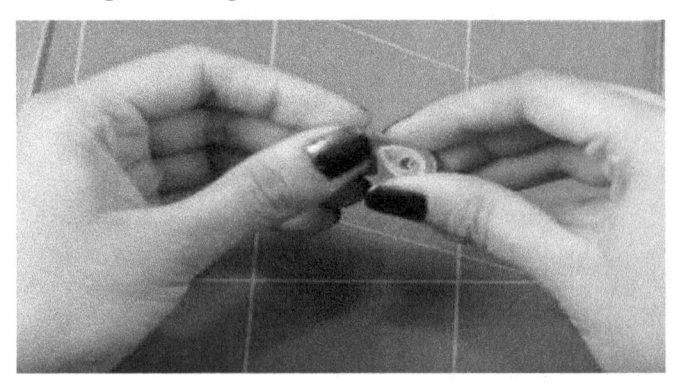

Step 4: From a variety of paper strips, get/pick for yourself one strip and coil the paper around the tip of the quilling tool, which in this case, is the slotted tool.

Step 5: Having done the above, gently pull the coiled strip off the slotted tool.

Then shaped your coil to the exact size you desire and then apply a small drop of glue to the end tail of the paper strip to close your to finish you the coiling process.

Step 6: Take any size of colored paper as in your predetermined color and quilting design. Ensure the paper you can use for this background has a considerable gram in thickness.

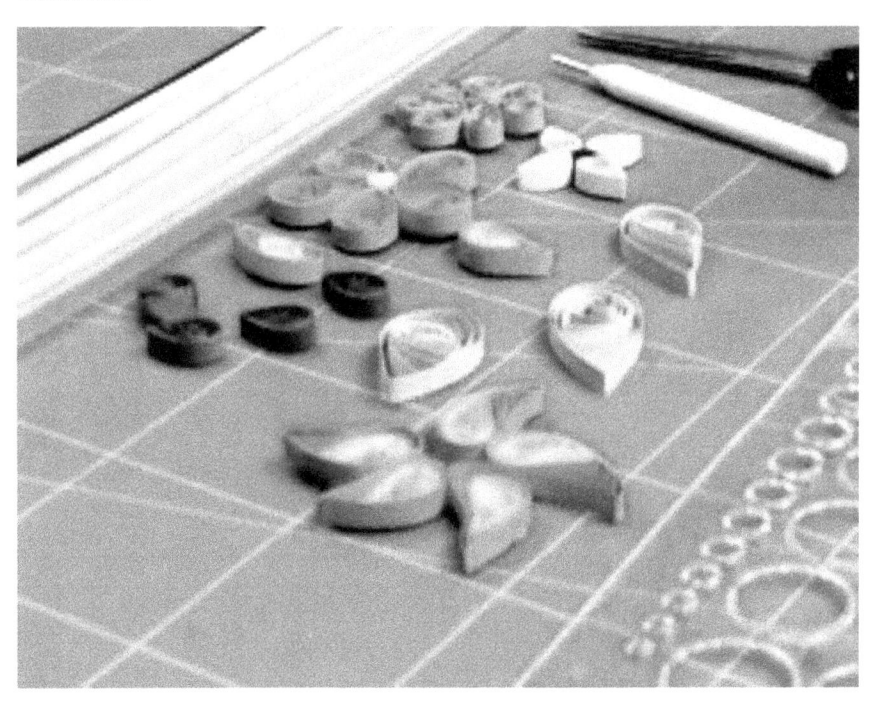

If you can lay your hands on a desirable colored A4 paper, then you are good to go. But if not, you can also get a paper of any length wideness and cut or trim to any size of your choice, then fold it in half to make the card of hard-back.

Step 7: This part entails the design and decoration of your card. The first type of design to be considered is to try and achieve the rose-like pattern of design by making small cuts on the quilling paper. Then, roll it on the slotted tool and pinching/bending the coil's edges outside to give it that shape of a rose.

You can even join more than one quilling paper to give your card that whimsical and alluring look that everybody might want. Make the same number of things as you need with various shapes and sizes, utilizing the opened instrument, tweezers device, pleating apparatus, pins, stick, and the whole quilling devices if important.

Fix all the objects of different styles and shapes on the front cover and the back of the card while keeping the card with more of the quilled shapes and designs is generally considered the front of the card. Make your arrangement be in a specific pattern or randomly place them depending on the design you intend to make or create.

From experience, it is always better you sketch your predetermined design faintly on your paper cover front for easy object placement, or you could choose to do the sketching on another paper sheet so to serve as a guide.

Don't forget to create a space for some write up. Or you can do your major write-up on the inside of the already made card by either writing directly on it or by attaching a paper-leave on the inside of the card to write on.

Quilled Letters

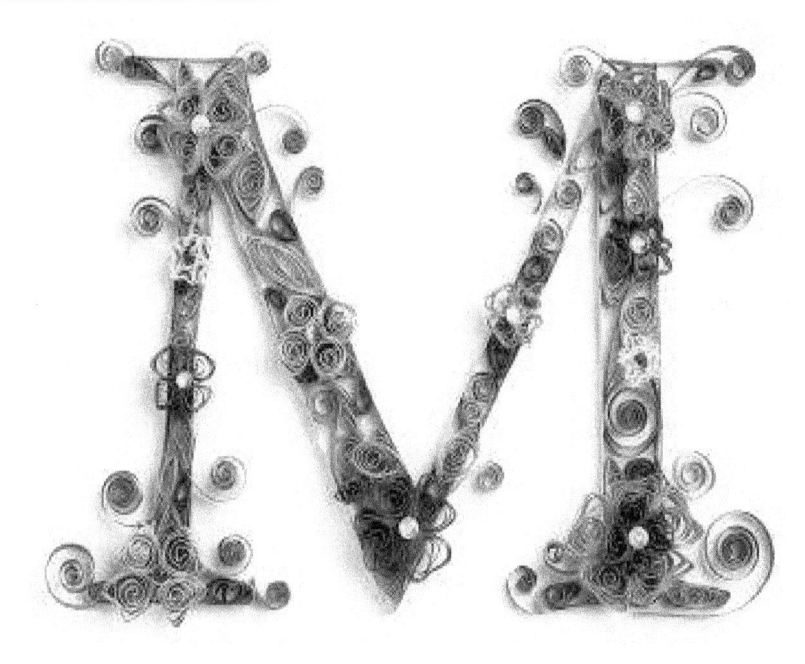

Quilled artworks featuring one letter are one of the most sought-after designs. It is called monogram quilling. When you look at them closely, though, you may get intimidated by the number and intricacy of the straight and curve lines required to form the letters. Fret not. This project is not that hard to make.

Materials:

- Precut quilling paper or self-made cardstock paper strips of the same width
- Board with white background
- A printed copy of any letter you want to make (the outline of the letter will do)
- Sharp pencil
- Craft glue

- Two tweezers
- Pins
- Scissors or thread snapper
- Cuticle nipper

Steps:

1. Place the printed copy of the letter you want to make on the board.
2. Using your sharp pencil, trace the outline of the letter.
3. Make the different coils you want to add to your artwork.
4. Trace the slightly etched outline of the letter using your preferred paper strip. It will be stand out from all of your artwork, so choose a color that looks bright and different from the ones you use for your coils.
5. Fold and curl your paper strip as needed. Attach a paper strip of the same color to cover the entire outline of the letter.
6. Use pins but keep them at least an inch apart.
7. Next, glue your paper strip into the board.
8. Leave it to dry. While you wait, plan the coils you will insert in the letter and the coils you will place on its sides and edges. You may also consider adding some wavy lines.
9. Cut the uneven parts of your outline with a cuticle nipper. Get rid of some visible dried glue as well.

Place the bigger coils inside the outline of your letter. Apply glue to the sides and bottom of your coils. You can insert them by hand. Use the tweezers to adjust their placement.

Next, insert the small coils inside. Apply glue to their sides and bottom as well. Use tweezers to put them in.

Add some open coils with tails on the sides of your letter. Glue them properly. Leave it to dry.

Remove the visible dried glue.

Are you satisfied with your artwork? Consider displaying it as wall decor. Has it framed to keep dust at bay?

Try the steps herein to make different letters and numbers as well. You can use your creations as decors for parties.

You may also draw the letters and numbers yourself. You may even draw landscapes, seascapes, silhouettes of people, or outlines of simple items. Find inspiration in your surroundings. You can certainly find one which you can use for your quilling artwork.

Birthday Card

RIBBON

Make two bunny eras and two arrowheads, using full-length grape purple strips. Wrap the center of the ribbon with a 1/8" (3 mm) wide strip.

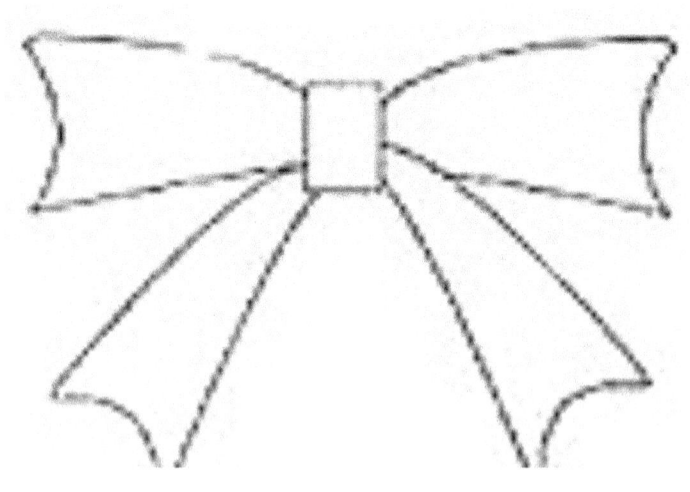

LAVENDER MARQUISE FLOWER AND FLOWER BUDS

Make four flowers for each flower. Roll three marquises, using 1/6 length lavender strips. Make six more marquises for buds. LAVENDER TIGHT COIL FLOWER BBUDS Make four tight coils using 1/8 lavender strips.

LEAVES

Make fourteen large and six small leaves. For each leaf, make three-loop vertical husking, using moss green strips. Make four more leaves. For each leaf, make two-loop vertical husking.

VINES

Make six loose scrolls with ¼ length yellow-green strips and two more with 1/6 length yellow-green strips.

POLLEN

Make six tight coils, using 1/16 length canary yellow strips.

HEART-SHAPED STEM

Fold one (21 cm) long moss green strip in half and curve the ends inward. Glue the ends at the same time to form a heart shape.

ASSEMBLY

1. Glue the heart-shaped stem in the center of the card.
2. Glue the large leaves outside the bottom of the heart-shaped stem and glue the small leaves above them.
3. Glue the lavender marquise flowers outside the heart stem and between the leaves. Glue the vines on the inside of the heart shape.

4. Glue the pollen between the flowers and leaves. Add the ribbon in the center of the heart shape.

5. Add a happy birthday to the center of the card.

Simple Flowers

Another simple flower is a cornflower.

Instruction:

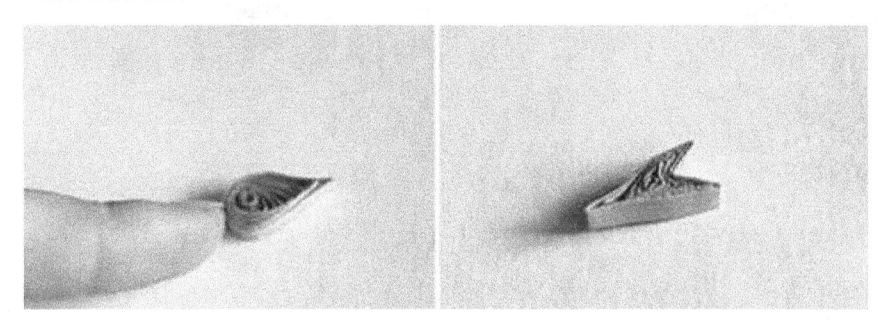

Imagine how delicate it is to get a handmade New Year card with a daisy applied to it! And you can make such a bouquet in an hour.

Instruction:

1. Cut out 8 mm wide and 20 cm long white paper strips.

2. Twist them with a drop.

3. Cut an 8 mm wide and 20 cm long strip from yellow paper.

4. We make it a close role.

5. We glue the elements - the chamomile is ready.

6. We should focus separately on creating volumetric colors. For your base, you need a special cardboard cone.

Instruction:

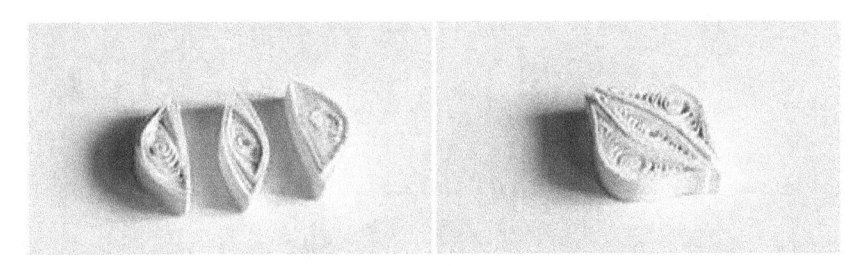

Water lily looks no less original and beautiful on crafts (especially in applications on notebooks). It also needs a cardboard floor.

Instruction:

1. We make 14 drops.
2. Glue 8 blanks onto the edge of the base cone.
3. We glue another five drops to the second stage.
4. The last element is defined in the middle. The water lily is ready.

Simple Heart

Overlay strip fifty-fifty, turn one end cycle a mixed drink stick at that point roll freely by hand until you have made one portion of a heart. Rehash this progression on the opposite end, rolling the strip the other way. For this quilling card, you will need:

- Strips of paper
- Cocktail stick
- PVA glue

Butterfly

Art is naturally appealing, and paper quills butterfly is an art. Therefore, paper quills butterfly is appealing to not just the eye but the mind. However, there seems to be something that ignites a deeper sense of artistic elegance in paper quills butterflies.

If you know how to make paper quills butterfly, you sure would be among the finest artists in the world. Would you not love to be a rewarded fine artist? I see you want to. Now, I will introduce you to the basics and equally expose the secret things that could make your paper quills butterfly unique.

Required Materials for Paper Quills Butterfly

To arrive at a decent paper quills butterfly. There are a few materials to put in place. The basic five materials include:

- The quilling paper
- Quilling pins
- Quilling stencil

- Slotted quilling tool
- Dispensing quilling glue

If you do not own any of the tools above, the chances of arriving at something elegant would be quite low. Some persons substitute for other papery materials as a replacement for the traditional quilling paper. But then, the result would either be a distorted finishing or a swaying design.

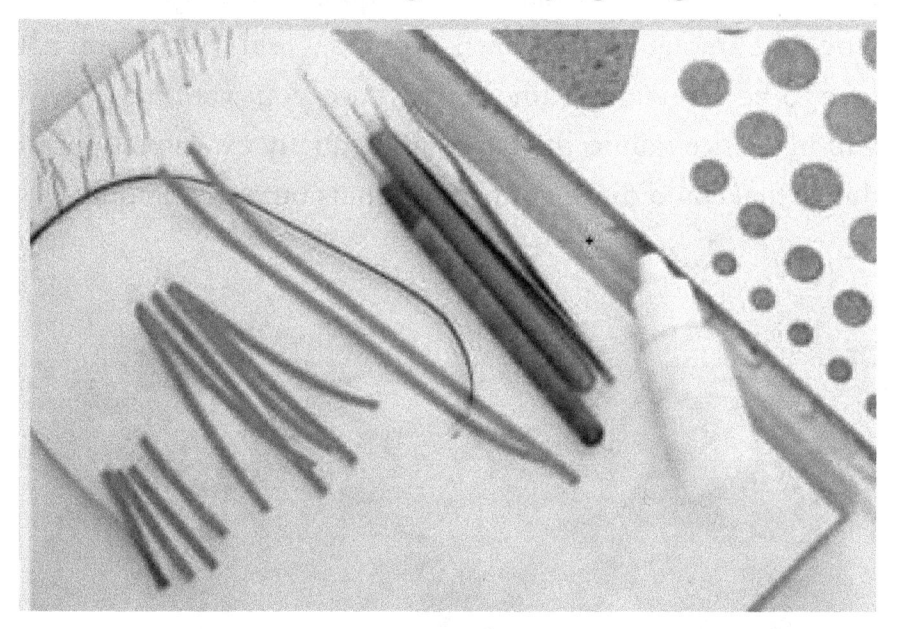

How to Make Paper Quill Butterflies

Gather the Required Supplies

For a small butterfly, the required supplies include:

(4) One and a half inch strips

(6) Three-inch strips

(2) Six-inch strips

A 12-inch strip of black slotted quilling tool glue

#Optional Tools

Needle tool

Tweezers

Circle sizing board

Corkboard and pins

Fold the Strips in the Corkboard

After you have the mentioned tools in place, punch holes on the corkboard. The hole may not necessarily have to be like what you have on this photo. You may design, however way you desire. In this photo, a pink strip is used because it is what I choose. There are more lovely colors, and if you do not mind, I will recommend some colors for you. You may go for something like royal blue, pitch color, or emerald green if you love pink, no problem.

Arrange the Strips as Shown Here.

At this point, take a studying look at the image above. You can see the looks of the quills. Now, here is how to achieve the design. I believe you have the glue with you because it is needed now. Just as in the picture above, arrange each pink (depending on the color you are using) strip to look the same. Once you have been able to do so, apply the quilling glue, and try not to hold the bottom of the strap tight. Since it may be difficult not to hold it while applying the glue, hold it with less pressure so that each wing would be pointy when the glue is dry.

Rose

It is easiest for beginners to sort out schemes with descriptions of the roses' quilling flowers, so recommend artisans.

Instruction:

1. Cut out a 20cm long and 10mm wide paper strip.

2. Insert the end of the strip into the eye and wrap three times around the axis.

3. Apply the adhesive with a toothpick and lay the tape at right angles to you.

4. Make another round with a bell on the needle and drip the glue again.

5. If you repeat steps 3 and 4, place the entire strip. Rose is done.

EASY 3D PROJECTS FOR BEGINNERS

Another way that quilling is changing this time around: It's going upward and off the page. Not, at this point, must quill be stuck down and fixed, a convention that truly restricts what can be refined. More up-to-date quilling paper brands offer more extensive and heavier weighted paper than was commonly accessible previously, accordingly permitting quillers to make paper design, useable, and curious things that would have been hard to achieve 30 years prior.

The capacity to make whatever is in your Materials' eye has countless favorable circumstances. Innovativeness can truly sparkle in unlimited manners. The little fish TV was, in the long run, made into adornment, and it would likewise make an amazing keychain or zipper pull for your #1 one.

Jewelry Box

The process of making a jewelry box is a lot like that of making a pen holder. Perhaps, the only difference is that the former requires a cover. But it should not be a problem. Designing the cover is the most enjoyable part of making a jewelry box.

Materials:

- precut quilling paper
- cardboard
- cutter
- scissors or thread snipper
- craft glue and tape

- circle sized ruler or board
- ruler
- paper and pencil (for creating a layout)

Steps:

1. Create a layout for your jewelry box with your paper and pencil. A square jewelry box is preferable, as this is your first time.
2. Indicate the dimensions for your jewelry box. It is best if you start small. You may want to use 4 inches for your jewelry box's length, width, and height.
3. Indicate the colors you want to see in the body of your jewelry box as well. Stick to one color for now. For the cover, you can use different colors for designing.
4. Cut a 4x4 inch piece of cardboard.
5. Decide the thickness of your coils. The recommended one for a 4x4x4 inches jewelry box is ¼ inch thick coils.
6. Make tight coils using a needle tool.
7. Make sure they are ¼ inch thick using your ruler, circle sized ruler, or moldboard.
8. Glue your coils of the same color to the 4x4 inch piece of cardboard that you cut earlier. It is for the bottom of your jewelry box. Start gluing for the middle parts. Cover the entire piece of cardboard. It is okay if the coils overlap the edges.
9. Next, glue coils for the body of your jewelry box. Instead of gluing the side of the coil by the side, place them in an

upright position. Attach them to the coils outlining the bottom of your jewelry box. Keep on gluing coils until the sides of your jewelry box are at 4 inches tall.

10. For the cover, measure the width of each side of your jewelry box. Because your coils overlap the 4x4 inch piece of cardboard, the width is likely to be beyond 4 inches.

11. Next, trace the base of your cover on your cardboard. Use the measurements from the last step. Add 1 mm to ensure that your cover fits nicely. Cut the base of your cover.

12. Trace and cut four additional pieces of cardboard for the sides of your cover. They should match the width of your cover, but they should only be ½ inch high.

13. Use tape to adjoin the cover's base and its sides.

14. Attach coils to the sides of your cover. This time, they should be attached side by side and not necessarily in an upright position.

15. Fill the topmost surface of your cover with coils. You may feature a heart or a flower pattern in the middle. You may put two teardrop-shaped coils at the top as well. Place them in the middle with their pinched ends together.

After trying out a square jewelry box, you may go after round-shaped and heart-shaped ones. Aside from boxes and pen holders, you should explore the construction of miniature houses, cakes, pianos, and the like by using coils alone. If you can visualize it in your head, you'll be able to make it genuine. Just keep on rolling and gluing paper strips.

Earrings

You know, paper quilling comprises quite a several mouth-watering designs. These designs evolve with time and become even better depending on their creativity and craftiness or artist handling it.

Earrings look good but using the paper quilling concept makes it look better. The daisy earring from paper quilling stands a chance against diamond-plaited sorts of earrings. And, this would solely depend on making and finishing. Together, let us uncover the appropriate way on how to make paper quilled daisy. The moment you coat with sealants, trust me, everyone would give it a second look. Ready to be proud of your craftiness? Then, follow this simple guide and be attentive to the photos.

Required Materials Paper Quilling Flowers

- A slotted quilling tool
- Quilling paper
- Quilling stencil
- Pins
- Paper glue
- Glue dispenser

How to Make Paper Quilled Flower Materials

Below are the basic materials required to do paper quilled flowers on your own. Refer to the photo if you can't identify the materials.

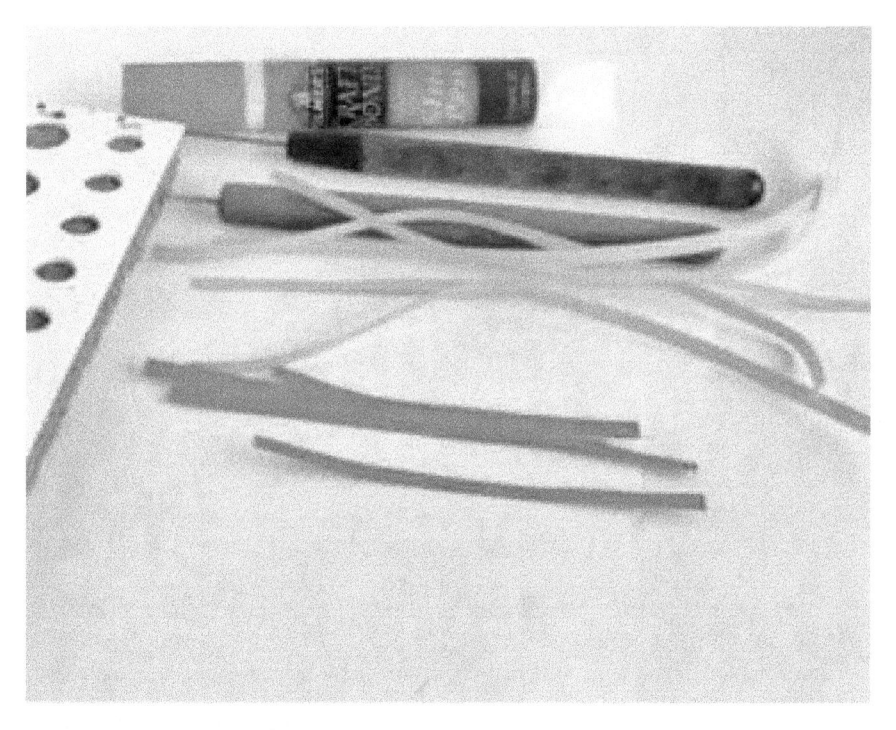

- Five paper strips (6 inches long)
- Another five paper strips (3 inches long)

- Slotted quilling tool
- Paper glue
- Corkboard
- Pins
- A circle-sizing tool (It may be aboard as well with hole)

The strips may be any preferred color as long as it suits the occasion.

1. Gluing Both Strips

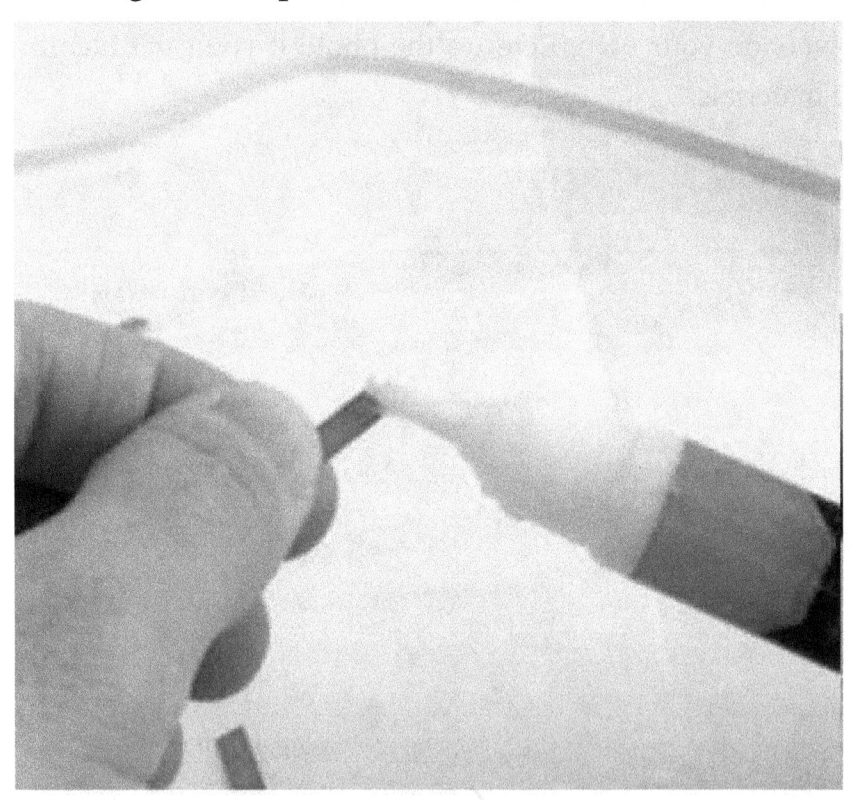

Apply paper glue at the preferred edges of each strip (3" and 6").

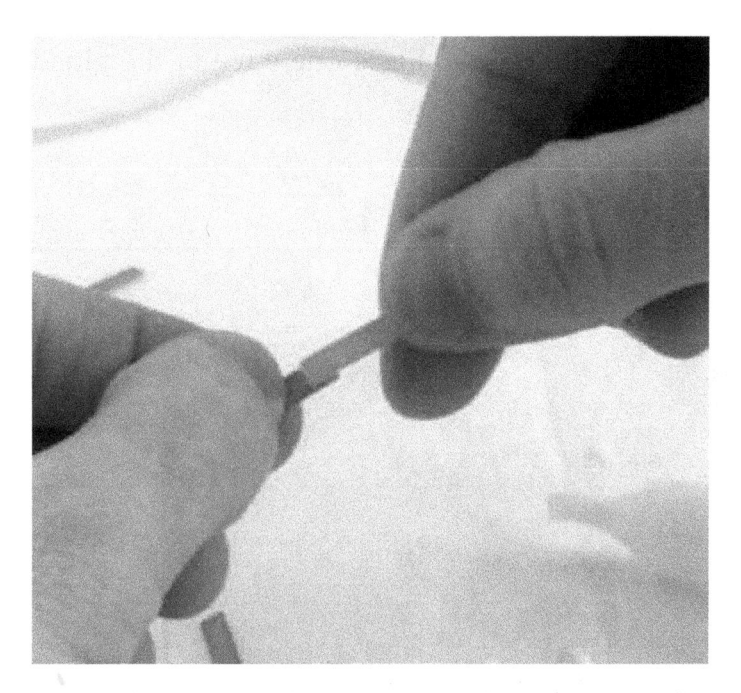

Bring the edges of each strip where you applied glue. Note, the strips you are gluing together must not be the same inches, i.e., only 3" strips must be paired with 6" strips.

2. Rolling the Quilling Paper

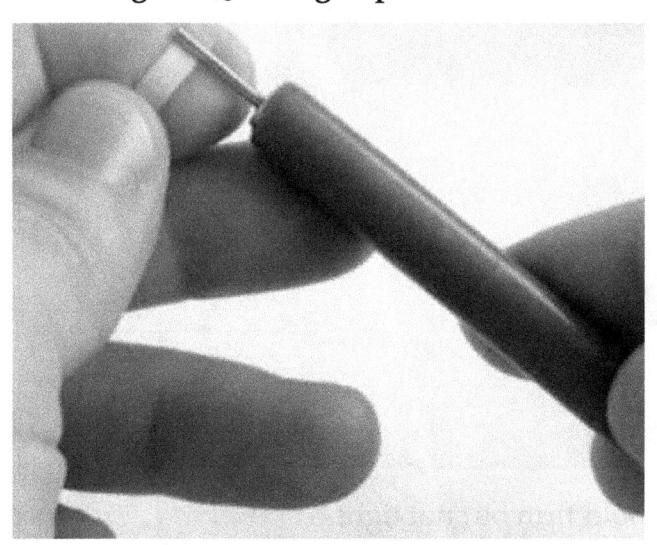

Pick up the slotted quilling tool. Place one edge of the glued strips at the tip of the tool.

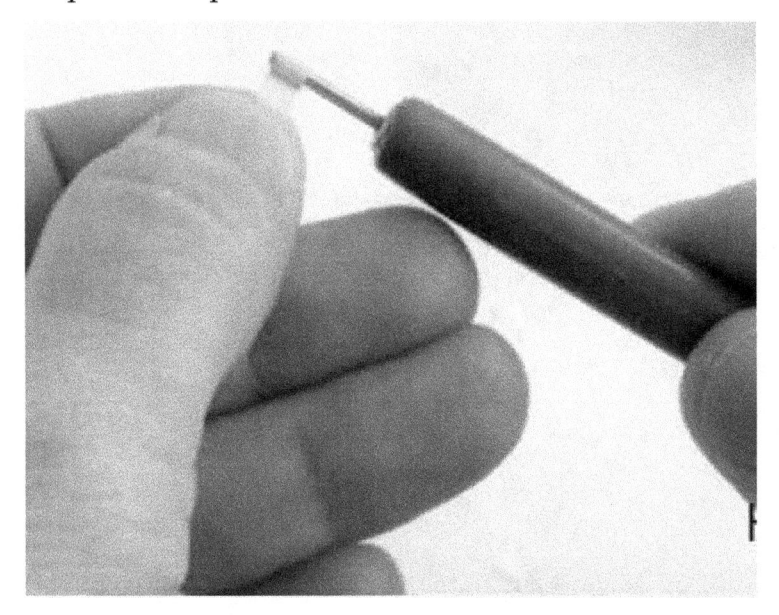

Start turning the quilling tool.

Ensure that you hold firm but not tight.

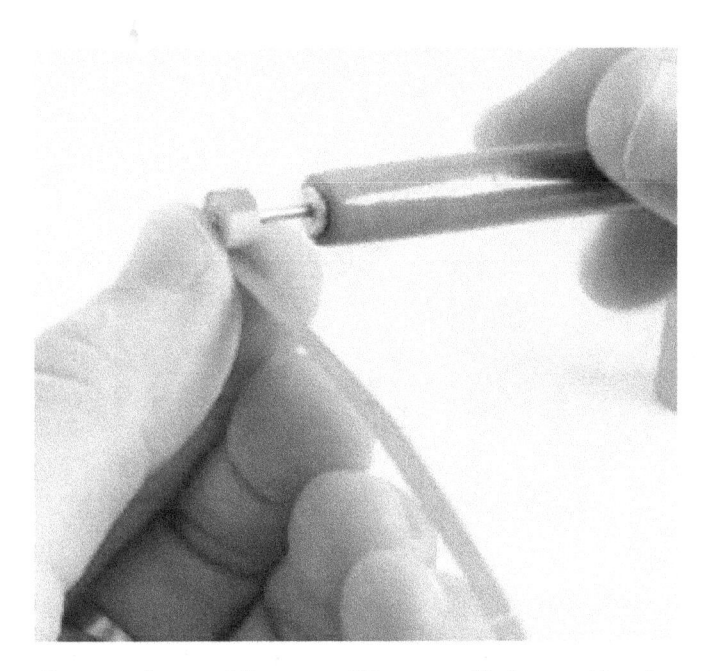

Go gently and keep rolling until the entire length of the strip is consumed.

3. Remove the Quilling Tool

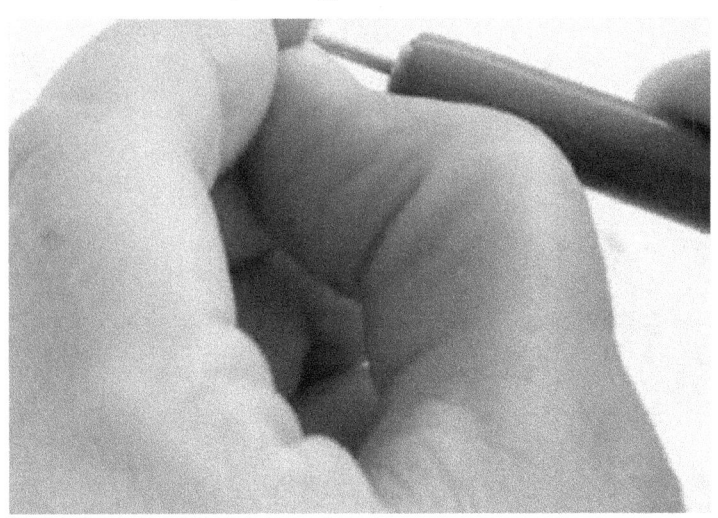

Add a light pressure using your forehand and thumb to press the strip to the quilling tool.

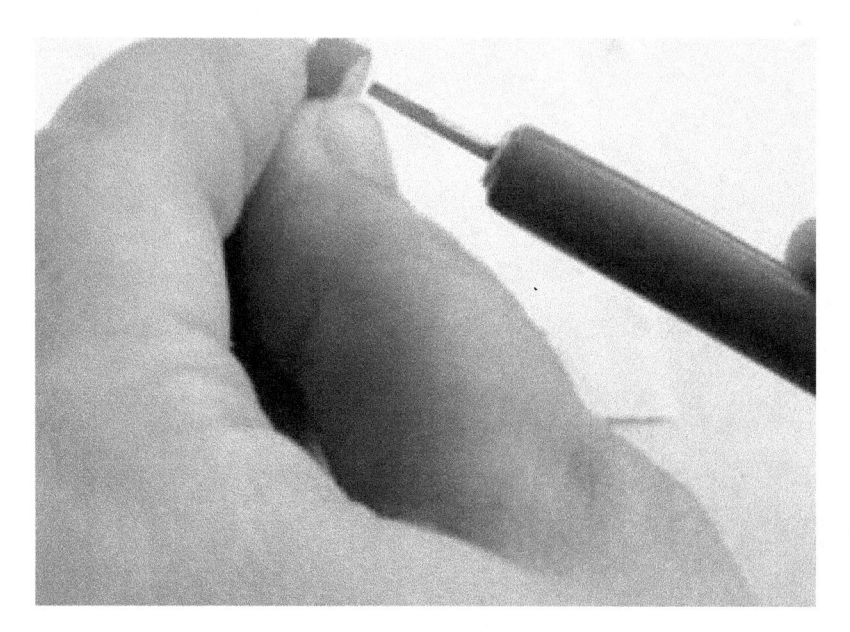

Carefully remove the scrolled paper from the quilling tool or whatever you're using. Ensure that the scroll is not scattered while retrieving from the tool.

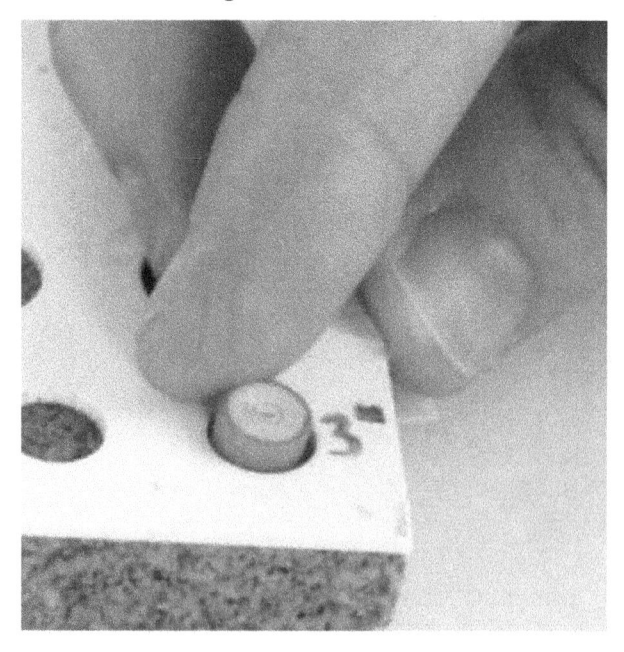

Gently place the retrieved scroll in the holes of the template. Be mindful of the hole size because the scroll will loosen when placed.

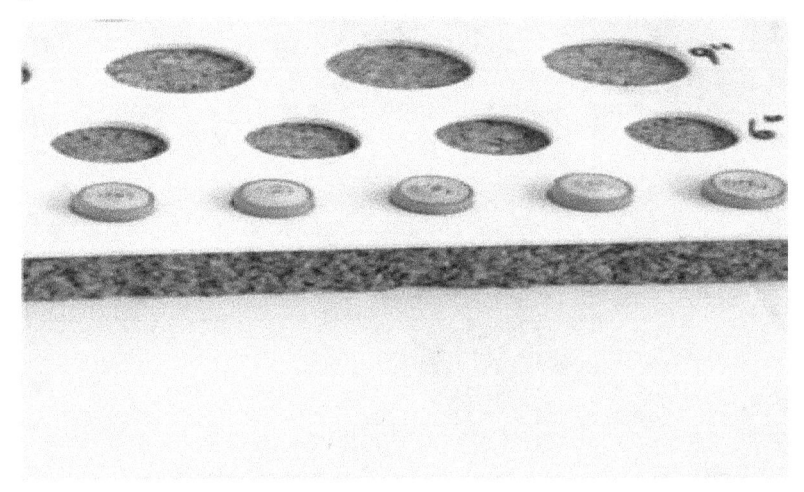

Repeat the process for all five scrolls.

4. Removing Scrolls from Template

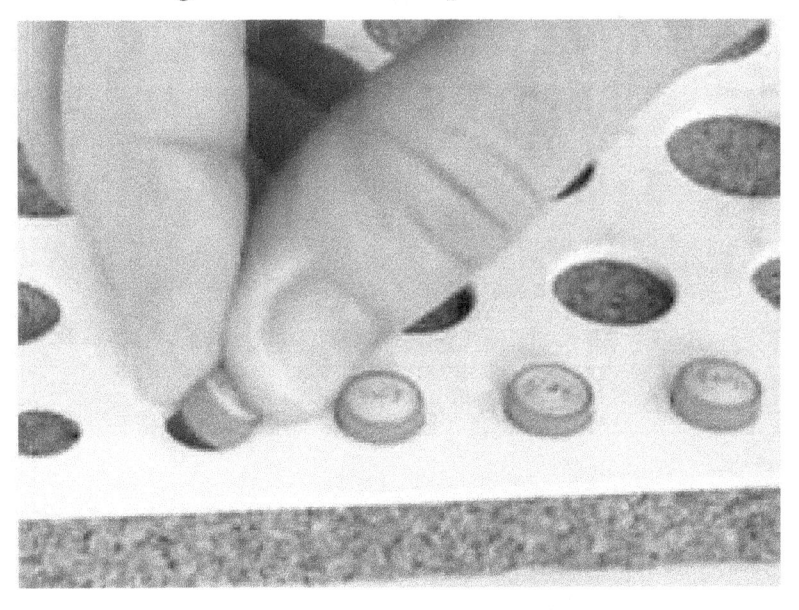

Carefully pick each of the five scrolls or whatever number of scrolls you're using.

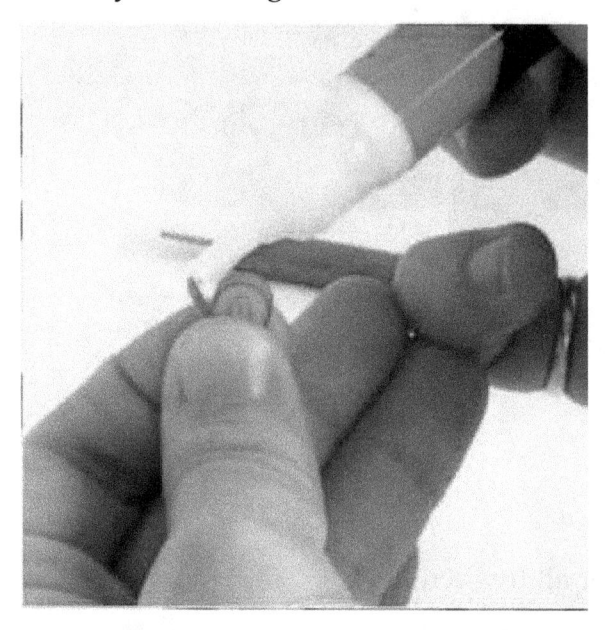

As you pick, glue the free edges of each scroll to lockdown the scroll against unfolding.

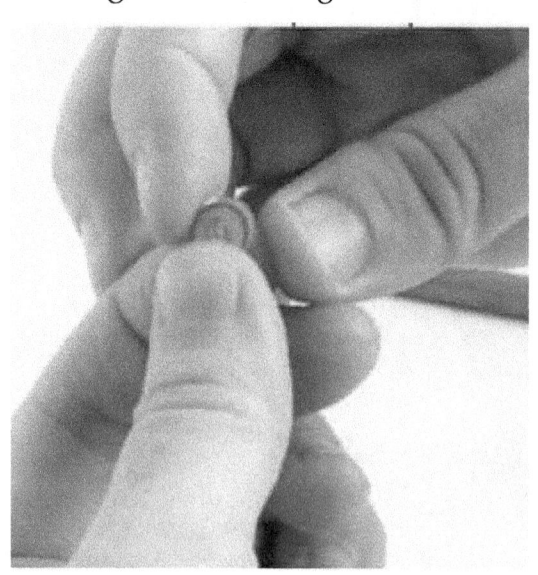

Allow scrolls to dry. Pick them out one after the other.

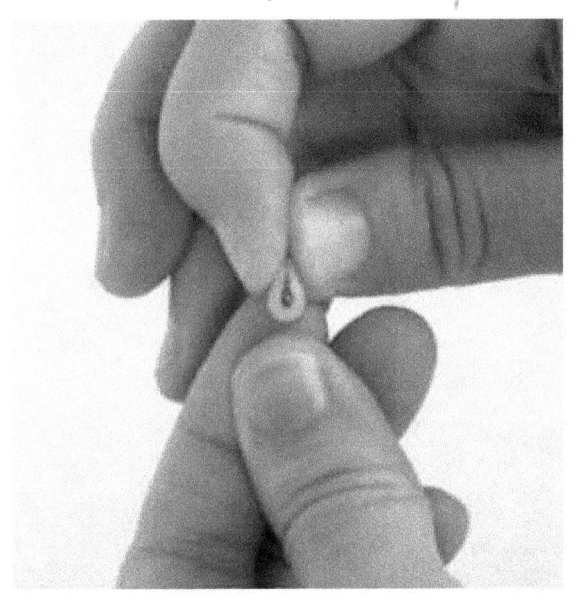

Hold the one edge of the scrolled quill down. Ensure that the held edge becomes somewhat pointy and gives a petal-like shape. Repeat this for all scrolls.

5. Gluing All 5 Petals

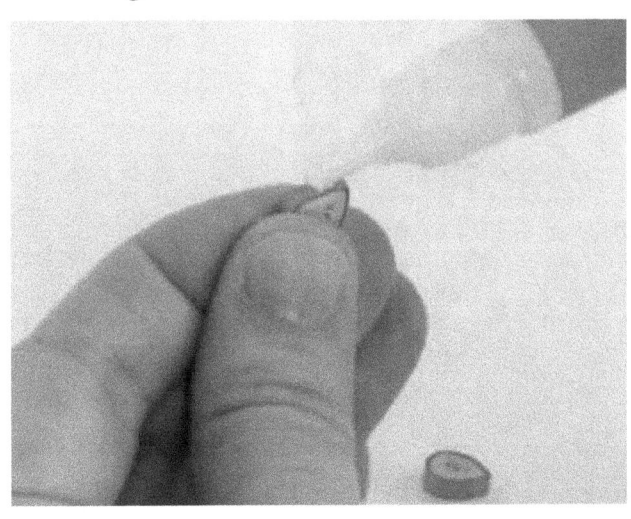

Apply glue using a glue dispenser towards the pointy part of every petal-shaped quill.

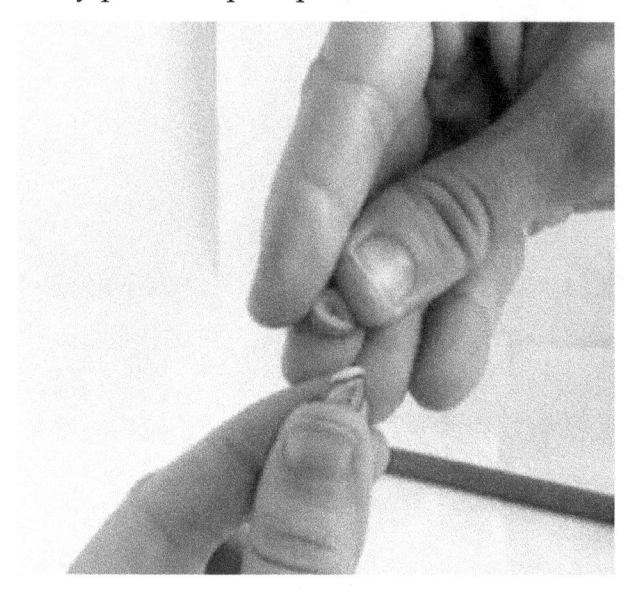

Place the glue parts together. Repeat the process until all five petals produce a star-like shape.

Ensure that the pointy edges of the petals face each other while making a placement.

In the end, you ought to have something like this. Place on a board and allow it to dry.

6. Arranging the Quill Daisy Earring with Pin

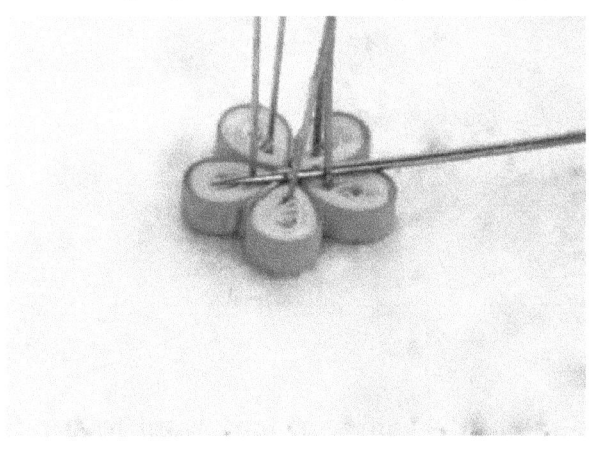

It is optional to give shape to the quilled daisy earring. While they are yet to dry, place pins on the areas with a distorted look. In my case, I do not have to place pins always. Sometimes, the quill comes out well arranged, and sometimes I have to use pins to give it shape.

If you prefer quill earrings with more opening, I recommend using 3" x 3" strips. Otherwise, use 6" x 3" strips for a tighter quilled earring.

Being that quills papers are delicate, you may want to apply sealants. I apply sealants on all my quilled earrings for them to resist water. If people using quilled earrings happen to find themselves out in the rain, they would have to worry less concerning their quilled earrings.

As straightforward and clear as this could appear, it is all you have to do to come up with a lovely quilled daisy earring. Simply follow the instructions and be attentive to the photos as well.

Would it be interesting if you choose to tweak this guide and maybe come up with something a bit different and unique? Of course, not. It is an art, and it is all about creativity. Besides, the making of paper quills evolves with time.

Wall Frames

This quilling project is very simple if you are just starting

Making your photo frames is a lot of fun. The great idea is to make watermarks of paper to outline the frame.

Christmas Time

The Christmas season is here, and alongside it comes the yearly race to convey and part with occasion cards to your loved ones. Regarding Christmas cards, a few of us like to go with the old reserve box sets (JAM offers a few exquisite choices) while others like to take the custom made course. If you are more inclined to place yourself into the latter classification, this post is for you.

The individuals who stay up with the latest with paper making patterns are presumably acquainted with quilling. For the individuals who are not, here is a short clarification. Quilling is the act of twisting and molding portions of the paper to make bigger ornamental shapes and plans. Here, I will tell you the best way to utilize quilling to make your own delightful and brightening Christmas wreath cards!

You will need:

- One standard quilling instrument (A sewing needle will likewise work.)
- Bright Hue Red Paper
- Dark Red Paper
- White Paper or Cardstock
- SCISSORS
- One hot glue gun (with glue)

Step 1:

Cut slim, 11 inch long portions of green paper. These strips ought to be generally even in width. However, they shouldn't be definite.

Step 2:

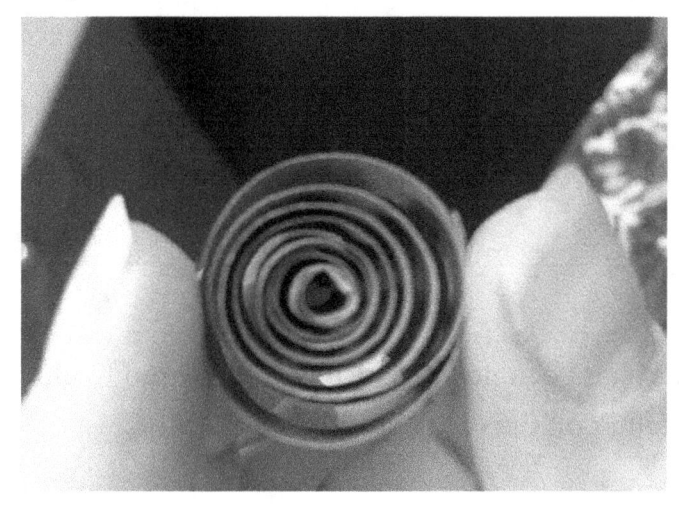

Utilizing your quilling device or needle, fold the initial segment of paper into a winding. After it is completely moved, eliminate it from the apparatus and let it mostly disentangle. It should resemble this.

Paste the remaining detail of the twisting set up with your paste firearm. Rehash this progression until you have enough green twisting's to frame a full wreath.

Step 3:

Pick a sheet of paper or card stock to use as the body of your card. For sturdiness, card stock is suggested. Before sticking it set up, lay put your green twisting's on your card surface as you might want to show up in your completed item.

After your design has been decided, use your glue gun to glue your wreath together on the card's surface!

Step 4:

Since your fundamental wreath shape is finished, you can proceed onward to making the bow. To start the bow, cut a few red and dim red paper pieces, and you did with the green paper in sync 1. After these strips have been cut, pick two similar tone segments to make into quilled tear shapes. These will turn into the inward most bits of the bow.

Step 5:

To make a teardrop shape, wind your segment of paper around the quilling instrument or needle similarly that you did to make essential circles. While eliminating the paper from the device, just permit it to disentangle part path instead of releasing it. How much you permit it to disentangle will influence the size of your tear shape.

After this winding has incompletely slackened, hold the focal point of this twisting with the forefinger and thumb of your non-prevailing hand while pulling tenderly outward and utilizing your predominant hand to pull the external bit of the twisting the other way while squeezing to shape a point (the head of the tear). Paste the remaining detail of the shape set up with your glue gun.

Step 6:

After you have made two teardrop states of a similar tone, take two pieces of another state of red and firmly fold them over these shapes. Paste the remaining details set up. Next, take two portions of the main shade of red you utilized and freely fold them over the external surface of the shapes you simply wrapped. Squeeze the head of everyone, so it coordinates the states of the focal points. To complete the two parts of the bow's head, do this again with the contrary shade of red. Appeared beneath is the teardrop shape you began with contrasted with a finished portion of a bow.

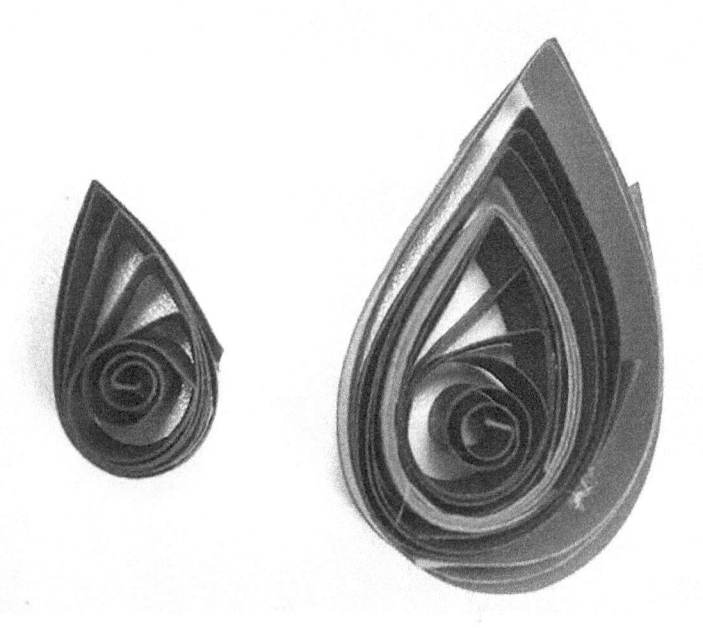

Step 7:

Make center for your bow by winding a tight, little hover of red paper and wrapping a piece of the other red shade around it. Paste this round shape along with your paste weapon and afterward stick all lace pieces onto the wreath in any capacity you might want!

After these are in place, loosely curl a few more red strips of paper and glue them in place to create the bottom/ excess bowstrings.

Your wreath card is now complete! If you wish, you may use writing utensils to include a message such as "Merry

Christmas," "Happy Holidays," or "Hi, Mom" within the wreath!

We hope that this craft helped to brighten up your season. Happy Holidays from all of us at JAM!

Snowflake

An artificially made snow should be enough to remind the young ones and the elderly of snow even during winter. Paper quills bring our imaginations to reality, and one of such is the cold snow. Instead of packing and feeling the roof with cold snow, make quills snowflake a companion. This paper quills pattern brings the snow close enough that you may not last long for natural snow any longer.

I know you would love to learn this art, and I am willing to show you how it is done. Do you fear this design would be the most difficult of all you have seen so far? Trust me; your mind is playing games because the snowflake paper quills are as easy as any other easy-to-do paper quill.

In this guide, you will learn to become a better quill artist rather than sit all day and be praising the quill creativity from others. It is time to get the praises too, and I trust you to do even better than what you find here.

Required Materials for Paper Quilled Snowflake

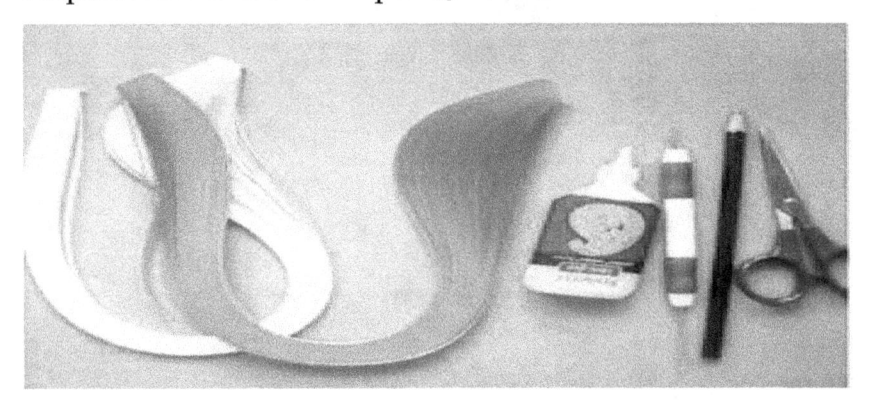

- Quilling paper strips
- Quilling pins
- Quilling stencil
- Glue and Glue dispenser
- A pair of Scissors
- Slotted quilling tool
- Pencil
- Ruler
- A geometric compass
- A plain paper sheet

Folds Needed for Snow Quilled Snowflake

Here are the number of folds and types of folds needed regarding the snowflake quilling done in this guide.

- Six blue 54cm length teardrops
- 6 white 54cm length marquis
- 6 white quarter-length marquis
- 6 white 54cm length tight coils
- 6 blue half-length tight coils
- 1 white half-length tight coils
- 18 blue quarter-length tight coils

You will see how to make marquis folds, teardrop folds, and tight coil folds as you read on.

How to Make Paper Quilled Snowflake Ornaments

1. Figure Out the Length

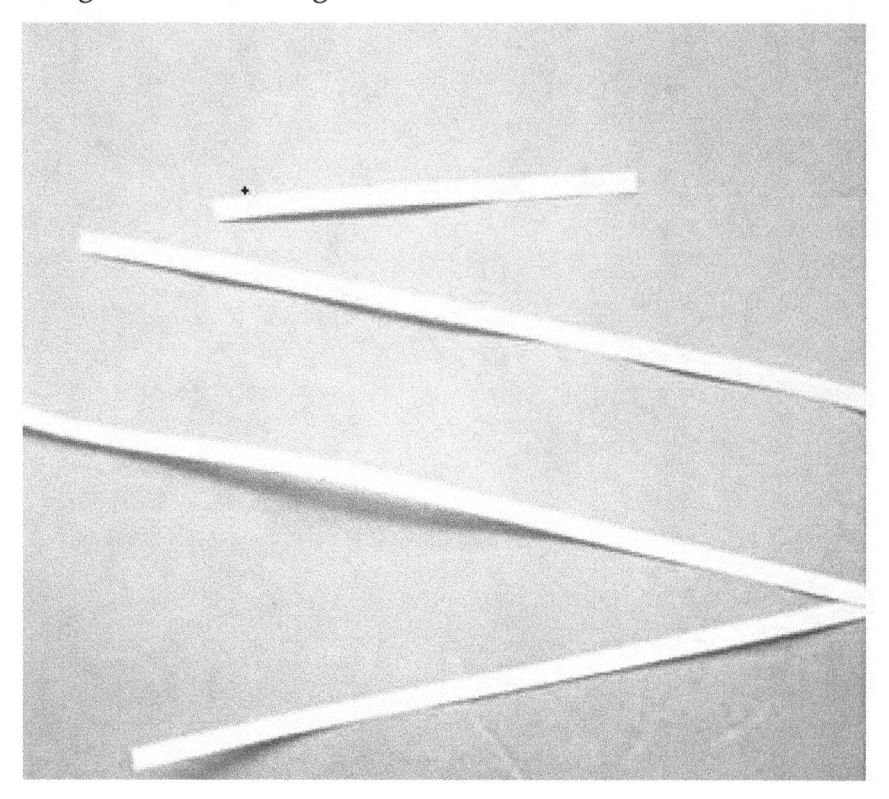

Pick a length that best suits the occasion. In this guide, we are using 5mm Width and 54cm length paper strips. Depending on your requirement, you may opt for something different. However, for this guide's purpose, use a paper strip of 5mm Width and 54cm length to follow up better.

2. Draw a Circle

Pick a compass from the materials and insert a pencil in it. Alternatively, use a well-rounded container or anything measuring just 5cm. Make a 5cm circle on the plain sheet and divide the circle into six equal parts, as shown in the picture.

3. Applying a Design

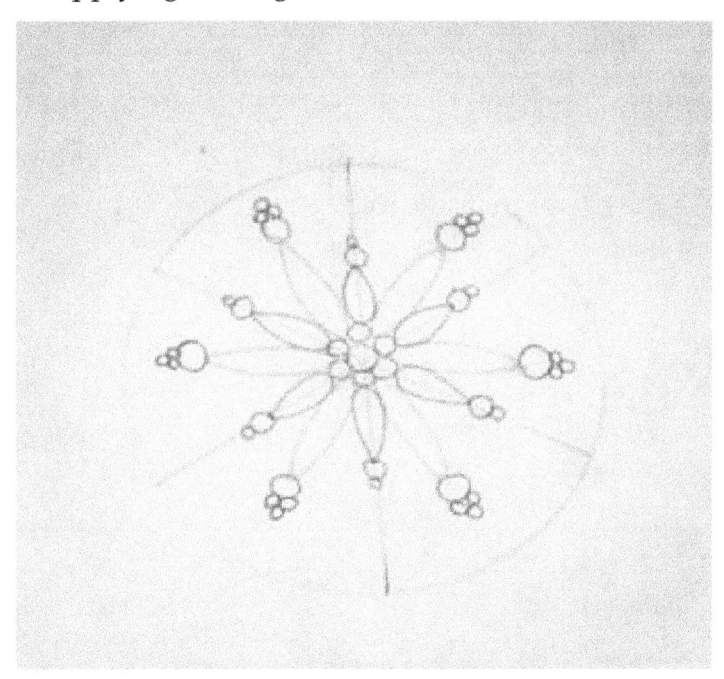

There are several designs you can decide to take on. For now, make exactly the design you find here unless you are an

~ 111 ~

expert willing to do something different. To come up with the snowflake design, you may visit online guides on how to draw a snowflake because several snowflake drawings could be used to develop the snowflake. If you are okay with what is on this photo, then follow suit.

4. Making the Folds

To develop a proper snowflake similar to what is on this photo, you need to make three different quilling folds, which include:

- Marquis
- Teardrop
- Coil

How to Make Marquis Fold

You can also call marquis the eye-shaped fold or the eye fold. This fold would look exactly like the shape of the eye. Below is how to make the eye or marquis fold.

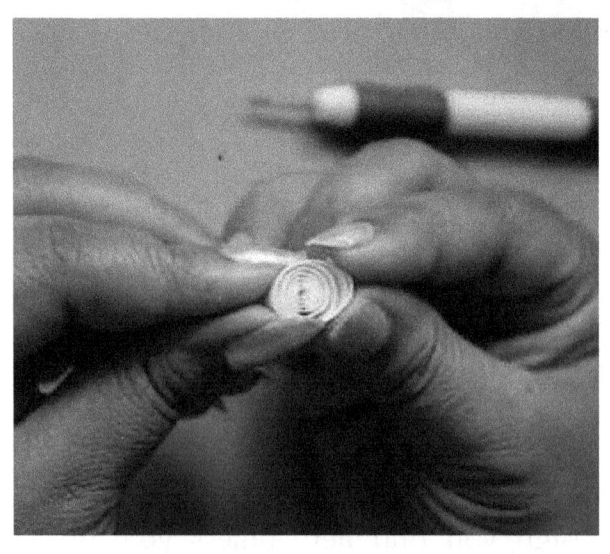

Pick a slotted quilling tool and use it to roll a paper strip. In place of a quilling tool, you may use any other tool, but a quilling tool makes the work more convenient. While rolling the strip around the slotted quilling tool, add a bit of pressure on the strip using your forefinger and thumb.

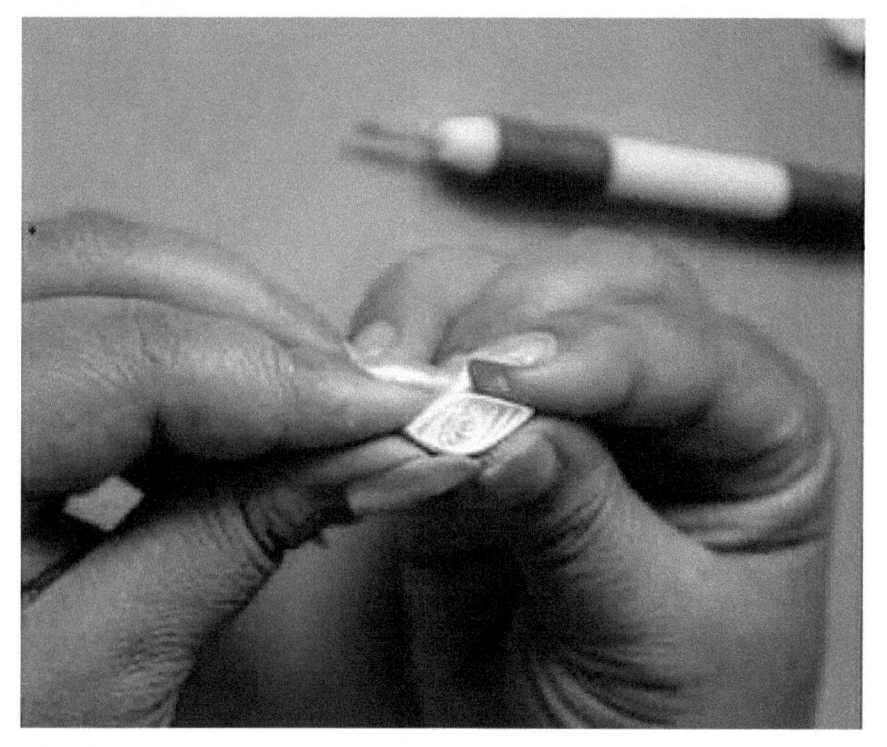

Gently retrieve the paper strip from the slotted quilling tool. Allow the paper strip to loosen a bit, then press two opposite ends to form an eye shape. Use the glue dispenser to apple a drop of glue to shut the strip together. Repeat this for all strips to be used as marquis.

How to Make Teardrop Fold

Roll the paper strip around a slotted quilling tool. Do not apply excess pressure but hold firmly to the strip.

Gently remove the strip from the quilling tool and press just one edge of the scroll to obtain a petal shape. Apply paper glue to stick the free edge together and allow it to dry.

How to Make Coil Fold

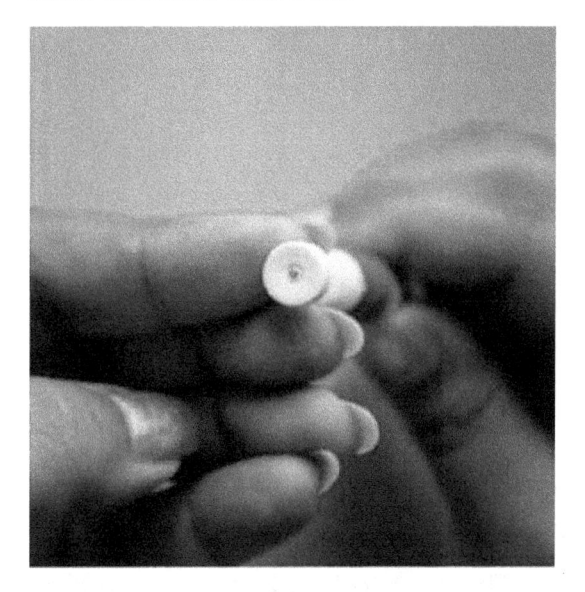

Roll the paper strip around the slotted quilling tool. Press firmly to make further the strip take shape.

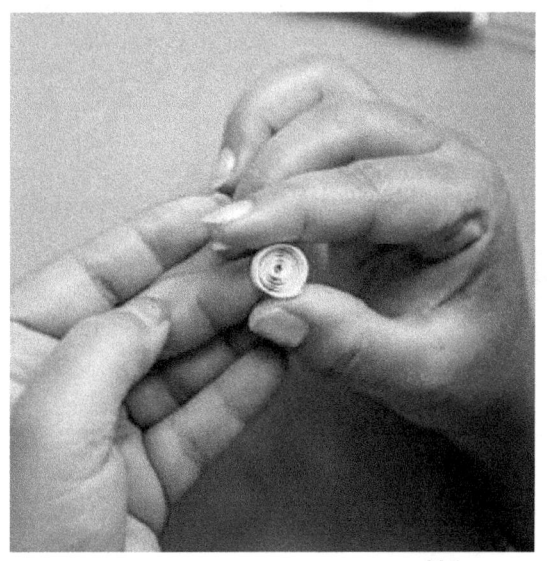

Gently, take off the strip without pressing any part of it. Apply glue to the open edge to glue it together. Place and allow drying.

5. Setting Up the Folds

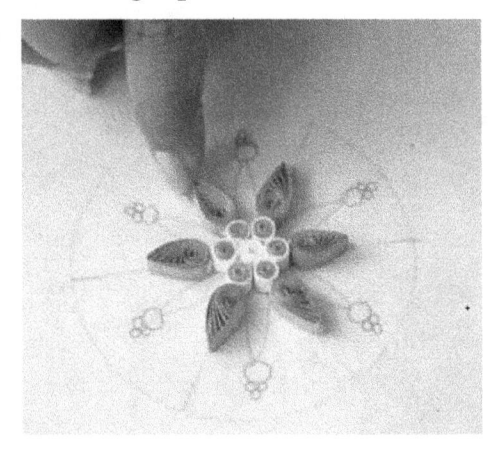

Drop appropriate folds on the corresponding drawing on the plain sheet. The first coil is the while coil, placed in the center of the snowflake diagram. The next to be placed are the blue quarter coil folds wrapped in while strips. Apply glue, if the glue is dry, and place all six blue teardrops on each blue quarter coils' outer edges.

Now, place the marquis or eye-shaped folds in the in-between every blue quarter fold. Go ahead and place the white folds on the edges of all six marquises.

You should be left with 12 blue quarter coil folds. Glue all 12 blue quarter folds in twos and attach them to the white folds, as shown in the picture above. Finally, attach the white half-length coil folds on the quarter length blue folds.

6. You are Done.

Place the paper quill and allow drying.

You may then choose to apply sealants, but coating with sealant may not be relevant since it is just a merry piece of art.

Other than this, retry this artwork but with a different design of snowflakes. It is not rocket science, and neither costs too many resources nor thinking to actualize.

Christmas Tree

Supplies needed:

- Green Craft paper
- Quilling strips in different colors

- Quilling Tool
- Pencil or pen
- Scissors
- Glue or glue stick

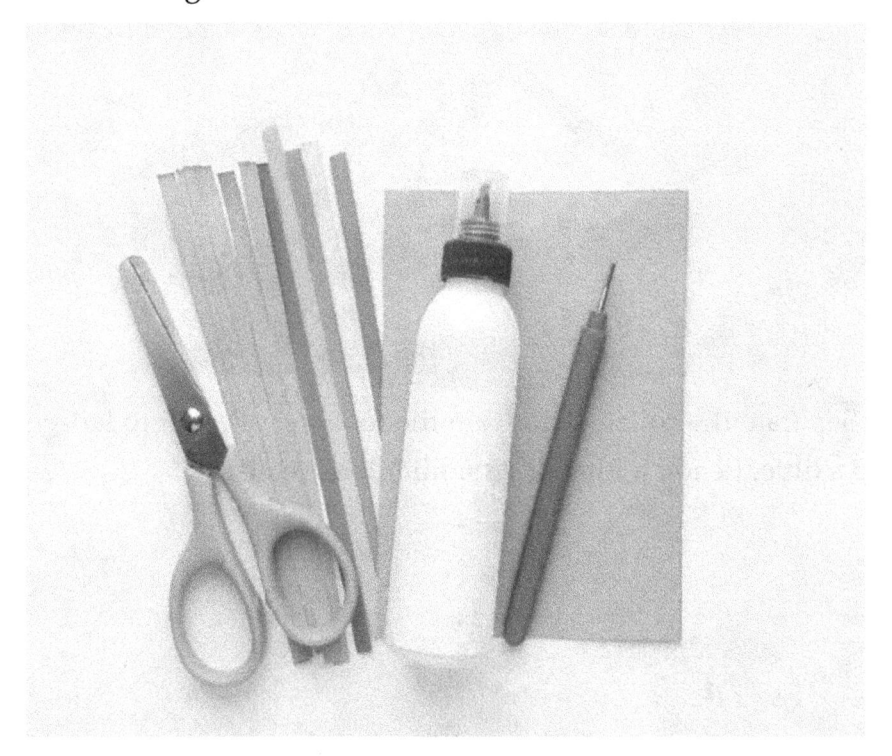

Instructions for making the Paper Quilling Christmas Tree Ornament:

1. Take 6 inches in length green quilling strip and utilize the opened quilling instrument to loop the whole strip into a tight curl.

2. Separate the coiled strip from the tool and allow it to loosen up a little. Ready a total of 15 similar loose coils.

3. Utilize 3.5 inches red strips to make little tear shapes.

4. Presently make a couple of loops utilizing quilling strips in arranged tones. You can make them free or tight – whatever you like. Make four earthy colored free loops too.

5. Take a rectangular bit of green specialty paper and accumulate all the green free loops arranged in sync 1 and 2. Use create a paste to stick five free curls in an orderly fashion towards the lower side of the green-hued make paper.

6. Keep staying lines of the free green curls, one over the other. As you move upward, continue lessening the number of curls in a line by 1, so you end up with a triangle design.

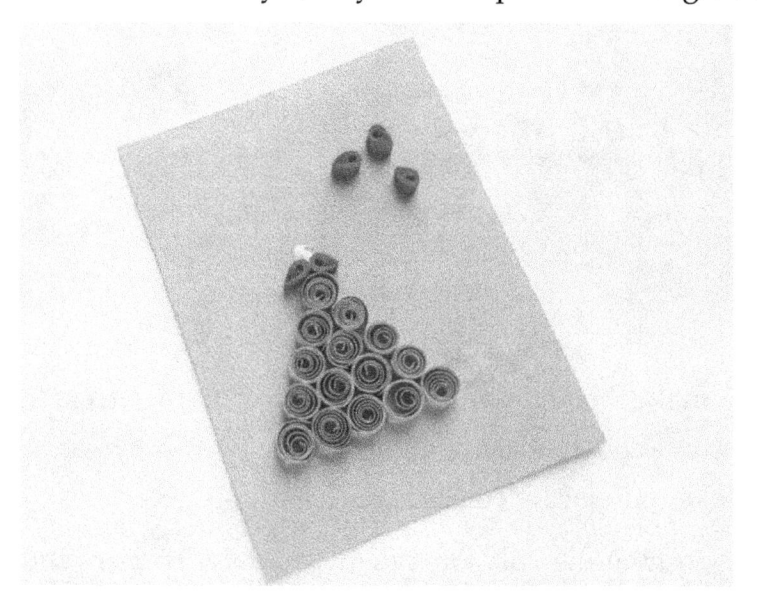

7. Stick the red tear shapes on the top finish of the triangle. Paste them along with the pointy end out, so you get a 5 point star design.

8. Cut the art paper along the external edge of the Christmas tree, including the red star.

9. Utilize the various brilliant loops to embellish the tree by essentially sticking them on either side. Include four earthy colored curls on the tree's base side in a square example to make the tree trunk.

10. At long last, include a little globule as the focal point of the star design if you like. Allow it to dry, and it's finished!

This Quilling Christmas Tree Ornament is very multipurpose. You can join a string and balance it on the tree with a similarly adorable Paper Quilled Wreath Ornament. However, you can likewise make a handcrafted Christmas Card with it. Or then again, why not connect it to a bit of card to cause it to go with these Christmas Gift Tags? It couldn't be any more obvious; a little exertion and a couple of strips sure go far!

Snowman

Christmas crafts are popular and good gifts. Right now, I will tell you how to create a Christmas paper quilling snowman.

There are many quilling paper Christmas ornaments on Panda hall. Most of them are cute and uncomplicated to make. The materials are quilling papers in different colors and some pearl beads. You need no other professional skills in making this DIY snowman craft.

Supplies needed:

- 3mm Pearl Beads
- Quilling Paper(Bright Red, Green, Yellow, Black, White)
- Model
- Scissor
- Tweezers
- White Glue
- Rolling Pen

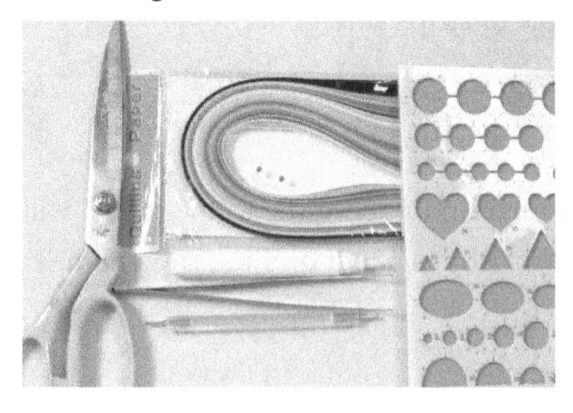

Step 1: Make a few paper quilling roundabout globules

Take around 4 bits of white quilling papers, fold them into enormous round dabs, and stick the end solidly. Take around 2 bits of white quilling papers, fold them into a round globule, make the other five white roundabout dabs and other two red round dots, and two green roundabout dots with a similar length. Stick all the little roundabout globules around the large round dab as envisioned.

Step 2: Include another roundabout example and pearl dots

Roll a white roundabout dot with around 3 bits of quilling papers; stick 2 bits of 3mm blue pearl dabs on it as eyes. Cut an off bit of yellow quilling paper, move it to a round globule, make guarantee the internal part higher than the external part, at that point take advantage of the white roundabout dot as a mouth as envisioned.

Step 3: Make an oval bead

Fold a dark quilling paper into a roundabout globule, placed it into the 10cm opening and stick the end, and squeeze the roundabout dot into an oval dab as imagined.

Stage 4: Make the final Christmas snowman plan

Stick the dark oval dot to the top of the snowman as a cap; at that point, roll other dark round dot and take advantage of the cap as envisioned. Cut an off red quilling paper and a dark quilling paper, move them a few circles and extricate them to make them as the image appeared. Stich the finish of the red quilling paper with the dark quilling paper together, at that point, sticks the conclusion to left round globules of the snowman, and stick three blue pearl dots on the enormous roundabout dab as envisioned.

Here is the last look of the Christmas paper quilling snowman:

Do you love this bright and charming paper, quilling snowman? I completed this DIY snowman make inside 15minutes. You can likewise find it out how to make a Christmas snowman at home. It fits for another comer to begin his/her quilling paper DIY venture. Presently, my instructional exercise on the most proficient method to make a Christmas snowman has concluded. Have a pleasant attempt!

Christmas Lights

Is it safe to pronounce that you are searching for a novel specialty to do with your children? It would even be an extraordinary specialty to do with kids for a winter or Christmas celebration. With only a couple of apparatuses, they can make this remarkable arrangement of lights to show for these special seasons!

List of Supplies:

1. Craft paperwhite
2. Quilling Strips
3. Slotted Paper Quilling Tools
4. Scissors
5. Craft Glue or glue stick

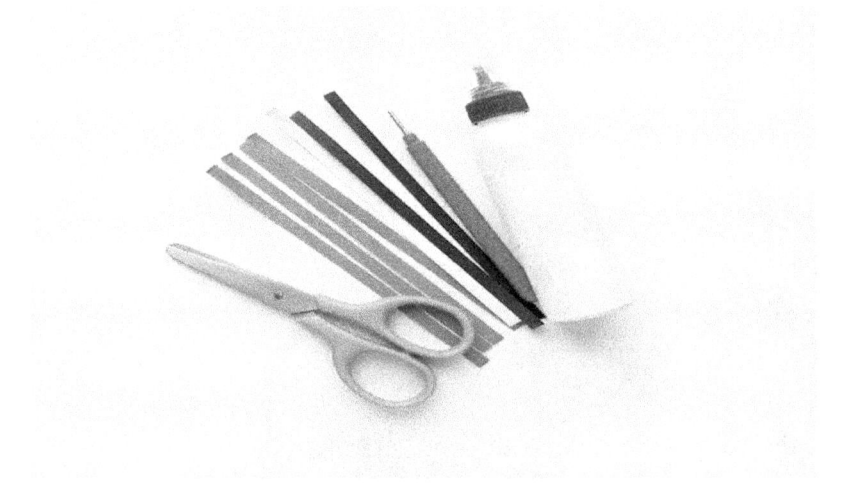

Instructions to make the craft:

Step 1: Take 20 inches since quite a while ago, hued quilling strip, and utilize the opened quilling device to curl the whole strip.

Step 2: Once the coiling is finished, take out the tool's coiled strip and allow it to let it out.

Step 3: Hold any one side of the release coil to form a teardrop shape and pasted the open end to secure the shape.

Step 4: Take 3 inches in length white shaded quilling strip and make a free loop shape with it.

Step 5: Press 2 inverse sides of the free curl to frame a focal point shape.

Step 6: Get the tear shape arranged in the last advances.

Step 7: Supplement the focal point shape made in sync five into the tear shape, through the hole of any loops close to the bent end; the bulb design is prepared. Also, make more bulb designs.

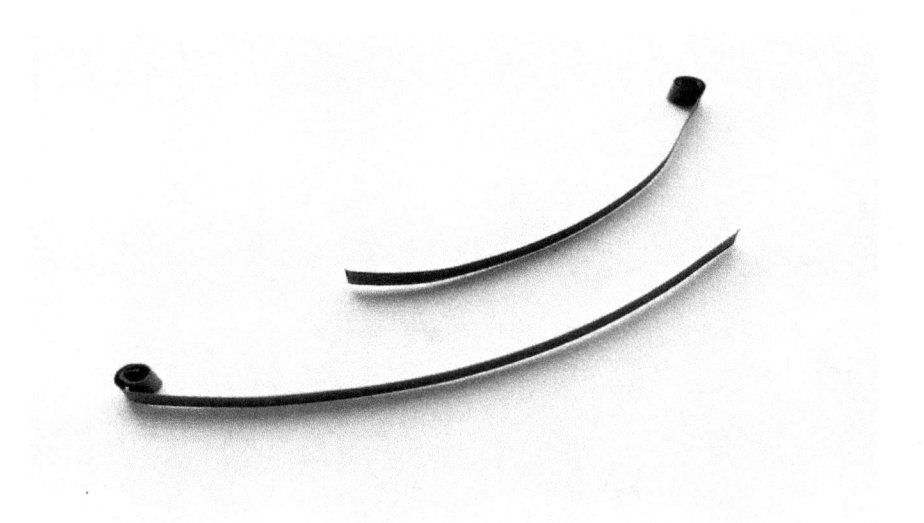

Step 8: Presently take 6 inches in length dark quilling strip and make a little whirl on any of its finishes. Use around 2 or 3 cm to make the whirl design.

Step 9: Cut out a white specialty paper or cardstock paper for the foundation, or you can pick any shading you need.

Step 10: Paste the two dark whirled strips on the paper by making a slight breathtaking example with them. Paste the two strips in 2 lines, keeping, in any event, an inch hole between them.

Step 11: Take a bulb example and paste it on the paper by keeping the bent end contiguous with the dark strip (the bulbs' fundamental wire).

Step 12: Individually include the remainder of the bulbs to fill the dark strip.

Allow the glue to dry and have fun!

TIPS AND TRICKS

As a beginner quilter or even as an expert/professional whose interest is to survive in the craft of quilling without much stress, here are few tips that could help you actualize this. They include;

Using a Background Platform that is Colored

If you use a quilling background that is attractively laden with colors, it will help boost the sight impression and improve your craftwork's attention after completion and while on display. If the kind of background paper you are using is void of color or colors, say a plain white sheet, you can easily color the paper to any color of your choice, and that's it; you've just made one for yourself.

Use Paper Strip (Shredder)

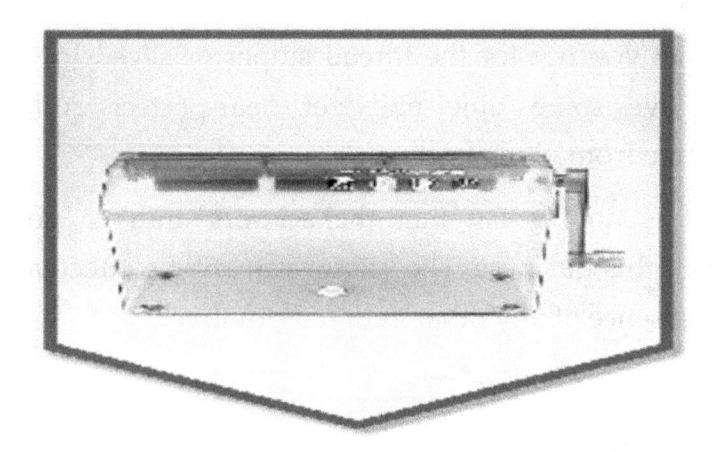

A shredder in paper quilling is a box-like tool normally made of plastic materials with a winding handle. The paper to be threaded is placed neatly in the opened allowable part of the box, and the handle is wind. It is the manual paper stripping method.

Using the scissors to do your quilling process could be cumbersome and tiring sometimes. Subsequently, it is suggested that you opt for the thread sniper or slicer. In this way, you save some time and get near-perfect quilled paperwork free from glue attachments.

However, it is not to say that the scissors aren't a good companion in this business. The scissor can still be effectively used in the absence of any other better alternative.

Use The Needle Before The Comb

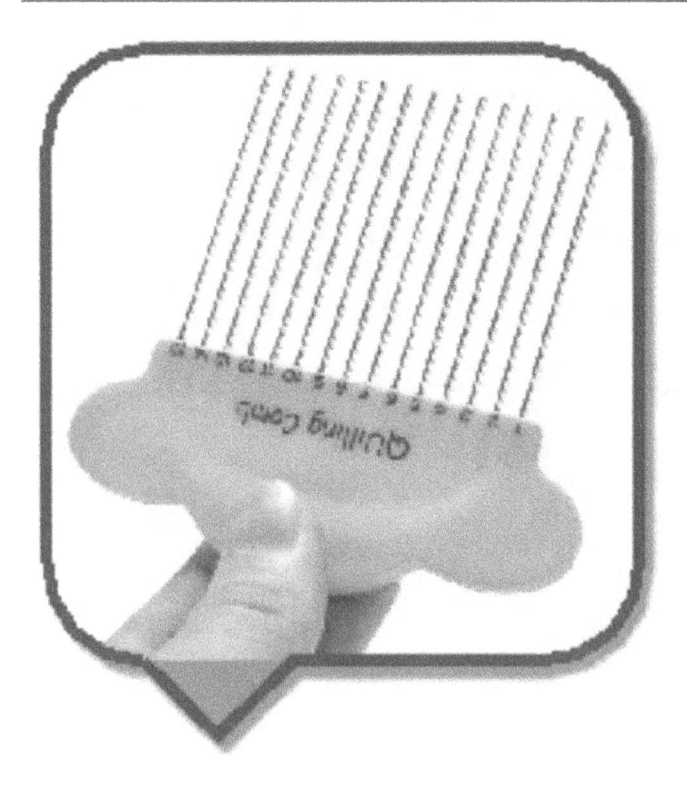

In this craft, the experience pays quite a lot! Some persons find the quilling comb quite difficult to use in the first place. Using the quilling needle tool first before applying the quilling comb would help save a lot, both time and energy, and help keep the middle of your rolled coil in check.

Learn To Roll Two Strips Together

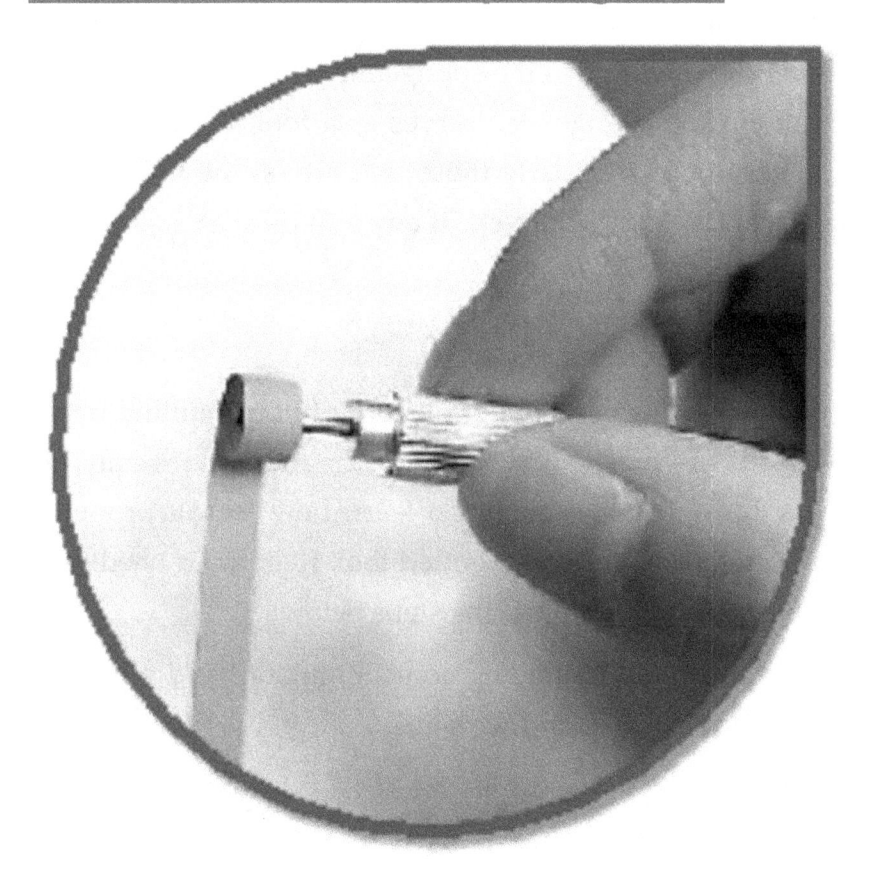

As you continue to grow in this craft experience, you will come to discover that rolling up just a single paper strip could lead to weariness. Still, it is advisable for you and the strip to always join at least two strips together before taking a manual hand roll.

Get a Quilling Sponge

The quilling sponge is more or less like a holding container that helps to hold the glue bottle while working to prevent unsolicited glue/gum spillage on a given job or project, as the glue bottle or container is normally placed or turned with its tip facing downwards on the sponge for easy access and quick application. The sponge also serves as a tool for cleaning up unwanted glue, particularly those that are on the fingers and palms, in addition to spillovers, if any.

Rolling Using a Slotted Tool

This technique lets you create coils out of your quilling paper strips. Coils are present in most quilt creations, so it only fits to know how to make them. To learn how to roll properly, grab a paper strip, and your slotted tool. Keep your needle-tip craft glue nearby and follow the steps below:

1. Hold the slotted tool using your dominant hand while the paper strip is in your other hand.
2. Putting the tip of your paper strip into the slit of your slotted tool's needle.
3. Hold the paper strip with your non-dominant hand's thumb and index finger.
4. Start rolling the slotted tool. It is the right way. Do not wrap the paper strip around the slotted tool's needle.
5. You may roll the paper strip up to the very end or leave something like a tail.

There are three types of coils you can create with the steps mentioned above. These are: open, closed, and tight.

- To make an open coil, gently remove the rolled paper strip from the slotted tool and put it down right away.

- To make a closed coil, gently remove the rolled paper strip from the slotted tool, let it loosen but apply a small amount of glue at the end of the paper strip.

- To make a tight coil, gently remove the rolled paper strip from the slotted tool and hold it lightly for 20 seconds. Apply glue at the end of the paper strip.

If you want your coils to be of similar size, make sure that the paper strips you use are also of the same size. Additionally, use your circle sizer ruler or board to measure your coils.

Creating as many coils as you can until you master rolling with your slotted tool. Do not throw your coils right away, though. No matter how displeasing they might seem, you can use them to try forming the basic shapes and learning how to insert small coils into big ones later.

You'd be surprised that you can master this technique in an hour or two. You should be warned, though. Rolling paper strips continuously may lead to cramps. To prevent this, relax your grip on your slotted tool and paper strip. Stretch and let your fingers rest every so often. You might want to consider holding a cloth or padding between your dominant hand and the slotted tool.

Rolling Using a Needle Tool, Toothpick, or Any Other Alternative

Rolling using a needle tool, toothpick, or any other alternative to the slotted tool is a little bit harder because of the lack of slit where you can place one end of your paper strip. Although tricky, this technique does not leave behind a crimp in the middle of your coil, which usually happens when you use the slotted tool. To start, keep your fingers a little bit moist and follow the steps below:

1. Use your dominant hand to hold your tool while your other hand is for the paper strip. You may add a quilling coach to your needle tool.

2. Curve the end of the paper strip around your tool. Do this near the tip of the tool for easy and speedy removal of coils later.

3. Gently press the end of the paper strip attached to your tool to keep it in place.

4. Start rolling your tool.

To create the three types of coils using a needle tool, toothpick, or any other alternative, follow through the same steps as those mentioned for rolling with a slotted tool. When you are done mastering the art of making coils, go to a whole new level by transforming your coils into basic quilling shapes. You can do this by hand alone. The following are some of the basic quilling shapes you can create with your paper coils.

Teardrop

To make a teardrop-shaped paper strip, pinch one part of your coil. Apply glue at the end.

Eye

Pinch two opposite ends of your coil. Make sure they are equally molded on each side. Glue the loose end of your coil.

Leaf

The leaf-shaped coil is similar to the eye. You also have to pinch two opposite parts of your coil. After that, push the pinched parts towards each other. Do not forget to apply glue at the other end.

Petal

To create a petal-shaped coil, you should also pinch two opposite parts of your coil. However, one of the pinched parts should be bigger than the other.

Practice making these basic shapes for as many times as you want. Experiment with wider and narrower paper strips, as well as with longer and shorter paper strips. You can also try modifying the techniques bit by bit.

Rolling Using a Border Buddy or Any of Its Alternatives

Some quilling border buddies have handles, so learning how to use them is easier. However, some do not have any handle at all. You have no other option but to hold the body of the border buddy. But this could be an advantage. You will be trained to use the border buddy and lids, small bottles, or any other item used as a molder.

The steps for rolling a paper strip using a border buddy or any of its alternatives are similar to rolling using a needle tool unless your molder is not round, oblong, or oval. Always start with round border buddies. Try creating big coils of different sizes. Once you are done with the round ones, proceed with the triangle and square border buddies. When you use a lid, make sure your paper strip is narrower. Otherwise, you will lead up with a coil full of crimps on the edges. Below are the steps in using a border buddy or any other molder for that matter:

1. Use your dominant hand to hold the molder while the other hand is for your paper strip.
2. Put one end of your paper strip into the molder. Press it with your thumb to keep it in place.
3. Start twisting your molder slowly but guide your paper strip using your non-dominant hand's thumb and index finger. If your molder has one or more corners, press your paper strip in those corners.
4. After the first roll, apply glue to the end of your paper strip that is affixed to your molder.
5. Continue rolling until you achieve your desired thickness. You may or may not leave something like a tail of your coil.

If you are going to make a closed coil, do not remove your paper strip from the molder right away. Apply glue at the other end of your paper strip while it is still on the molder. After that, remove your paper strip and hold it for 20 seconds (or until the glued end is not likely to slide) to maintain its shape.

Create coils of different colors, shapes, sizes, widths, and lengths. Try out various plastic and glass bottles, jars, and other containers. Use wood blocks to make big squares, rectangles, or triangles. You may transform your coils into other shapes by pinching them or just leave them as they are.

Gluing Coils Together

Gluing coils is made easy and less messy with needle-tip craft glue. But for your practices, it might be a waste to use such glue right away. As an alternative, you may use regular glue and a pin.

You are going to use the glue to join coils together. For now, you can glue the different coils you just created. Do not obsess about forming patterns in the meantime. Below are the steps in applying regular glue using a pin.

1. Prepare your tweezers, cuticle nipper, and a piece of scrap paper.
2. Squeeze a little amount of glue to the piece of paper. Close your glue to keep it from drying.
3. After that, get a bit of glue using your pin and spread to one side of the coil. You may use your hands to hold big coils, but you should use tweezers for the small ones.

4. Get another coil and affix it to the glued part of one coil. Hold it together for at least 20 seconds or until the glue dries.

Practice gluing coils that are of the same width. Use your cuticle nipper to get rid of dried glue or to cut some uneven parts.

Gluing Coils on a Medium

One of the simplest quilled artworks you can make is card designs. You do not need to glue coils together for this. You can attach the coils directly to your card or any other medium. For this, you just need to put a small amount of glue at the bottom of your coils and glue it to paper. Try gluing coils of different shapes individually. After that, try to put coils together. To do this, follow the steps for gluing coils together first. Apply glue to the bottom of your adjoined coils and affix it to your paper.

Inserting Small Coils into Big Coils

One of the toughest steps in creating a quilled artwork is inserting small coils into big ones. To help you stay sane throughout the entire process, get your two tweezers and a handkerchief for your sweaty hands. Prepare your big coils and small coils as well. Below are the steps in inserting small coils:

1. Glue your big coils on a paper. Do not worry about forming figures or patterns for now. Just glue them.
2. Next, apply glue to the bottom and sides of your small coils.
3. After that, use your tweezers to insert the small coils to fill up the big coils' holes. Start inserting the slightly bigger ones first.
4. If there are some noticeable spaces left, make small coils that can fit into those. You may cut the coils you already need to form the small coils.

For the loose and open coils, you can place them beside the big coils. Put a paste to the bottom and sides of the coils that are going to be linked to the other coils. It is quite tedious to apply glue to the bottom of loose coils, especially if they have tails.

Here is an important reminder when applying glue: It is better to apply a little more than a little less. If you apply a too small amount, your coil may get detached easily. If you apply a little more, you can simply remove the excess dried glue with a cuticle nipper or a pin. A pin works best for the dried glue in the inner parts of the coil. If it is quite difficult to reach, though, it is better to leave the dried glue in peace.

CONCLUSION

Thank you for making it to the end of this quilling guide. In today's modern world, quilling is on the rise as more people are becoming interested in the art of quilling. Most of us can relate to quilling as it has a history, and it has been around for years. Many people are going back to the old days of quilling, and more people are showing interest in quilling. It is important that people know what quilling is, and how to get started quilling. By the time you are finished reading this quilling guide, you will be on your way to knowing the basics of quilling, and you will be well on your way to becoming a professional quiller.

Quilling is sometimes used for Christmas, greeting cards, scrapbooks, decorating wedding invitations, birth announcements, and boxes. Quilling can be found in numerous craftsmanship exhibitions in the United States and Europe, and it is an artistry that is presently rehearsed the world over.

Quilling is quite uncomplicated to learn compared to other crafts, and with many resources available today, it can be learned by almost anybody interested. I have given out the basic quilling techniques, and I suggest that you also visit YouTube and join many life classes to improve your skill. Other corresponding books focus on just projects you can develop by quilling. If you have kids, you can introduce this craft to them as it teaches fine motor skills and a great craft to improve hand-eye coordination.

Quilling lessons are quite a tedious job, requiring perseverance, diligence, precision, and patience. For newbies, learning can be very difficult. To master the techniques, you should begin with the slopes more easily. The primary concern is to assist in this business, and even the most unpredictable specialties should be possible rapidly and absent a lot of exertion.

I believe that with all these we have seen, you can start with the technique of quilling. The truth is that when you see works, on the one hand, you feel like running out to roll strips, and on the other hand, a huge fear comes up because we may feel that we won't be able to do anything like that. Surely not, but quilling offers us the possibility of developing our creativity and gives us the freedom to express ourselves with colors and shapes as we feel.

Do not hesitate to resort to looking out for resources about this craft. On the Internet, you will find patterns, designs, and all the step-by-step tutorials so that you do not look lost. On YouTube, you can find illustrative videos of how to do what you want with paper strips.

I hope this book was able to help you know how to roll and shape paper strips to form beautiful quilled artworks. Hopefully, it taught you how to get, take care of, and use your materials properly. I hope you can make lots of creative quilled artworks with the help of the patterns, projects, and ideas in this book.

The next step is to keep on applying and trying out new shapes, patterns, and projects. You can find a lot of free templates online. You can even design your own.

Thanks so much for purchasing, and I believe you've learned quite a lot. Don't hesitate to seek me if you have any questions to ask.

I wish you more of luck in your paper quilling craft and beyond.

Cheers!

CW01116635

מסורה

ArtScroll Mesorah Series®

Expositions on Jewish liturgy and thought

Rabbis Nosson Scherman / Meir Zlotowitz
General Editors

rosh hashanah

rosh
hashanah

ROSH HASHANAH — ITS SIGNIFICANCE, LAWS, AND PRAYERS / A PRESENTATION ANTHOLOGIZED FROM TALMUDIC AND TRADITIONAL SOURCES.

Published by

Mesorah Publications, ltd

ראש השנה

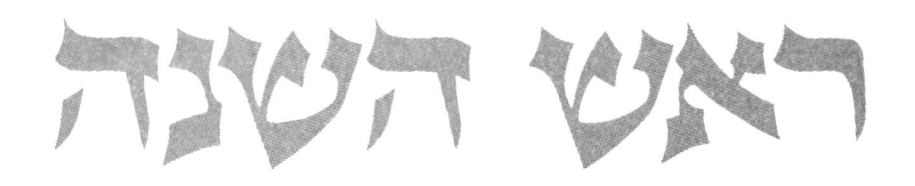

Overview by
Rabbi Nosson Scherman

Laws by
Rabbi Hersh Goldwurm

Insights and Prayers by
Rabbi Avie Gold

FIRST EDITION
First Impression ... July, 1983

Published and Distributed by
MESORAH PUBLICATIONS, Ltd.
Brooklyn, New York 11223

Distributed in Israel by
MESORAH MAFITZIM / J. GROSSMAN
Rechov Bayit Vegan 90/5
Jerusalem, Israel

Distributed in Europe by
J. LEHMANN HEBREW BOOKSELLERS
20 Cambridge Terrace
Gateshead / Tyne and Wear
England NE8 1RP

ARTSCROLL MESORAH SERIES®
"ROSH HASHANAH" / Its Significance, Laws, and Prayers
© Copyright 1983 by MESORAH PUBLICATIONS, Ltd.
1969 Coney Island Avenue / Brooklyn, N.Y. 11223 / (212) 339-1700

ALL RIGHTS RESERVED.

This text, the new translation, Overviews, instructions, prefatory and associated textual contents and introductions — including the typographic layout, cover artwork, and ornamental graphics— have been designed, edited and revised as to content form and style.

No part of this book may be reproduced **in any form** without **written** permission from the copyright holder, except by a reviewer who wishes to quote brief passages in connection with a review written for inclusion in magazines or newspapers.

THE RIGHTS OF THE COPYRIGHT HOLDER WILL BE STRICTLY ENFORCED.

ISBN
0-89906-195-8 (hard cover)
0-89906-196-6 (paperback)

סדר במסכרת
חברת ארטסקרול בע״מ

Typography by Compuscribe at ArtScroll Studios, Ltd.
1969 Coney Island Avenue / Brooklyn, N.Y. 11223 / (212) 339-1700

Printed in the United States of America by Moriah Offset

לזכר נשמת
Dedicated in Memory of
Our Father and Grandfather

Mr. Louis Yager

ר' יהודה אריה בן ר' אהרן הלוי ז"ל

נפטר כ"ט ניסן תשמ"ג — April 12, 1983

ואהבת את ה' אלקיך
שיהא שם שמים מתאהב על ידך (יומא פ"ו.)

If a Jew addresses others in a gentle and friendly manner, receives them with a happy countenance, does not offend them even if they insult him, honors even those who make light of him, acts honestly in his dealings, moreover, if he always acts towards his fellow men beyond the strict demands of the law, then this Jew truly sanctifies the Divine Name. Of him it is said (Isaiah 49:3), "You are my servant, Yisrael, through you I will be glorified."

ר' יהודה אריה בן ר' אהרן הלוי ז"ל — from his early years in Poland through the awesome Shoah to the building of a family in America — personified this ideal of Kiddush Hashem throughout his life.

Robert and Roselin Vegh,
David, Jeffrey and Shalom

May his memory and midos be an inspiration

ת.נ.צ.ב.ה.

ᴥ§ Preface

The Days of Awe begin with Rosh Hashanah, the festival that is such a delicate balance between the Jew's eternal confidence in God's mercy and his fear that the inadequacy of his deeds makes him fall far short of the minimum threshold of performance. The sound of the shofar, the taste of the apple dripping with honey, the emotion-packed services, the firm handshake and fervent wishes for a good and healthy year — these are Rosh Hashanah memories that remain warm and vivid all life long.

In this volume, Mesorah Publications is proud to pluck a selection of Rosh Hashanah highlights and offer them to the reader. The goal of the book's authors is to provide color, background, meaning, and authenticity to observances and aspects of this profound and meaningful festival. It is often said and just as often forgotten that people let the most important activities of their lives become habitual. This dismal part of human nature is particularly disturbing at times like Rosh Hashanah, when Jews are called upon to examine themselves, shed their failings, and elevate their awareness, aspiration, and performance.

A new year begins on the anniversary of the creation of man, not the creation of the physical world — that began five days earlier. So Rosh Hashanah is the time when man is judged to determine how well he lives up to the Divine expectations implicit in the declaration "Let us make man!" It is our profound hope that this book will help its readers explore and absorb the message of Rosh Hashanah — and even more, that it will help them personify the goals of the day.

The book contains four sections:

☐ The **Overview**, like the others in the ArtScroll Series, presents a hashkafah/philosophical perspective on major concepts of the day.

☐ The **Insights** offers a fascinating collection of rabbinic thought, homilies, and interpretation.

☐ The **Laws and Customs** offers a digest of the laws that apply to the individual, at home and in the synagogue.

☐ The **Prayers** concentrate on the Shofar service and the meal, and are complete with the original translation and anthologized commentary that are unique to the award-winning ArtScroll Series.

The Laws and Customs were written by RABBI HERSH GOLDWURM, whose breadth of scholarship has been displayed in many tractates of the ArtScroll Mishnah, the Book of Daniel, and the ArtScroll History Series. It is a rare privilege to be associated with him and bring his writings to the public.

The Insights and Prayer sections are by our colleague, RABBI AVIE GOLD. In his modest, unassuming way, he has become a major — indeed, an indispensable — part of the ArtScroll Series.

We are deeply grateful to ROBERT and ROSELIN VEGH who dedicated this book in memory of MR. LOUIS YAGER. That this warm, sensitive couple chose the vehicle of Torah to memorialize a loved one is the most eloquent testimony to their scale of values. May the accomplishments of this book be an eternal source of merit to the niftar.

RABBI YAAKOV MARCUS of the Young Israel of Staten Island is the mentor of hundreds of families, the Veghs among them, and a long time friend of the ArtScroll Series. We are proud of that friendship and greatly admire his mushrooming accomplishments for Torah life.

MR. AARON L. HEIMOWITZ has been a pillar of support and a source of imaginative leadership for a host of institutions. We are gratified beyond words that he has chosen so many ArtScroll publications as vehicles for Torah dissemination. He has been a friend, confidant, and counselor. We are deeply grateful and hope that we can remain worthy of his confidence.

Like scores of its predecessors in the ArtScroll Series, this volume is a tribute to the graphics artistry of REB SHEAH BRANDER. His skill is a jewel in the crown of Torah.

We are grateful to the entire ArtScroll staff, who cope with pressures, deadlines, and inconvenience with an aplomb that is surely born of their dedication to the ideals we are privileged to serve: MR. STEPHEN BLITZ, MR. YOSEF TIMINSKY, MRS. FAYGIE WEINBAUM, CHANEE FREIER, LEA FREIER, EDEL STREICHER and MRS. ESTHER FEIERSTEIN.

Rabbi Nosson Scherman / Rabbi Meir Zlotowitz
GENERAL EDITORS

Tammuz 5743 / June 1983

Table of Contents

܀§ An Overview / That You Make Me Your King

I. King or Ruler	15
II. The Judgment of Rosh Hashanah	20
III. God's Remembrance	28
IV. Ashes and Life	31
V. The Shofar	35

܀§ Background and Insights

Rosh Hashanah / The Day and the Month	43
Day of Shofar Blowing	49
Determining the Day	51
Significant Omens	55
The Shofar	58
To Confound Satan	62
Order of the Shofar Blasts	65
Its Composition and Its Shape	67
The Persons Obligated	68
Some Aspects of the Prayer Service	68
Talmudic Teachings	74

܀§ Observance / Laws and Customs

The Month of Elul	79
Selichos	80
Erev Rosh Hashanah	81
Night of Rosh Hashanah	82
Day of Rosh Hashanah	85
Sounding the Shofar	86
Second Day of Rosh Hashanah	88

܀§ Observance / Prayers and Ritual

Eruv Tavshilin	92
Kindling of Yom Tov Lights	92
LeShanah Tovah	94
Kiddush	96
Significant Omens	104
Sounding the Shofar	110
Kiddusha Rabba	124

৺ An Overview /
That You Make Me Your King

    King or Ruler
    The Judgment of Rosh Hashanah
    God's Remembrance
    Ashes and Life
    The Shofar

—Rabbi Nosson Scherman

An Overview/
That You Make Me Your King

אָמַר הקב"ה ... אִמְרוּ לְפָנַי בְּרֹאשׁ הַשָּׁנָה מַלְכִיּוֹת זִכְרוֹנוֹת וְשׁוֹפָרוֹת: מַלְכִיּוֹת כְּדֵי שֶׁתַּמְלִיכוּנִי עֲלֵיכֶם, זִכְרוֹנוֹת כְּדֵי שֶׁיַּעֲלֶה זִכְרוֹנְיכֶם לְפָנַי לְטוֹבָה. וּבַמֶּה? בַּשּׁוֹפָר.

The Holy One, Blessed is He, said ... on Rosh Hashanah recite before Me [verses that speak of God's] Sovereignty, Remembrance [of all events] and Shofar blasts: Sovereignty so that you should make Me your King; Remembrance so that your remembrance should rise up before Me for [your] benefit. And through what? — through the Shofar (Rosh Hashanah 16a, 34b).

I. King or Ruler*

God's sovereignty is the primary theme of Rosh Hashanah and the Ten Days of Judgment it inaugurates. The service of the day is filled with references to God as King and with prayers that His mastery be acknowledged by all human beings. The *shofar* service of the *Mussaf Amidah* begins with ten Scriptural verses speaking of God's 'Kingship' and, as the Talmud teaches, we recite these verses so that we should proclaim Him as our King. It would seem that the title King carries with it a dimension beyond that expressed even by the Name HASHEM, with all the infinite power and perfection that it implies. What is meant by God's Kingship and how is it enhanced by our noble proclamations? Moreover,

> The title king carries with it a dimension beyond that expressed even by the Name HASHEM, with all the infinite power and perfection that it implies.

---

* Sections I-III of the Overview are based on the writings of Rabbi Gedalyah Schorr, as found in *Ohr Gedalyahu*.

does the All-powerful, Omnipresent, Omniscient God need puny man to declare, 'Long live the King'?

Creation Begins

We can find a clue to the significance of God's Kingship in the Rabbinic tradition that the day we celebrate as Rosh Hashanah — the day we call the beginning of Creation — is not the anniversary of the Creation of heaven and earth; rather it is the day when Adam and Eve were created. [This and the Talmudic discussion of the date of Creation are cited on pages 43 and 74.] Thus, the first five days of Creation began on 25 Elul, five days before Rosh Hashanah. The first of Tishrei, Rosh Hashanah, was the *sixth* day of Creation, but because it was then that human life came into existence, we say of that day: זֶה הַיוֹם תְּחִלַּת מַעֲשֶׂיךָ, *This day was the beginning of Your handiwork (Rosh Hashanah Mussaf).*

Creation did not begin in a meaningful sense until God gathered particles of earth, shaped them, breathed a soul into them, and said, 'This shall be called Adam.'

Clearly Creation did not begin in a meaningful sense until God gathered particles of earth, shaped them, breathed a soul into them and said, *'This shall be called Adam' (Genesis 5:2).* Before that moment, everything was in place: the celestial worlds of the angels and other spiritual beings; the cosmos in which our solar system is but a speck; the uncountable number of living species; the vegetable world; towering mountains, fertile plains, fearsome deserts, powerful rivers and vast oceans. Everything was created earlier, but none of it was worthy of being called even the *beginning* of God's handiwork until man opened his eyes to see it, his mind to comprehend it, his heart to guide it.

Kings and Rabbis

The Hebrew word מוֹשֵׁל, *ruler, refers to a sovereign who reigns against the wishes of his subjects; a* מֶלֶךְ, *king, on the other hand, rules with the consent and recognition of his subjects.*

What was added to the universe with the birth of humanity? — the possibility for God to be proclaimed King. *Vilna Gaon* explains that there is a fundamental difference between the words מֶלֶךְ, *king,* and מוֹשֵׁל, *ruler.* The Hebrew word מוֹשֵׁל, *ruler,* refers to a sovereign who reigns against the wishes of his subjects; he is someone we would call a dictator or tyrant. A מֶלֶךְ, *king,* on the other hand, rules with the consent and recognition of his subjects. This aspect of kingship does not imply anarchy or even democracy. His rule may be strict, even harsh. He is not subject to recall or reelection, and his rule is dynastic. Nevertheless, he rules wisely and his power is buttressed by the citizenry's acknowledgment that he is worthy of his rank and that a rudderless and leaderless society cannot function. Consequently, a 'king' can degenerate into a 'ruler' if he becomes corrupted by the pomp and power of his position. Indeed, Scripture tells us of righteous kings whose heirs proved unworthy of their heritage, and history shows us presidents and leaders who became hated burdens upon their countries when power-lust and greed changed them into self-centered rulers who accumulated wealth and/or power like a magnet clutching metal filings. Conversely, a 'ruler' who imposed his authority can become a 'king' if he proves his dedication to the welfare of his country and wins the regard of his subjects. Human nature being what it is, this breed is rare, but not unknown.

A 'king' can degenerate into a 'ruler' if he becomes corrupted by the pomp and power of his position.

The difference between the concepts implied by the words מֶלֶךְ and מוֹשֵׁל is not symbolized by purple robes and a chest-full of medals on the one hand and a business suit or a cardigan on the other. The difference between 'kings' and 'rulers' does not even lie in whether or not there are constitutional restraints on their powers: David was a 'king' though his authority was as absolute as many a modern day despot. The difference is in the attitude of the people. Israel accepted David and submitted to him as the *anointed of the God of Jacob (II Samuel* 23:1), so he was their king rather than their ruler.

When the Sages say, 'The rabbis are called kings,' they refer to a nobility without scepters or armies, only with the authority of God's word.

When the Sages say רַבָּנָן אִיקְרִי מְלָכִים, *the rabbis are called kings (Gittin* 62a), they refer to a nobility without scepters or armies, only with the authority of God's word and the loyalty of a nation willing to accept it. The Talmud records that at the conclusion of a Yom Kippur day, multitudes of Jews escorted the *Kohen Gadol* [High Priest] from the Temple until they saw Shemaya and Avtalyon, the leading sages of the nation. Instinctively, and immediately, the people left the *Kohen Gadol* and walked with the sages. Shemaya and Avtalyon had no distinguished lineage — they were descendants of proselytes — but they bore the jewels and ermine of Torah knowledge. Such was Jewish royalty.

When Roman oppression and Jewish factionalism stripped the Sanhedrin of its authority, the court went into voluntary exile.

In stark contrast, when Roman oppression and Jewish factionalism stripped the Sanhedrin of its authority in the dismal period before the end of the Second Temple Era, the court went into voluntary exile forty years before the Temple was destroyed. Lacking the sovereignty that had once been inherent in their mastery of the Torah, the members of the Sanhedrin refused to maintain to facade of their noble office when they were prevented from carrying out its mission.

Man's Uniqueness

God lacked no power before the creation of man, but there was no one *voluntarily* to proclaim him King. The keyword is 'voluntarily.' The angels had been created before man, and God can create infinite numbers of them at will. But angels have no evil inclination. They are purely agents of God's will; the possibility of doubt or rebellion does not exist among them. Consequently they are no more capable of free-willed acceptance of God's sovereignty than is an army of robots. It is not that they are coerced to sing, 'Holy, Holy, Holy,' like a captive population reelecting its leader in an election supervised at riflepoint. Rather they are spiritual beings that see the goodness of truth so vividly that there is no room for doubt. To the angels, God is a Ruler, a Creator, a Master — but not a King.

The purpose of Creation was so that there would be a species that was capable of freely choosing to recognize and obey God.

The purpose of Creation was so that there would be a species that was capable of freely choosing to recognize and obey God. If this creature were so to choose, it would be worthy of Heavenly reward — and God wanted to confer His largesse on someone who had *earned* it by rising above temptation and choosing wisely. There had to be a being with the capacity to seek alternatives and be seduced, a being with physical drives and immoral temptations. That creature was man.

Everything in the universe — the sun, the moon and the stars, even the most sublime angels — had no

An Overview / That You Make Me Your King   [18]

value in the Divine scheme except as a prelude to the creation of man. As the Sages put it, כָּל הָעוֹלָם כֻּלּוֹ, לֹא נִבְרָא אֶלָּא לְצַוֵּת לָזֶה, *the entire universe was created only as companionship for [man] (Berachos 6b)*, because man could not survive alone without the entire infrastructure of the universe.

When was the world created? That depends what one considers its purpose.

When was the world created? That depends what one considers its purpose. If it is an immense parcel of real estate whirling about its sun among untold galaxies, then it came into existence on the first day of creation and was shaped and filled in the succeeding days. But if the world exists in order to proclaim God King, then it was created on the sixth day when Adam and Eve pointed and said, 'This is our King!' In this sense, Rosh Hashanah is *the beginning of Your handiwork*, and this is the only sense that really matters, for it is the reason for Creation.

This idea is expressed in the psalms chosen to be sung during the Temple service. The Sages explain why the various psalms were chosen to be sung by the Levites on the respective days of the week:

בַּשִּׁשִּׁי הָיוּ אוֹמְרִים: ,,ה' מָלָךְ גֵּאוּת לָבֵשׁ,'' עַל שֵׁם שֶׁגָּמַר מְלַאכְתּוֹ וּמָלַךְ עֲלֵיהֶם.

On the sixth day [of the week] they [i.e., the Levites] would recite: 'HASHEM will have reigned, He will have donned grandeur' (Psalms 93), because He completed His labors and reigned over them (Rosh Hashanah 31a).

God's power was no greater on day six than on day one — or in the infinity that existed before Creation. What happened on the sixth day was that man came into being.

Clearly, God's *power* was no greater on day six than on day one — or in the infinity that existed before Creation. What happened on the sixth day was that man came into being; man with his free will and choice; man who can be blinded by his own intelligence; man who can respond to the grandeur of the sun, the vastness of space, and the promptings of his desires; man who can accept God as his King or deny His existence; man who can even be fool enough to acknowledge that there is a God only on the condition that He is accommodating enough to be a mirror image of current fads in politics, morality, or progressive' religious thought.

Man's importance is not in his physical strength — any number of animals can outfight him

Man's importance is not in his physical strength — any number of animals can outfight him; even an ant is relatively stronger than man. Nor is man unique in his spiritual perception, which cannot compare to that of the angels. Man's greatness is in his power of choice. Because he can deny God, man's recognition of His sovereignty has value. That is why the sixth day was the climax of Creation, and why its anniversary is Rosh Hashanah.

II. The Judgment of Rosh Hashanah

Anniversary of Purpose

This explains why Rosh Hashanah is a day of judgment. Any intelligent plan must be evaluated from time to time to see how well it has succeeded, whether the individual actors have carried out the roles assigned them, and whether its goal is being realized. Since it was God's desire that man proclaim Him King, He chose the anniversary of the day when it all began to review the results of the previous year and determine how to proceed in the next. It is essential in our understanding of the Jewish calendar to know that each of the festivals offers an opportunity for us to renew the function, the spiritual gift and challenge, represented by that particular event.

Jewish religious observances are not mere memorials of ancient events

Jewish religious observances are not mere memorials of ancient events. To follow the modern secular vogue and shift the date of a festival to create a conveniently long week-end would not only be distasteful, sacrilegious, and halachically impermissible. It would miss the point entirely. Once the New Moon has been established, the festivals follow uncontrovertibly on their assigned dates. Emanations of holiness reach the world on the Sabbath, of forgiveness on *Yom Kippur*, of freedom on Passover, of Torah on *Shavuos*. Dates can be manipulated by legislatures and calendar manufacturers, but the heavenly cycle of Creation is unchanging and unchangeable. The distinct and particular forms of holiness represented by each sacred and festive day can be perceived and felt, depending, of course, on the level of greatness of the individual. Even those unable to reach the highest plateau can perform their observances knowing that they are significant cogs in a Divine scheme, that their good deeds matter, and that, although they may not consciously feel them, the unique emanations of each day make their way into the people's souls.

There are times of joy and times of reflection; times like *Shavuos* when the Jew can more easily absorb Torah and times like *Pesach* when he can free himself from the yoke of slavery to material masters — whether without or within himself. God has not created the universe to be a never-changing series of days distinguished only by climate, weather, and season.

Past and Future

One of those spiritual seasons is Rosh Hashanah: it is the season of God's Kingship, the time when God brings man to judgment on how well he has carried out the mission of proclaiming ה' מֶלֶךְ, *HASHEM is King*.

The judgment looks in two directions, at the past and at the future. During the past year, each man and woman had it in his ability to add in some degree to God's sovereignty. People with power and influence could have influenced multitudes, the humblest folk could have accomplished little more than improve themselves or make a slight change in the behavior or faith of a few close friends and relatives. No one is expected to do more than he can, but neither is he pardoned for doing less.

And what of the future? God's kingdom is infinite, but everyone has some share in it. The judgment of Rosh Hashanah determines what each individual can be expected to contribute. If he has something to offer, he is alive and vibrant. If not, though he may be living and breathing and exercising authority over many employees and associates, he has no life in terms of the Divine scheme.

This is the sense in which our Sages proclaimed their famous dictum

צַדִּיקִים בְּמִיתָתָם נִקְרְאוּ חַיִּים, רְשָׁעִים בְּחַיֵּיהֶם נִקְרְאוּ מֵתִים.

The righteous are considered alive even when they are dead; the wicked are considered dead even when they are alive (Berachos 18a,b).

Sometimes a person's role in God's Royal scheme requires him to cope with the tests of success, sometimes to accept adversity unbowed. Sometimes he will serve God in life, sometimes by giving up his life — even the righteous die. These and untold other possibilities are weighed in the scales of God's justice. But because the primary message — the goal — of the day is to proclaim God's sovereignty over all of creation, the fate of individuals is important primarily as part of the universal scheme. That is why the fervent prayers of Rosh Hashanah contain no mention of individual needs. It is certainly true that in their heart of hearts, people think of their sick parents, ambitious children, business problems, domestic hopes, and so on, but these smaller goals are subordinated to a greater end — that of bringing all the world to the acceptance of God's kingship. Everything else pales besides that, just as a mother praying for the survival of her badly injured child gives no thought to his bloodstained and torn trousers. Therefore, the major prayers of the day ask that all mankind fear God, that His Name be sanctified, and that Israel become privileged to lead all peoples to serve Him.

This explains a difficulty that troubles many commentators. There is a general rule that no personal requests may be made in the first three blessings of *Shemoneh Esrei*; if so, why do we insert in the first of those blessings, during the Ten Days of Repentance, a prayer that God remember us with life and inscribe us in the 'Book of Life'? And why on Rosh Hashanah do we insert a long series of requests in the third blessing of *Shemoneh Esrei*? The answer is that on Rosh Hashanah we do not pray for ourselves as individuals. We ask for life and for universal recognition of God's greatness only because these are

An Overview / That You Make Me Your King [22]

means toward the general goal of bringing about the unanimous proclamation that God is King.

Individual and Group

The decisions of Rosh Hashanah involve each person as an individual and as a part of the larger group. It may well be that as an isolated unit a particular human being may add little or nothing to God's glory — at least not enough to make him deserving of a reprieve in the Heavenly judgment. But man does not stand alone. He is part of a group, and his actions and his very presence affect others as well. Perhaps he is found wanting as a solitary human being, but his family or community may function better because he is there. He may be the corner merchant who eases the life of a great *tzaddik*, or he may be one of those whose company, smile, or helping hand helps lighten the burden of someone else's loneliness.

There are myriad ways in which someone can be part of a group that contributes to God's goals, because the combination of many efforts produces a desirable result. This too can be sufficient to earn someone abundant blessings in the Heavenly Tribunal of Rosh Hashanah.

As we say in the *Unesaneh Tokef* prayer, one of the emotional highlights of the *Rosh Hashanah* and *Yom Kippur Mussaf*, God judges all people individually as if they were sheep going single file through a narrow opening in the corral, and He also views them as a shepherd surveying His entire flock. These are two distinct facets of judgments: someone may earn beneficence for his private accomplishments or as a member of 'God's flock.'

Satellites of a Tzaddik

There is another aspect of the Jew's role that extends beyond himself. The world is the vehicle for the execution of God's will as it is expressed in the Torah. Since Israel was chosen to receive the Torah and to bear the sole responsibility for the fulfillment of its commandments, it is clear that the entire universe is elevated if Israel carries out its mission, and vice versa.

This is a difficult concept because we cannot perceive the spiritual dimensions of existence. We cannot touch, smell, or measure holiness; to the contrary, when a society's quality of life is enhanced we can always manage to explain why by pointing to such factors as favorable agricultural conditions, wise statecraft, technological progress and so on. It is hard enough to ascribe such longed for conditions as peace and prosperity to such seemingly extraneous factors as religious observance; it is even harder to give the credit to the deeds of one tiny nation or a small number of that nation's righteous people.

Perhaps we can find a helpful, though not perfect, analogy in the phenomenon of large organizations that revolve around the fortunes of a single star — an athlete, an entertainer, or an artist. If he performs well, then a surge of excitement enlivens everyone in the organization, from executive to janitor. The prosperity engendered by the star's success will benefit everyone, and the rave notices he wins will elevate everyone's morale. If only all mankind could realize that the true servant of God is its 'star' and that its success is intertwined with his ability to serve God as well as possible, it too would thrill at the achievements of the lone Jew who masters the Torah's knowledge and succeeds in sublimating his body to become an equal partner of his soul. Just as every member of the great performer's entourage basks in the glow of his success, so would every member of a *tzaddik's* society feel ennobled and take pride in his achievements.

The Sages teach that Aaron, the first Jewish High Priest, raised the level of his brethren through his fellowship with them. When he encounterered a less than virtuous person, Aaron would befriend him. Later, when Aaron's 'friend' wished to sin, he would reproach himself, saying, 'If so great a man as Aaron considers me his friend, how can I remain the same sinner I used to be? How will I be able to face Aaron the next time I see him?' *(Avos D'R' Nosson* 12:3). Just as the company of an Aaron changed people, so the spiritual ascent of Israel, whether as a nation or

An Overview / That You Make Me Your King [24]

of its individuals, enhances the stature of all humanity.

Man Makes the Difference

But the effects of Jewish virtue go far beyond this, for it has spiritual reverberations that are beyond man's ability to fathom. The Torah teaches that in Noah's time, all humanity except for Noah and his family became morally and ethically corrupt. It began with private denial of God in the form of covert idolatry that later became public. It spread to thievery and violence of all sorts, reaching a level of decadence that, in a way, was best expressed by cunningly taking even insignificant amounts of property in such ways that the money could not be recovered in the courts. Sexual debauchery and perversion became the norm.

The ill effects were not limited to man: וַיַּרְא אֱלֹהִים אֶת הָאָרֶץ וְהִנֵּה נִשְׁחָתָה, *And God saw the earth and behold it was corrupted (Genesis 6:12)*. Most commentators understand this as a reference to the quite foreseeable and understandable ill effects of moral corruption on the *inhabitants* of the earth, although the lifeless land was not affected by their behavior. As *Sforno* puts it, the immorality of adults corrupts children and violent robbery corrupts the social order.

The immorality of adults corrupts children and violent robbery corrupts the social order.

Zohar, however, interprets the verse literally: the very earth was corrupted, that is, man constitutes the essence of the earth so that his corruption infects the earth itself. The earth which failed to please God by raising up for Him righteous children was ashamed, like a faithless wife who hides her face from her husband, as it is written elsewhere *(Isaiah 24:5): and the earth was defiled under its inhabitants ...* Here, too, '*the earth* was corrupt.' Why? As the Torah continues *because all flesh had corrupted their way.* The Midrash comments that human immorality brought as its by-product sexual perversion among animals and even a degree of 'lewdness' in the vegetable kingdom, in the sense that wheat would be sown and the earth would yield weeds. [See ArtScroll *Bereishis* 6:1-12 for a full commentary on this Midrash.]

Human immorality brought as its by-product sexual perversion among animals and even a degree of 'lewdness' in the vegetable kingdom.

The Torah seldom tells us so vividly how man's failure has cosmic repercussions. Like many chapters in the Torah, this one teaches a phenomenon that is a permanent part of creation: the law that human actions affect everything in the universe, a law as binding as any law of physics. Having been told of its existence, we are expected to apply it to all future experiences.

> *The law that human actions affect everything in the universe is as binding as any law of physics.*

Ramban (Leviticus 26:11) explains, not surprisingly, that such an outcome is miraculous. We would expect the results of spiritual labors to be spiritual in nature. A sinner would become corrupted and gradually lose his ability to comprehend sanctity and spiritual beauty. Conversely, one who dedicates himself to spiritual pursuits would sublimate his nature and become increasingly receptive to spiritual stimuli. This is entirely in line with our constant experience. One who studies the Talmud intensely becomes a Talmudic scholar. One who is preoccupied with playing the violin becomes as accomplished a violinist as his talent permits. The Torah has no need, therefore, to list the spiritual rewards of one who carries out God's will; it is only natural that he be rewarded with the splendors of the World to Come and the ineffable pleasures of closeness to God. The Torah need not tell of these rewards for spiritual activity. Instead it tells us what is not obvious:

> *The Torah has no need, therefore, to list the spiritual rewards of one who carries out God's will; instead it tells us what is not obvious.*

> *If you go according to My statutes and observe My commandments and perform them — I shall provide your rains in their proper time and the earth will give its produce ... I shall provide peace in the land and you shall go to bed and none shall cause fear ... the sword shall not traverse your land. You shall pursue your enemies, and they shall fall before you to the sword ... (Leviticus 26:3-12).*

On Rosh Hashanah

In the same mysterious way, Israel's obedience to the Torah is the dynamo that drives all creation to the zenith for which it was intended. Just as the Torah assures us that the study hall full of scholars well past midnight and the generosity of a community that refuses to overlook the plight of its needy contribute to tranquillity and prosperity in *Eretz Yisrael*, so, too, the deeds of Israel are instrumental in benefiting the rest of the world.

This is what we are called upon to do when we proclaim God's sovereignty on Rosh Hashanah. The fullest expression of kingship is the complete obedience of all subjects to the will of the monarch. A king's greatest measure of majesty comes when his subjects freely, intelligently, and enthusiastically *choose* to serve him. God's Kingship, too, should flow from mankind's free-willed decision that it best fulfills its own destiny by submitting to God's will. To achieve this end, God put man at the center of the universe and tied the fortunes of every creature to his choice. The sins of Noah's generation corrupted even the animals; the virtues of Noah saved enough of them to begin anew. Each Rosh Hashanah, Israel can pull together and mesh all the cogs of creation into a unified machine in the service of its king. Or, if only a part of the nation is capable of declaring from its heart, 'Hashem is King,' whatever fractions of the universe correspond to the respective missions of those enlightened Jews will thrive. And if there is only *one* righteous Jew ready to stand alone against a hostile world and declare in word and deed that man is not a prince but a servant — well, the Patriarch Abraham was all alone, and he became the father of the nation that received the Torah.

The theme of Israel's expanding influence on ever wider circles of people is symbolized in the progression of prayers in the Sanctification section of the Rosh Hashanah *Shemoneh Esrei*: 'May Your Name be sanctified upon Israel your nation; ... place Your dread, HASHEM, our God, upon Your entire handiwork; ... may all [creatures] form a single band to do Your will; ... May You reign ... speedily, all alone, over all Your handiwork ...'

The context indicates that first Israel must succeed in acknowledging God as *its* king. That will be the starting point, to be followed by growing recognition of Him by others until all creatures unite to serve Him.

III. God's Remembrance

Conglomeration of Events

Human memory takes many forms. We remember some experiences vividly and others hardly at all. Often we block out unpleasant events, while sometimes they remain to haunt us and to give us nightmares. Often our lifelong perception of a person or place is colored by the indelible memory of a particularly powerful experience. If someone proves his loyalty in very trying circumstances, it would take heaven and earth to convince us that he is capable of betrayal. People go through life with memories of 'the old neighborhood' or 'the old country' that often seem out of touch with reality, but some old memories are stronger than present reality. It is no idle figure of speech when people say their memory is playing tricks on them. It does, more than we are capable of knowing and admitting.

People go through life with memories of 'the old neighborhood' or 'the old country' that often seem out of touch with reality.

God's memory is of another kind entirely. It is perfect in terms of accuracy, of course, but that is not all. God is not limited by time. To Him, past, present, and future are not imperative considerations. This means that when God sees a person, He sees the total conglomeration of everything the subject has ever done — and even the potential, drives, ambitions, and values that will shape his future actions.

The *total* person is shaped by the sum of all his experiences, regardless of the thousands of diary pages that would be needed to record them. One might liken this to an accountant's reckoning of a client's net worth. The fact that the transactions contributing to the aggregate were of many varieties and occurred over many years is not important when one is concerned with the 'bottom line.' The ten-year-old profit or loss might just as well have happened this morning, because it is still a part of the subject's net worth. Similarly, God views a person as a total

The ten-year-old profit or loss might just as well have happened this morning, because it is still a part of the subject's net worth.

entity. Everything he has ever done has shaped him, so God sees the total man as if he were living his whole life at that instant.

The same holds true for what he will do in the future. The human being who is capable of performing heroic deeds ten years hence is not the same as someone else who will never rise above his present state of distinction or mediocrity.

Seeing it All One of life's truly interesting experiences is to look through a class yearbook thirty or forty years after the graduation. The fresh, smiling faces, lists of awards and honors, and semi-serious predictions the graduates make about one another will give us some idea about what to expect of each student as he battles his way through the 'real' world. Then, let us compare the dream world of the yearbook with the reality of the intervening decades. Many of the expectations are exceeded, many are disappointed, few are matched. Even the 'experts' are rarely right. True, lives are affected by events and circumstances beyond the control of the participants, but that explains only part of the discrepancy between fact and expectation. Some people surmount circumstances and display personality and character traits that professors and teachers never detected. When God looked at those graduates, however, He saw their complete lifetimes, including all the potential that mortal eyes would not detect for years to come.

Let us compare the dream world of the yearbook with the reality of the intervening decades. Even the 'experts' are rarely right.

Not only that, He sees the qualities that each person will impart to future generations. So it was that Lot deserved to be saved from the destruction of Sodom because Ruth, Naamah, and the Davidic dynasty were destined to descend from him *(Bava Kamma* 38b, *Bereishis Rabbah* 50). Lot would not have been worthy of such a great miracle had he not had within him the seeds of a great future. The Talmud and commentators often explain God's forbearance in the face of intolerable sins on the basis of future events. A nation or family may seem to be irredeemably evil and we question their claim to existence in the scheme of Divine justice. The answer

The Talmud and commentators often explain God's forbearance in the face of intolerable sins on the basis of future events.

[29] **ROSH HASHANAH** / Its Significance, Laws, and Prayers

may never be known to us, but often our Sages explain it in terms of past merit or future events.

The extraordinary success of a nation may sometimes be understood in retrospect as God's way of preparing for the future. Or the extraordinary success of a nation may sometimes be understood in retrospect as God's way of preparing for the future. Some contemporary Jewish thinkers have conjectured that the United States was showered with unprecedented Heavenly bounty because the Jewish communities of Europe, Israel, and elsewhere from World War I to the present would be so dependent on help from overseas. Thanks to the American tradition of fair play and generosity, the nation's prosperity has helped people and countries overseas to an extent undreamed of in international relations. The American Jewish community has responded to a much greater extent to the deprivations of its brethren. This is not to excuse the failure of the American government and so many individuals to rise to the challenge of the Holocaust; that is a tragedy that God's judgment will measure and remedy, but we cannot fail to be grateful that Divine Providence prepared America as a refuge and helping hand during generations when it was needed desperately.

Sadly, the sins of the future cast a pall on the present as well. Sadly, the sins of the future cast a pall on the present as well. After defeating the marauding kings who overran Canaan and kidnapped his nephew Lot, Abraham pursued them until the future territory of Dan *(Genesis 14:14)*. There he was forced to halt because his strength was sapped when he foresaw that one day — centuries in the future — his descendants would erect an idol there *(Sanhedrin 96a)*. Did Abraham become weaker militarily because of transgressions that would not occur until hundreds of years later? Yes, because his successes were built on his merit in God's eyes, and his stature was diminished by the sins that would become part of his heritage.

Rosh Hashanah Calculation The verses of Remembrance in our Rosh Hashanah service express this concept, because they tell how God remembers everything that ever was: זֵכֶר כָּל הַיְצוּר לְפָנֶיךָ בָּא, *the remembrance of every creature comes before You.* As we have seen, in God's remembrance all events are simultaneous because their effects still exist. Thus, God judges our total lives, and He judges all the world in its totality.

God remembers and calculates more than actual deeds. In the Rosh Hashanah prayer of *Zichronos*, Remembrances, we speak also of God's knowledge of our thoughts and plans. We conclude the prayer with a plea that God remember עֲקֵדַת יִצְחָק [the *Akeidah*], *the Binding of Isaac* on the altar, by his father Abraham. The *Akeidah* theme is primary in our Rosh Hashanah prayers and it is the Torah reading of the second day. A reading of the Talmudic sources makes clear that God thinks of Isaac as if he had actually been sacrificed and his remains burned on the altar. As we shall explain in detail below, in the Divine scheme a person's absolute willingness to undergo an ordeal for God's sake is equivalent to his having done it. Since inner resolve is so vital in the eyes of Heavenly justice, the *Akeidah* is an eloquent challenge to every Jew to strengthen his resolve to crown God and serve him to the maximum extent humanly possible. Abraham and Isaac did it, and we cling to their merit to this day.

> *The Akeidah theme is primary in our Rosh Hashanah prayers and it is the Torah reading of the second day.*

IV. Ashes and Life*

וְזָכַרְתִּי אֶת בְּרִיתִי יַעֲקוֹב וְאַף אֶת בְּרִיתִי יִצְחָק וְאַף אֶת בְּרִיתִי אַבְרָהָם אֶזְכֹּר וְהָאָרֶץ אֶזְכֹּר. וְלָמָה לֹא נֶאֱמַר זְכִירָה בְּיִצְחָק? אֶלָּא אֶפְרוֹ שֶׁל יִצְחָק נִרְאֶה לְפָנַי צָבוּר וּמוּנָח עַל הַמִּזְבֵּחַ.

And I shall remember My covenant with Jacob, and also My covenant with Isaac, and also My covenant with Abraham and I shall remember the Land (Lev. 26:42). Why does it not specify 'remembrance' in connection with Isaac? Because [God says], 'The ashes of Isaac are visible before Me, gathered together, lying atop the Altar' (Toras Kohanim).

---

* This section is taken from the Overview to *Vayeira, Bereishis/Genesis,* Vol. II.

Everpresent Ashes

Isaac's *ashes* lay before God. The Talmud teaches that when the Sages had to determine where to place the Altar when they were building the Second Temple, the site was indicated by the ashes of Isaac, which lay there *(Zevachim* 62a). But how can the Sages speak of Isaac's ashes when Isaac was never slaughtered and never burned? There can be no *ashes* of an Isaac who never became an actual sacrifice, yet the halachically specified placement of the Altar was determined by the 'ashes of Isaac.' A strange paradox! Isaac lived, but his ashes mark the place of his sacrifice.

Abraham prayed that the sacrifice of the ram be considered as if Isaac had remained upon the altar *(Bereishis Rabbah* 56:14). The plea was not rhetorical. Both Abraham and Isaac came with all their hearts to complete the offering. There was no hesitation, no attempt to seek a reprieve. In every sense except the physical, Abraham *did* slaughter Isaac and burn his remains as an offering. As the commentators note, the purpose of every offering is to demonstrate in a tangible manner that a Jew dedicates all his faculties and resources to God and His service. Animals were created to serve man. They do so by providing labor, food, hides. When used as an offering, they serve him by being the vehicle to show the owner's complete deference to God. Theoretically, it would seem that the best way for someone to prove his devotion would be to sacrifice himself or whomever he loves the most, but a person has no right to demonstrate this awareness by sacrificing himself or another human, because every human being comes to earth with a mission and the potential to fulfill it. Were he to become or to offer a human sacrifice, he would *fail* to serve God, because genuine service can be done only by utilizing every available means to carry out His will, not by ending a life that can still make contributions. It is not for us to say when God's gift of life should be returned to him.

When an offering is brought with proper intentions, it is truly a substitute for its owner, as if he were declaring that he would mount the Altar himself if that were God's will. Forbidden to do so himself, he offers his living possession to represent his own dedication. No human being had ever done this as Isaac did. He truly became Abraham's offering. He mounted the altar and the knife was at his throat. It took a Divine command to gain his release. When he descended the altar, he was no less an offering than he was when he ascended it. When God commanded Abraham to substitute a ram for Isaac, it became his substitute in a more tangible way than even the purest ordinary sacrifice because Isaac had actually been on the altar. The ashes of the ram were on the altar not only to symbolize Isaac's intentions but in place of the *real* Isaac. Thus the ashes of the ram *were* Isaac's ashes in a very real sense *(Michtav MeEliyahu).*

Those Who See

We may see this on a deeper level by exploring the phenomenon of light. To the prisoner in a dungeon, light is the bare bulb hanging over his head, to the draftsman it is the lamp illuminating his work, to the vacationer it is the brilliant sun, to the scholar it is the wisdom of Torah. Which is the *true* light? We may well say that the answer is relative, or that the true light is the sun, and the others are either approximations or allegories. But that is not true. The spiritual person knows that the only true light is Torah — God's wisdom. All the others are material representations, just as a child's mathematics beads and blocks are but symbols of real numbers and more mature concepts. We refer to this idea as the 'different worlds': the spiritual world and physical world (see *Overview* to *Bereishis).* In a higher world, Isaac surely can be seen as ashes. His willingness to become a sacrifice never left God's cognizance. The spiritual effect of his deed remained imprinted on the top of Mount Moriah.

People attuned to spirituality see things that others do not see. When Abraham and Isaac approached the mountain, they knew without being told that they had found *the* place where God had directed them to climb to a spiritual zenith. How did they know? They saw a beautiful mountain covered by a pillar of smoke — the *Shechinah* [God's Presence]. Their two attendants looked at the same mountain and saw only a desert *(Pirkei dR' Eliezer)*. Were all four in the same place? Geographically, yes. But in the truest sense they were worlds apart. Abraham and Isaac were at the Mountain of God, but Ishmael and Eliezer were in the Canaanite desert. From that perspective, the participation of Abraham and Isaac at the *Akeidah* created *his* ashes, for he was truly sacrificed in every world but the material one. Only in the material world did the ram take his place.

Were all four in the same place? Geographically, yes. But in the truest sense they were world's apart.

The Men of the Great Assembly had spiritual sensors that could see Isaac's 'ashes' on Mount Moriah. It was as clear to them where the Altar had to be as it was to Abraham and Isaac that they had arrived at the mountain. And if we don't see those ashes — well, neither did Ishmael and Eliezer see more than a desert.

To Remember Dedication

As we noted above, God speaks of 'remembering' His covenant with Abraham and Jacob, but the term *remember* is not associated with Isaac. The word remember implies thinking about something that happened in the past, but is no longer present. One must remember what happened last week, last year; he need not remember what he sees at that very moment. God promised to *remember* the covenants of Abraham and Jacob, which had been sealed many centuries before, but there was no need to bring the covenant of Isaac back from the past. Isaac's ashes are before Him *always*, a living reminder of Isaac's covenant — because an ascent to such spiritual heights as the *Akeidah* never dies.

Isaac's ashes are before Him always, a living reminder of Isaac's covenant.

Therefore, too, Isaac's life after the *Akeidah* was of a different order than any other. He was a living sacrifice, sanctified and spiritual. For that reason he was forbidden to leave the Holy Land. Before him, Abraham had gone to Egypt and after him Jacob would go to Charan and Egypt. But when famine struck in Isaac's time, God ordered him not to leave *Eretz Yisrael;* he was a holy offering — and offerings may not leave the holy soil.

Among his ten reasons for the blowing of the *shofar* on Rosh Hashanah, *R' Saadiah Gaon,* writes that the *shofar* is made of a Ram's horn as a reminder of the *Akeidah* (see *Insights,* p. 61). Meaningfully, this aspect of the *shofar* commandment calls our attention to the magnitude of commitment and sincerity in spiritual advancement. R' Saadiah urges that just as Isaac was ready to sacrifice himself to sanctify God's Name, so should we be ready to give ourselves up for God's sake. R' Saadiah uses the term מְסִירַת נֶפֶשׁ, which is usually understood to mean the literal giving up of one's life. Indeed, it often *does* mean that, but not always. Certainly R' Saadiah means more than literal death. Giving up one's 'life' for God's sake means also to remain alive while subjugating one's personal preferences and desires to God's will. The word נֶפֶשׁ means not only soul, but *will* (as in *Genesis* 23:8). A person's 'soul' is the sum total of his desires, hopes, goals — and the true dedication to God is to say, 'God — I am Yours, my will is Yours, even my life is Yours.' R' Yosef Yoizel Horowitz of Novardok captured this idea pithily when he said, 'It is easier to die as a Jew than to go on living as a Jew.' Thus, when we remember Isaac's ordeal and triumph, we remember also that our own goal is to identify completely with God's will, that He is our King and we are His servants.

Giving up one's 'life' for God's sake means also to remain alive while subjugating one's personal preferences and desires to God's will.

V. The Shofar*

Of Sins and Stains

In describing the framework of the *Mussaf* service, the Talmud states that the verses of *shofar* have the effect of bringing before God the remembrance of the Jewish people for their benefit *(Rosh Hashanah* 16a, 34b). It is sobering, even frightening, to contemplate the requirement that we accept the absolute

---

* This section of the Overview is based on *Resisei Laylah,* by R' Tzaddik HaKohen, chs. 8, 50.

sovereignty of God and to realize that His total and timeless recall brings before Him all our deeds with vividness and immediacy. If this is what God's judgment entails, then who can survive it? How can the Jew temper the inevitable verdict that he has fallen far too short?

> *How can the Jew temper the inevitable verdict that he has fallen far too short?*

Scripture likens sin to a stain on a garment. Depending on the extent and depth of a stain, it can be rubbed off, soaked until it loosens, or vigorously scrubbed until the garment becomes clean. Similarly, depending on the extent of the spiritual 'stain,' repentance of various degrees and sorts can cleanse the Jew of his sin. Sometimes a stain becomes so set in the material that it goes through and through. Scripture *(Jeremiah* 2:22) speaks of this as נִכְתָּם, *an indelible stain.* This symbolizes a person who has become so mired in sin that it has become so much a part of him that he has forgotten even the language of repentance *(Rosh Hashanah* 18a).

> *Scripture speaks of an indelible stain that symbolizes a person who has become so mired in sin that it has become a part of him.*

We meet people to whom the basic concepts of Judaism are so foreign that they cannot identify with them to any degree; or people who, though they are generally observant, often have a family of sins, so to speak, that have become so ingrained that the transgressors no longer consider them even to be wrong. A common example is the sin of לָשׁוֹן הָרָע, *gossip* and *slander* [literally *evil speech*]. Gossip has always been a serious problem, but in modern times it has become so prevalent that witty innuendo is a mark of distinction, and character assassination is a constitutionally protected right that is regarded as an essential safeguard to a free society. In polite society, only gross abuses of the right of free speech are even frowned upon. Can an honest person help but feel embarrassed when he pronounces the empty words of confession that he has sinned by bearing tales, when he knows that to him it is not a sin but a virtue and the key to popularity — and certainly the best protection against boredom?

Such sins, whether they are many or few, are indelible stains that do not lend themselves to ordinary cleansing. Lacking proper recognition of their

Lacking proper recognition of their seriousness, we may even find it impossible to discuss them as true shortcomings. seriousness, we may even find it impossible to discuss them as true shortcomings; if we did, we would be at least *part* of the way toward improvement, because 'lip-service' *does* mean something. We often speak piously of the 'right thing to do' even though we do not practice what we preach. If we *preach* a virtue, then at least we acknowledge it as a standard of behavior, but if an improper attitude or practice is so habitual, so ingrained, that we can barely survive without it, we lack even the words to begin propelling ourselves out of the muck.

Wordless Hope For such people, too, there is hope. The Sages assure us that at essence the Jewish soul remains pure, and that even the most indifferent — and antagonistic — Jew can be reached. In the most awful periods of Jewish suffering, there have been Jews who responded to persecution and slaughter by stepping forward and joining hands with their brethren and acknowledging their Jewishness, instead of running away to anonymity and safety.

True, they lack the words to express their inner stirrings, but sometimes there is the wordless groan of an aching heart that longs to return to its spiritual origins.

Sometimes there is the wordless groan of an aching heart that longs to return to its spiritual origins. This is the sound of the shofar.

This is the sound of the *shofar*.

It is a primitive instrument, barely capable of modulating its tones or shifting notes. Can anyone play a symphony or even a song on a *shofar*? No, but its piercing sound symbolizes the inarticulate cry of the indelibly stained soul that longs to be cleansed but does not know how. It is a cry that only God's ear can comprehend and translate into the plea רְצוֹנֵנוּ לַעֲשׂוֹת רְצוֹנֶךָ, *it is our desire to perform Your desire* — but we do not know how. The constant poundings of the Evil Inclination, of society, culture, habit, surroundings have numbed us to Your touch, have deafened us to Your message. As *Rambam* puts it, perhaps we do not know the intellectual reason for the commandment of *shofar*, but it has a symbolism that we *can* comprehend. It is like a bugle blowing a reveille for a slumbering soul, saying, 'Wake up, you sleepers, from your sleep, and you slumberers, rouse yourselves from your slumber and return to God.'

Refuge and Belonging

Where does a Jew *really* belong in his heart of hearts? This is symbolized beautifully in a mishnah that discusses the laws of ritual purity and contamination, which are not the same for fish and land animals. The mishnah *(Keilim* 17:13) discusses the case of an amphibian called כֶּלֶב הַיָּם, *walrus* [lit. *sea dog*]. Since it inhabits both sea and land, does it have the laws of a fish or of an animal? The mishnah rules that since in time of great danger it flees from the water and takes refuge on land, it is a land animal. Similarly, even an estranged Jew remains Jewish, so long as he returns 'home' when threatened. The *shofar* is his homing signal, the cry from the Jewish heart that says, 'I belong here,' and the echoing cry from God's heart that says, 'Yes, the door is open.' That is why there was an intense *shofar* sound when the Torah was given and that is why the *shofar* will sound again to herald the final redemption. It is the instrument that says that when no words are possible, no words are needed.

> The shofar is his homing signal, the cry from the Jewish heart that says, 'I belong here,' and the echoing cry from God's heart that says, 'Yes, the door is open.'

That is what the Sages mean when they say that we recite verses of God's Kingship to acknowledge his total sovereignty and verses of remembrance to bring our remembrance before God — but בַּמֶּה, *with what?* The very question 'with what?' implies that we lack the righteous deeds that would entitle us to place our case before God. Indeed, often we do. Often, all the words we can say are meaningless, are empty, because we are so impregnated with outward stains.

But then the *shofar* sounds. It blares out, proclaiming that even the fastest stains can be removed because there is an area of the heart that they have not penetrated.

That is why, as the Talmud says *(Rosh Hashanah* 16b), the sound of the *shofar* confuses the accusing Satan. The *Great Shofar* of Messianic times is really an accumulation of all the heart-cries of all the generations of the Jews that Satan thought were his.

Many a Rosh Hashanah may have gone by without even a murmur of inner recognition from who knows how many slumbering hearts. But there are always hearts that open a bit, that hear and respond to a greater or lesser degree. Every Rosh Hashanah there are more. Some day there will be enough — so many that the inner sounds of, 'It is our desire to perform Your desire,' will blast through the insulation of habit and apathy.

Satan knows that. He knows that then, all the little sounds of individual Jewish longing will accumulate to form the awesome sound of the *Shofar of Messiah*.

וְהָיָה בַּיוֹם הַהוּא יִתָּקַע בְּשׁוֹפָר גָּדוֹל וּבָאוּ הָאֹבְדִים בְּאֶרֶץ אַשּׁוּר וְהַנִּדָּחִים בְּאֶרֶץ מִצְרָיִם, וְהִשְׁתַּחֲווּ לַה' בְּהַר הַקֹּדֶשׁ בִּירוּשָׁלָיִם.

And it will be on that day that a great shofar will be blown and they will come: those who were lost in the land of Assyria and the outcasts in the land of Egypt; and they will prostrate themselves before HASHEM in the holy mountain in Jerusalem (Isaiah 27:13).

Rabbi Nosson Scherman

ט"ז תמוז תשמ"ג

✢ Background and Insights:

The Day and the Month
Day of Shofar Blowing
Determining the Day
Significant Omens
The Shofar
To Confound Satan
Order of the Shofar Blasts
Its Composition and Its Shape
The Persons Obligated
Some Aspects of the Prayer Service
Talmudic Teachings

—Rabbi Avie Gold

❦ Background and Insights:

Rosh Hashanah / The Day and the Month

When was the World Created?

❦ According to R' Eliezer, the universe was created in Tishrei while according to R' Yehoshua it was created in Nissan *(Rosh Hashanah* 10b-12a). This disagreement extends to many other events as well and each of these Sages offers numerous proofs from Scripture to support his view (see p. 74). The Talmud's conclusion is in favor of R' Yehoshua's view that the world was created in Nissan and it is for this reason that halachic astronomical calculations assume that the heavenly bodies came into existence in Nissan (ibid. 12a; *Rashi* s.v. ולתקופה כר״י).

If so — the Talmud asks (ibid. 27a) — how can our Rosh Hashanah prayers include the declaration: זֶה הַיּוֹם תְּחִלַּת מַעֲשֶׂיךָ, *This day was the beginning of your work,* a statement that seems to say clearly that creation took place in Tishrei rather than Nissan? In explaining that passage, *Rabbeinu Tam* sets down two fundamental theses regarding the question of Nissan versus Tishrei:

1. The Halachah indeed assumes that the Creation took place in Nissan. The reference to Rosh Hashanah as the 'beginning of [God's] work' refers to His work of judging the world and deciding upon its continuing survival. This, too, is a 'creation' to a significant degree.

2. In the case of disputes between the Sages of the Talmud, the rule is often stated that אֵלּוּ וָאֵלּוּ דִּבְרֵי אֱלֹקִים חַיִּים, *these and those are the words of the Living God,* meaning that every opinion of people of such lofty stature is solidly based on well-founded principles of Torah exegesis and principle. Thus, even though the opinions seem mutually contradictory, each one is true in its own way. Consequently, *Rabbeinu Tam* reasons, the world was created *both* in Nissan and Tishrei; it remains for us to understand how this is possible in practical terms. *Rabbeinu Tam* submits that in Tishrei God formulated His intention, as it were, to create the universe, but He did not put His plan into effect until Nissan. [See Overview for a further elaboration of this concept.]

The Day Denotes the Purpose

◆§ *Pirkei d'R' Eliezer* teaches that the 'day of creation' — whether the first of Nissan or the first of Tishrei — was actually the day when Adam and Eve were created. The six days of creation began five days earlier with the creation of heaven and earth. This demonstrates that God's purpose in creating the universe was not to bring the vastness of the galaxies into existence, but to create the one intelligent being among all the species who has the ability to fulfill the commandments.

The Seventh Month

◆§ The Torah refers to Tishrei as the *seventh* month even though it is the beginning of a new calendar year. In his commentary to *Exodus* 12:2, *Ramban* elaborates that the verse, *This month* [Nissan] *shall be unto you the head of the months; it is the first for you of the months of the year,* is a commandment to refer to the months by number and to begin that count from Nissan, as a constant reminder of the great miracle of the Exodus which occurred in Nissan. Therefore, Jews did not designate special names for the months.

In accordance with the commandment constantly to remember the Exodus, the Torah refers to Tishrei as the *seventh month,* even though it marks the beginning of the new year. This is similar to the Jewish practice of referring to days of the week by number — e.g., Sunday is called *'the first day to the Sabbath'* — in fulfillment of the commandment constantly to remember the Sabbath.

The Months Get Names

◆§ The currently used Hebrew names of the months are of foreign origin. As the Talmud *(Yer. Rosh Hashanah* 1:2) explains, 'The names of the months came up with [Israel] from Babylon,' meaning that the names of our months are not Hebrew but Babylonian, and that they are, in effect, a vestige of the Babylonian exile. Why did the Jewish people suddenly discard their reminder of the Exodus and adopt a set of heathen names?

Ramban cites Jeremiah (16:14,15): *And it will no longer be said* [in an oath] *'By the life of HASHEM Who brought up the Children of Israel from the land of the North* [Babylon].' In other words, the miracle of the return from Babylonian Exile will supplant the miracle of the Exodus to some degree (but not completely) in the memory of the Jewish people. This, says *Ramban,* is the reason for the Talmud's statement that the names of the months are of Babylonian origin. After the return from Babylon it was incumbent upon the Jews to remember the miracle of that deliverance by referring to the months by their Babylonian names.

□ Harav Yaakov Kaminetzky finds in this practice of calling the months by foreign names an attempt by the Sages to preserve Jewish allegiance to the goal of the Messianic era. Since some of these months, such as Tammuz, were the names of idols *(Yechezkel* 8:14), it seems doubly strange that the Sages authorized their use as part of Jewish observance. In this case, too, the Sages wished to establish constant reminders for a principle of Jewish belief. There was a danger that the returnees from Babylon, having built the Second Temple, might have deluded themselves into thinking that the period of גְּאוּלָה שְׁלֵמָה, *complete redemption,* had arrived. To dispel this notion, the Sages of the period decreed that the Babylonian names of months — including the blatantly pagan ones — should be used. This would emphasize to the Jews that even though they were back in *Eretz Yisrael,* Israel was not yet considered to be free from its exile status.

Tishrei

◈§ According to *Pesikta Rabbasi* the term תִּשְׁרֵי, *Tishrei,*[1] is derived from the Aramaic root שרי, which can mean *to loosen, to untie* or *to dissolve.* Thus the name of the month implies the theme of its first day, Rosh Hashanah, 'Dissolve and pardon our iniquities.'

☐ The word תִּשְׁרֵי also means *you shall begin* (see *Targum Onkelos* to *Deuteronomy* 16:9) and implies the beginning of the year.

The Month of Eisanim

◈§ In the First Book of Kings, Tishrei is entitled יֶרַח הָאֵתָנִים, *the month of the Eisanim* (8:2). The Talmud explains the aptness of the title 'Month of the *Eisanim.*' An *eisan* is a mighty one, and the month of Tishrei is mighty in the sense that it is replete with *mitzvos:* Rosh Hashanah, shofar, Yom Kippur, Succos, *lulav* and *esrog,* Hoshanos *(Rosh Hashanah* 11a; see p. 75).

☐ An alternative opinion in the Talmud (ibid.) defines the *Eisanim* as those of powerful faith, i.e., the Patriarchs — Abraham and Jacob — who (according to this view) were born in Tishrei. *Maharsha* comments that they are called powerful because the world exists in their merit.

☐ *Targum* has a third interpretation of this phrase. The verse reads: בְּיֶרַח הָאֵתָנִים ... הוּא הַחֹדֶשׁ הַשְּׁבִיעִי, *in the month of the Eisanim ... that is the seventh month.* In *Targum's* paraphrase this is rendered: 'In the month that the ancient ones called the first month ... but now it is called the seventh month.'

---

1. The vocalization תִּשְׁרֵי, *Tishrei,* throughout this book is based on the commonly heard pronunciation of the name. In punctuated editions of *Targum* the word appears as תִּשְׁרִי, *Tishri.*

A Kabbalistic Interpretation of the Name Tishrei

◆§ The Hebrew alphabet contains twenty-two letters beginning with א and ending with ת. Each letter has, in addition to its pronunciation, a *gematria*, or numeric value. The letters א through ט represent one to nine respectively; י through צ stand for the tens from ten to ninety; and ק through ת equal 100 through 400. Stated in other words, the *gematrias* of the letters follow an ascending order. As such this alphabet, called the *alef-beis*, represents man's ideal aspirations to continuously reach for higher, more exalted, spiritual levels. These aspirations take concrete form in the counting of the Omer, the days leading from the Exodus and release from slavery to the Receiving of the Torah at Mount Sinai. Beginning in the month of Nissan, we count the days and the fifty spiritual levels they symbolize. For this reason Nissan is called the month of אָבִיב, *Aviv*. The word אָבִיב begins with the letters א and ב, indicating an ascending order — from the depths of slavery to the heights of spirituality *(Zohar)*.

□ In the timeless realms before Creation, however, the alphabet existed in a sequence opposite to that of the *alef-beis*. Then, the letters began with ת and proceeded in the order ת,ש,ר,ק. The last letter in the alphabet was א. This is the order in which the letters appeared on the Crown of God *(Sefer Yetzirah)*. Called *tash-rak*, this alphabet descends in *gematria* from 400 down to one. As such it represents God's plan of Creation. His glory fills the heavens, yet He reaches down to man to assist him in his quest for spiritual elevation. The letters of the name תִּשְׁרֵי, *Tishrei,* begin with the *tash-rak* order. It is, so to speak, God's month; the month in which His Kingship is proclaimed throughout the world. It is the month in which He is especially receptive to prayers of repentance, and reaches down to aid the penitent *(Zohar)*.

□ Following this line of reasoning, Zohar explains why בִּרְכַּת הַחֹדֶשׁ, the *Blessing of the New Moon*, which precedes the recitation of *Mussaf* on the Sabbath before a new month, is omitted on the Sabbath before Rosh Hashanah. All months except Tishrei are represented by the אָבִיב-*Aviv* concept of Nissan, which calls upon man to elevate himself step by step up the ladder of spiritual accomplishment. This is implied by the commandment introducing Nissan to the Jewish people: הַחֹדֶשׁ הַזֶּה לָכֶם, *This month shall be for you* (Exodus 12:2), suggesting that the months represent man's potential. That is why we introduce each month with a prayer for success and achievement. Before Tishrei, however, we omit the prayer, because Tishrei symbolizes God's flow of beneficence to man.

The Name Rosh Hashanah in Scripture and Mishnah

◆§ Strangely, the only time the name Rosh Hashanah appears in Scripture it refers not to the New Year's Day but to Yom Kippur — *In the twenty-fifth year of our exile, on Rosh Hashanah on the tenth of the month, in the fourteenth year after the city had fallen ... (Ezekiel 40:1).* Although the day is identified as 'Rosh Hashanah,' which falls on the first day of Tishrei, the verse gives the date as 'the tenth of the month.' The Talmud *(Arachin* 12a) explains that the year described by Ezekiel was *Yovel,* the Jubilee Year (see *Leviticus* 25:8ff). Because many of the special laws related to *Yovel,* such as the freeing of the slaves and the returning of fields to their original owners, take effect on Yom Kippur of that year (ibid. v. 10), that day — Yom Kippur, the tenth of Tishrei — can, in a sense, be considered the beginning of the *Yovel* year.

☐ In Mishnaic usage the term Rosh Hashanah is applied both to the first day of Tishrei, and, by extension, to any day which, for one purpose or another, marks the start of a new annual cycle. To cite a modern-day example, we find that the calendar year begins on the first day of January, while the beginning of the fiscal year may be on the first of July or October, and the school year begins in September. Such arbitrary designations of "new years" nevertheless may serve as a helpful analogy for understanding the Mishnah's use of the term Rosh Hashanah for certain functions other than that of the calendar year.

☐ The Mishnah *(Rosh Hashanah* 1:1) reads:
There are four Rosh Hashanahs:

1. On the first of Nissan is the Rosh Hashanah for [reckoning the reigns of Jewish] kings and for [establishing the order of] the pilgrimage festivals. [No matter when a Jewish king acceded to the throne, we say that a "new year" of his reign begins on the first of Nissan. This was of pivotal importance in pre-Mishnaic times when legal documents were dated according to the year of a king's reign. In the case of festivals, Pesach, which occurs in Nissan, is regarded as the first festival of the year.]

2. On the first of Elul is the Rosh Hashanah for the tithe of animals — R' Elazar and R' Shimon say: [It is] on the first of Tishrei. [The Torah commands that animals, like crops, are to be tithed. However, only animals born in the same mating season. This season ends on either the first of Elul or the first of Tishrei.]

3. The first of Tishrei is the Rosh Hashanah for [reckoning] the years [in the reign of non-Jewish kings], the Sabbatical years, the Jubilee years, the planting [of trees] and the vegetables. [The first three cases are obvious. The need for a "new year" with reference to tree planting and vegetables is as follows: The Torah ordains special restrictions on fruit during a tree's first three years (עָרְלָה) and special requirements on the fourth year crop (נֶטַע רְבָעִי). The anniversary date for the first three years is

the first of Tishrei. Regarding vegetable tithes, all crops picked before the first of Tishrei belong to the previous year and may not be intermingled with crops picked afterwards.]

4. On the first day of Shevat is the Rosh Hashanah for the trees, according to the words of Beis Shammai; Beis Hillel say: On the fifteenth thereof. [The laws of the fourth year of new trees begin in Shevat. Similarly, regarding tithes, the first or fifteenth of Shevat is the dividing line between one year's crop and the next.] (A full explanation of this passage can be found in the *Yad Avraham* commentary appearing in the ArtScroll edition of the Mishnah.)

□ The Mishnah's application of the term Rosh Hashanah to each of these days is more than a mere lexical convenience. R' Mordechai ben Hillel in his halachic compendium *Mordechai (Rosh Hashanah §701)* states that a community that wishes to decree a series of public fasts should not schedule a fast that would coincide with any of these days. He cites two reasons for this decision: (a) The Mishnah refers to each of these days as Rosh Hashanah and fasting is forbidden on Rosh Hashanah; and (b) all the days are combined into one grouping [with the words "there are four Rosh Hashanahs"], and just as fasting is prohibited on most of them [because they fall on the first of their respective months, on Rosh Chodesh], so is fasting prohibited on the fourth one [the fifteenth of Shevat].

An Incomplete Beginning

◈§ In describing *Eretz Yisrael* to the generation of the Wilderness, Moses called it, *'A land that HASHEM, your God, seeks out; the eyes of HASHEM, your God, are perpetually upon it,* מֵרֵא[שִׁ]ית הַשָּׁנָה וְעַד אַחֲרִית שָׁנָה, *from the beginning of the year until [the] year's end* (Deuteronomy 11:12). The word מֵרֵא[שִׁ]ית, *from the beginning* [related to רֹאשׁ, *head* or *start*], appears with an incomplete spelling, מֵרֵשִׁית. *Baal HaTurim* sees this deficient spelling as an allusion to the month of Tishrei, for the letters of מֵרֵשִׁית may be rearranged to read מִתִּשְׁרֵי, *from Tishrei*, i.e., the beginning of the year is Tishrei.

□ A different explanation is given in the Talmud *(Rosh Hashanah* 16b): R' Yitzchak says: A year that is רָשׁ, *poor*, at its onset, will be wealthy at its conclusion — as Scripture states: "מֵרֵא[שִׁ]ית הַשָּׁנָה, *from the beginning of the year"* but spells the word [deficiently, as if it read] מֵרֵשִׁית, *from poverty;* "וְעַד אַחֲרִית, *until [its] end"* implies that it will have a pleasant end. *Rashi* and *Tosafos* explain that the poverty at the year's outset refers to Israel's sincere prayers and repentance, in which the people sincerely declare that they are sorely lacking in merit (see *Proverbs* 18:23). As a result, God shows them compassion.

The Day of the Week: Lo Adu Rosh

לֹא אַדּ״וּ רֹאשׁ, *Lo adu Rosh,* is the concise halachic statement for the principle underlying the formulation of the calendar, namely, Rosh Hashanah may never fall on Sunday, Wednesday or Friday. [The word אַדּ״וּ is a combination of the letters א=1; ד=4; and ו=6, which stand for the first, fourth, and sixth days of the week.] This principle is stated by *Rambam* (*Hil. Kiddush HaChodesh* 7:1) who explains it with a series of astronomical considerations (ibid. 7:7). *Ravad* finds a much simpler explanation based on certain Talmudic discussions (*Rosh Hashanah* 20a; *Yer. Succah* 4:1). Stated tersely, *Ravad* teaches that if Rosh Hashanah were to fall on Sunday, then Hoshana Rabbah (on the twenty-first of Tishrei) would be on a Sabbath, and we would not be able to fulfill the ceremony of *Hoshanos.* If Rosh Hashanah were on Wednesday, then Yom Kippur (the tenth of Tishrei) would fall on Friday, and if Rosh Hashanah were on Friday, Yom Kippur would be on Sunday. Both cases would entail the observance of two consecutive days — the Sabbath and Yom Kippur — on which it would be forbidden to cook fresh food and to bury the dead. The year is therefore fixed in such a manner that such occurrences are avoided.

Day of Shofar Blowing

A Day and a Remembrance

The Torah refers to Rosh Hashanah in two ways: as זִכְרוֹן תְּרוּעָה, *a remembrance of [shofar] blowing* (Leviticus 23:24), and as יוֹם תְּרוּעָה, *a day of [shofar] blowing* (Numbers 29:1). The term "remembrance of blowing" implies that the *shofar* is only *remembered* but not actually blown. This is a Scriptural support for the Rabbinic prohibition against blowing the *shofar* on Rosh Hashanah that falls on the Sabbath [see *Rosh Hashanah* 29b]. Consequently, a weekday Rosh Hashanah is described in *Kiddush* and the *Amidah* as יוֹם תְּרוּעָה, *a day of blowing,* since the *shofar* is sounded on weekdays. On the Sabbath, however, Rosh Hashanah is זִכְרוֹן תְּרוּעָה, *a remembrance of blowing,* because the *shofar* is recalled in the day's prayers, but not sounded.

□ The contexts of the verses can be taken as a further Scriptural allusion to the Rabbinic injunction against blowing the *shofar* on the Sabbath. The verse in *Leviticus* reads: שַׁבָּתוֹן זִכְרוֹן תְּרוּעָה, *a rest day a remembrance of [shofar] blowing.* The term *rest day* [שַׁבָּתוֹן] may also mean the Sabbath. In *Numbers,* where the word 'remembrance' is omitted, the word שַׁבָּתוֹן, *rest day,* is also absent. Thus the respective verses carry an allusion to the Rabbinic decree *(Tosefes Berachah).*

God and Israel Praise Each other

◆§ In Scripture, God refers to the first day of the year as a day of *shofar* blowing, yet Israel calls it Rosh Hashanah. Why the discrepancy? Should the day not have one name used universally? The same questions arise regarding the holiday of Pesach. In Scripture the festival is called 'the festival of *matzos*,' while we refer to it as Pesach, or Passover.

R' Levi Yitzchak of Berditchev finds in this fact a parallel to the difference between the *tefillin* which we wear and to the figurative *tefillin* that the Holy One, Blessed is He, wears. The Talmud *(Berachos 6a)* tells us that God and Israel praise each other; for in our *tefillin* are found the words 'Hear, O Israel, HASHEM is our God, HASHEM is one,' while in the *tefillin* of the Master of the universe is written, 'And who is like Your people Israel, one nation on the earth?' It is the same with the name for Pesach. The Holy One, Blessed is He, praises Israel by referring to Pesach as 'the festival of *matzos*,' because Israel was so eager to carry out the command of God that there was not even time for its dough to ferment. Israel, for its part, refers to the festival by a name that implies praise of the Holy One, Blessed is He, for He 'passed over' *(pasach)* the houses of the Children of Israel in Egypt — thus the name Pesach.

A similar explanation may be given regarding Rosh Hashanah. In praise of the Jewish people, God calls the day by the name of the *mitzvah* so fervently performed by them. The Jews, on the other hand, call the day *Rosh Hashanah,* which does not mean 'the New Year,' but 'the beginning of the year.' This name implies that there is a 'beginning' — that Creation began at a particular point in time. Humanity did not evolve from some earlier form of life during some hazily defined period untold millennia ago. If that were the case, no day could be referred to as הַיּוֹם הֲרַת עוֹלָם, *Today is the conception of the world;* nor could we say in our prayers, זֶה הַיּוֹם תְּחִלַּת מַעֲשֶׂיךָ, *This day was the beginning of Your works.* By calling the day Rosh Hashanah, the Jew testifies that God is the Creator and we crown Him as our King on the anniversary of the Creation (R' Yaakov Zicherman in *Nachalas Yaakov*).

Determining the Day[1]

◈§ Rosh Hashanah contains an area which is unique to it, and which is irrelevant to any other festival — the problem of fixing the day on which the *Yom Tov* occurs. Unlike the other festivals which fall later in their respective months, Rosh Hashanah falls on the first day of the month, Rosh Chodesh; and during the period when the proclamation of Rosh Chodesh was dependent upon the testimony of witnesses who had observed the first appearance of the moon, the dating of the first day of each new month always remained in doubt pending events in the Sanhedrin, or *beis din,* in Jerusalem. A lunar month can be no less than twenty-nine days and no more than thirty days. Thus the thirtieth day since the previous Rosh Chodesh might or might not be proclaimed the first day of the new month, depending on three possibilities: (a) witnesses would come and Rosh Chodesh would be proclaimed based on their testimony; (b) no witnesses would come; or (c) would-be witnesses might have their evidence rejected for one reason or another. In the latter two cases, Rosh Chodesh would be proclaimed for the following day, the thirty-first day since the previous Rosh Chodesh.

This means of determining the date, however, gave rise to serious problems with regard to Rosh Hashanah. Since no one knew at the beginning of the day whether or not it would become Rosh Hashanah, how was it to be observed until the *beis din* convened? As, we shall see, this problem became the reason why Rosh Hashanah could be observed for two days even in *Eretz Yisrael,* as it is today.

The laws governing the fixing of the day of Rosh Hashanah (with regard to whether Rosh Hashanah is to be observed for one day or for two) have been affected by the four epochs through which our calendar has passed.

The First Era: Eyewitness Reports

◈§ The Mishnah teaches: *Originally, they accepted testimony regarding the new moon all day (Rosh Hashanah 4:4).* This mishnah characterizes the first of the four eras of Rosh Hashanah observance. During this era — within the bounds of the city of Jerusalem — Rosh Hashanah was observed sometimes for one day, and sometimes for two.

☐ Every year, with the onset of the evening which began the thirtieth of Elul, the people would desist from labor and behave as though the

---

1. The section entitled 'Determining the Day' is for the most part condensed from a much broader discussion of the topic appearing under the title 'Rosh Hashanah in Four Eras,' in *The Festivals in Halachah,* vol. I, pp. 67-84. Other ArtScroll publications that discuss the make-up of the calendar are: Mishnah, *Rosh Hashanah; Bircas HaChammah;* and *The Festivals in Halachah,* vol. II, pp. 321-323.

sanctity of the festival had begun — because there was a strong possibility that on the next day witnesses would testify regarding the new moon, and be accepted. Were that to occur, the preceding evening would turn out to have been, indeed, Rosh Hashanah, the first of Tishrei. In that case Rosh Hashanah would have been observed for one day and the next day would be the second of Tishrei, an ordinary weekday. If, on the other hand, the thirtieth day passed without the appearance of witnesses, then the thirty-first day would be Rosh Hashanah. In the latter case, the residents of Jerusalem would have observed two days of Rosh Hashanah: the thirtieth, because of doubt up to the very end of the day as to whether witnesses would come; and the thirty-first, because it was the true Rosh Hashanah.

☐ In addition to these two possibilities (that the witnesses might or might not come on the thirtieth day), there was a third possibility — that the *beis din* would not wait for witnesses at all. If, by calculation, they knew that the new moon could not possibly appear on the thirtieth day, then they would declare the month of Elul 'full,' i.e., to contain thirty days [a thirty-day month is called מָלֵא, *full;* a twenty-nine day month is called חָסֵר, *deficient*]. If so, even if witnesses were to testify that they had seen the new moon, the *beis din* would not accept them, since they were certainly false [or mistaken] witnesses. In this case, it seems reasonable to assume that the festival was observed on the thirty-first day only. In such a case, as *Rambam* states, the *beis din* did not even sit on the thirtieth day *(Hil. Kiddush HaChodesh* 1:6). Why, then, observe the thirtieth day as *Yom Tov* for no reason? *(R' Shlomo Yosef Zevin).*

We find, then, that in the time when the month was sanctified by means of eye-witnesses, there were three possibilities for fixing the day of Rosh Hashanah in the city of Jerusalem: the thirtieth day after Rosh Chodesh Elul only, the thirty-first day only, or both days together.

☐ But how, in this same era, did all Israel outside Jerusalem observe the festival? For the Talmud tells us that all who were beyond Jerusalem's boundary could not have known which day the *beis din* had declared as Rosh Hashanah. How did places distant from Jerusalem observe Rosh Hashanah? *Rashi* and *Tosafos* disagree about the answer to this question.

Rashi maintains that those outside Jerusalem observed only one day of Rosh Hashanah, and always on the thirtieth — for in the overwhelming majority of years Elul has twenty-nine days. Not knowing when Rosh Chodesh had been proclaimed, they must go according to the majority of years.

But *Tosafos* writes that they observed two days of Rosh Hashanah because of doubt as to which day the *beis din* had declared Rosh Hashanah.

☐ Our most ancient record of a two-day Rosh Hashanah during this early era is found in Scripture (Nechemiah 8:2,13): *And Ezra the Kohen brought the Torah before the congregation, both men and women, and all who had understanding to hear, on [day] one of the seventh month* [i.e., on Rosh Hashanah] ... *and on the second day* [of Rosh Hashanah (Rashi)] *were gathered the chiefs of the fathers' houses* ...

The Second Era: Early in the Day

◆§ The Mishnah *(Rosh Hashanah 4:4)* tells us that, due to confusion over whether or not a day would be proclaimed Rosh Hashanah, a mishap occurred in the course of the Temple service. At the time of the afternoon offering, the Levites did not know whether to sing the weekday psalm or the Rosh Hashanah psalm. According to some, they sang no psalm at all; according to others they sang the weekday psalm, which turned out to be wrong because witnesses appeared afterwards *(Rosh Hashanah 30b)*. The Sages responded to this mishap by decreeing that they would no longer accept witnesses who did not come before *Minchah* (i.e., the time of the daily afternoon offering). In that case, Rosh Hashanah would definitely be two days; the first day actually unsanctified, but treated as holy until *Minchah* because of doubt, and the second day holy by proclamation of the *beis din* as the true Rosh Hashanah. This solved the problem of a disrupted Temple service. However, this decree gave rise to a fresh problem. If witnesses had not arrived before *Minchah,* it was known that the day would not be sanctified. This produced two contradictions. First, work had been forbidden nearly all day and now at the end of the day it became permitted. Second, if witnesses finally appeared after *Minchah,* it would mean that even though the day would normally have been proclaimed Rosh Hashanah in accordance with the Torah, nevertheless it was not so proclaimed. Hence, the Sages added a second part to their decree — even though the day was definitely not *Yom Tov* in terms of the Temple service, it was to be treated as holy in terms of the prohibition of work.

Rashi explains the reason for the decree: Lest people come to treat [the day] lightly the following year, and perform labor the whole day, thinking, 'Last year we needlessly treated the day as if it were holy, and from *Minchah* on we went back to treating it as a weekday.'

The Third Era: Rabban Yochanan ben Zakkai

◆§ When the *Beis HaMikdash* was destroyed, the decree we have been discussing lost its relevance; the Temple service having ceased, there was no longer, alas, any danger of mishap. Thus begins a third era with regard to fixing the day of Rosh Hashanah. The Mishnah states: *After the Beis HaMikdash was destroyed, Rabban Yochanan ben Zakkai decreed that testimony about the new moon would be accepted all day long (Rosh Hashanah 4:4).* At first glance, it would seem that this simply restored the original situation, reestablishing the arrangement that had been in force before the decree. In fact, however, there are differences between the earliest period and the era instituted by Rabban Yochanan ben Zakkai. These differences are discussed in *Beitzah* (5b), where the question is asked: Does not Rabban Yochanan ben Zakkai admit that if the witnesses come after *Minchah*, that day is treated as holy, and the next day, holy?

□ According to *Rashi*, this passage means that the decree of Rabban Yochanan ben Zakkai affected only the determination of the calendar. If the witnesses came after *Minchah*, their testimony was heard and the *beis din* proclaimed the first day of *Yom Tov*, i.e., the thirtieth, as the first day of Tishrei. But, all the same, the previous decree was not abolished and the nation continued to observe a second day of Rosh Hashanah.

□ *Tosafos* disagrees with *Rashi*, asserting that Rabban Yochanan ben Zakkai nullified the first decree entirely, thus restoring the law that there would be only one day of Rosh Hashanah even when the witnesses came after *Minchah*.

The Fourth Era: A Fixed Calendar

∞§ The period beginning with Rabban Yochanan ben Zakkai extended from the Destruction until the time when Rosh Chodesh ceased to be determined on the basis of testimony. At that point the fourth era begins, the era of a calendar predetermined by calculation. Realizing that the rigors and persecutions of exile would soon make it impossible to constitute courts qualified to proclaim Rosh Chodesh, R' Hillel HaNasi, in the year 4119 (359 C.E.) formulated and proclaimed the present calendar.

There were those who argued, quite logically, that since the present calendar is mathematically calculated thus leaving no doubt as to when Rosh Hashanah begins, only one day should be observed in *Eretz Yisrael*. To this, Rav Hai Gaon replied in a responsum to R' Nissim Gaon: 'The law is that they should do as their predecessors did [that is, observe two days of Rosh Hashanah as in the third era], and not change the tradition of their forefathers.' This explains why Jews in *Eretz Yisrael* observe other festivals for only one day, but Rosh Hashanah for two. In both cases the Sages ordained that Jews should maintain the custom of their ancestors, as a reminder of the time when we were able to establish the calendar in the Scripturally ordained manner: through the sighting of the moon by witnesses and the proclamation by the *beis din*.

The very fact that our current, astronomically-based calendar includes provision for doubts, even those that existed only in times when the months were in doubt until the court acted, is eloquent testimony to our faith in the coming of the Messiah and the return of the *beis din* to the position of primacy in Jewish life.

Significant Omens

◈§ We anoint kings only at a spring, in order that their sovereignty be extended [like the stream that flows from the spring] *(Horayos* 12a; *Kerisus* 5b). Thus begins the Talmudic discussion regarding the efficacy of symbolic acts. After mentioning a series of other omens, the Talmud continues:

> Abaye taught: Now that you have said that an omen is significant, each person should habituate himself to eat [some versions read: to see] at the beginning of the year, קָרָא, *gourds* [e.g., cucumbers, pumpkins], רוּבְּיָא, *fenugreek* [an herb indigenous to western Asia], כָּרָתֵי, *leeks,* סִילְקָא, *beets,* and תַּמְרֵי, *dates.*

Rashi (Kerisus 6a) explains the symbolism of these five species in two ways. Some of them grow and ripen early and rapidly [and thus represent increased merits] while others are sweet-tasting [and signify a sweet year].

☐ A different rationale for eating these particular foods is evident from *R' Hai Gaon's* custom of reciting a short prayer which contained a wordplay on the name of the respective foods. When eating leeks [כָּרָתֵי], R' Hai would say, 'יִכָּרְתוּ שׂוֹנְאֵינוּ, *May our enemies be decimated';* over the fenugreek [רוּבְּיָא] he would recite, 'יְהִי רָצוֹן שֶׁיִּרְבּוּ זְכִיּוֹתֵינוּ, *May it be [Your] will that our merits increase' (Mordechai, Yoma,* as understood by *Beis Yosef,* 583).

Abudraham and *Kol Bo* carry the prayer one step further and begin each short prayer with the formula: יְהִי רָצוֹן מִלְּפָנֶיךָ ה' אֱלֹהֵינוּ וֵאלֹהֵי אֲבוֹתֵינוּ, *May it be Your will, HASHEM, our God and the God of our ancestors* ... This latter form is accepted by the *Halachah (Mishnah Berurah* 583:2). The symbolism of each food and the prayer associated with it are discussed below in the section on Prayers (pp. 104-109).

☐ R' Alexander Zusslein HaKohen, author of the halachic compendium *Agudah,* objects to R' Hai Gaon's view. He reasons that every food could then be eaten as a symbol. If the food or the connotation of its name is good, it will be taken to represent Israel; if bad, then it will be taken as an allusion to Israel's enemies.

☐ *Siddur Sha'arei Shamayim* replies to the *Agudah's* objection. Certainly only good, sweet foods should be eaten. Then, if the name or nature of the food indicates beneficence, it should be applied — verbally, with the recital of a prayer — to Israel; if the food alludes to evil, the prayers should relate the symbolism to Israel's enemies.

☐ *Pri Megadim* interprets the term 'our enemies' not as an allusion to the external enmity of the nations. Rather it refers to the מְקַטְרִיגִים,

accusing angels, created by the commission of sins. This is based upon the Mishnah's teaching *(Avos* 4:11): One who performs a *mitzvah* acquires for himself a *sanegor* (an angel who speaks in his behalf); and one who commits a sin acquires for himself a *kategor* (accusing angel).

Rich Foods and Sweet Beverages

◆§ *Maharil* finds an allusion to the custom of eating sweet delicacies on Rosh Hashanah in each of the three divisions of Scripture: *Torah* (Pentateuch), *Neviim* (Prophets) and *Kesuvim* (Writings or Hagiographa).

Torah: In *Exodus* 15:24 it is recorded that when the Jews arrived at Marah and complained about the bitterness of the water they found there, Moses was commanded to hurl a stick into the waters. וַיִּמְתְּקוּ הַמָּיִם, *Then the waters became sweet,* שָׁם שָׂם לוֹ חֹק וּמִשְׁפָּט, *there He gave him* [i.e., Israel] *a decree and a judgment*. This latter phrase refers to Rosh Hashanah, the Day of Judgment. [Additionally, it refers to the *mitzvah* of *shofar* about which it is written *(Psalms* 81:5): כִּי חֹק לְיִשְׂרָאֵל הוּא, *because it is a decree for Israel,* מִשְׁפָּט לֵאלֹהֵי יַעֲקֹב, *a judgment for the God of Jacob*.] Thus on Rosh Hashanah the nation was furnished with sweet drinks.

Neviim: David and his troops sent a message to Naval the Carmelite, *'We have come here for Yom Tov, please give us of that which is to be found in your hand' (I Samuel* 25:8). According to *Rashi*, the day was the eve of Rosh Hashanah and David lacked food for the festive meals for his retinue. Although Naval refused David's request and heaped insult upon him, Naval's wife Abigail supplied ample provisions, including wine, raisins, and pressed figs (ibid. v. 18). Thus sweet fruits were served at David's Rosh Hashanah meals.

Kesuvim: The same Psalm (81) that tells us to *blow the shofar at the New Moon, at the time appointed for our festive day* (v. 4), concludes with the words: *He would feed him from the cream of the wheat, and from a rock I would sate you with honey* (v. 17).

Furthermore, it was on Rosh Hashanah that *Nechemiah* (8:10) dismissed the Jews gathered in Jerusalem: *'Go, eat rich foods, drink sweet beverages, and send portions to whoever has nothing prepared for himself, for holy is this day to our Lord.'*

Additional Omens

◆§ R' Z'vid taught: The first day of Rosh Hashanah — if it is hot, the entire year will be hot; if it is cold, the entire year will be cold. What is the [halachic] implication [of this statement]? — The prayer of the *Kohen Gadol (Bava Basra* 147a).

Rashbam explains that, upon leaving the Holy of Holies during the Yom Kippur service, the *Kohen Gadol* [High Priest] would recite a brief prayer for the Jewish people, which included the request, 'If the year be hot, may it [also] be rainy [to counteract the heat]' (see *Yoma* 5:1 and 53b). Since, as R' Z'vid teaches, the year's weather is indicated by that of Rosh Hashanah, the *Kohen Gadol* would adapt the wording of his prayer to reflect the conditions prevailing on Rosh Hashanah.

□ A homiletical interpretation is given to this Talmudic passage by *Nachalas Shimon*. It is a reference to man's manner of serving his Creator. If his personal prayers and performance of *mitzvos* on the first day of the year are carried out with deep fervor and a burning desire to fulfill the will of the Holy One, Blessed is He, then the Heavenly Tribunal will assist him by adding sanctity to his sanctity and thus enable him to maintain and expand his fiery Divine service throughout the year. But if on Rosh Hashanah his prayers and *mitzvos* are done perfunctorily, as if only out of habit and without commitment, then the entire year he will find himself in the same situation. The rule is that the rest of the body follows the head — and so it is with the days of the year.

A Sleepy Beginning

◆§ There is an acceptable custom not to sleep during the daytime of Rosh Hashanah. This custom is based on a dictum of the Jerusalem Talmud (not found in extant editions): הַאי מַאן דְּדָמִיךְ בְּרֵישׁ שַׁתָּא דָּמִיךְ מַזְלֵיהּ, *If one sleeps at the beginning of the year, his mazal [guardian angel or, destiny] will sleep (Darkei Moshe).*

□ Another reason for the custom of not sleeping on Rosh Hashanah is quoted by *R' Yehoshua ibn Shuiv* in the name of *Ramban*. The *shofar* is a clarion call to judgment: 'Awake, O sleepers, from your slumber!' (see p. 59. This is a time that requires an awakening — as it is written *(Amos 3:6;* see p. 61): *Can a shofar be blown in a city and the people not tremble?* This is the basis for the Jerusalem Talmud's statement (see above). Additionally, daytime sleep is a sign of laziness — as it is written *(Jonah 1:6): How can you sleep? Up! Call to your God ...* (cited in *Bach).*

□ R' Yitzchak Luria (better known as the *Arizal*) permits a nap in the afternoon because the angel (see above) has already been aroused through the sounding of the *shofar* and the prayers. Similarly, *Bach* cites *Tashbatz* who attests that *Maharam* of Rothenburg would nap as was his habit on every other festival.

Anger

◆§ Now that we have seen the extent to which the Talmudic Sages have admonished us to be scrupulous with regard to the symbolic foods we eat on Rosh Hashanah — all for the sake of good omens — how much more so must one control his anger on this day. Self-control on this day is especially important not only because of the sin of anger, but additionally an even temper will serve as a significant omen for a good year. Therefore one should be of happy heart, righteous and confident in his faith in God, in his repentance, and in his good deeds *(Chayei Adam).*

The Shofar

For the Good of Israel

🎗️ Tanna deBei Eliyahu records the words of R' Yehoshua ben Karchah:
> The *shofar* was not created except for the good of Israel. The Torah was given to Israel with the blowing of the *shofar* — as it is written *(Exodus 19:19): The sound of the shofar continually increased ...*
> The wall of Jericho collapsed with the blowing of the *shofar* — as it is written *(Joshua 6:20): And it was when the people heard the sound of the shofar ... that the wall collapsed in its place ...*
> The advent of the Messiah will be announced with the *shofar* — as it is written *(Zechariah 9:14): Then HASHEM will appear upon them* [i.e., Israel], *and His arrow will go forth as the lightning; HASHEM, God, will blow on the shofar ...*
> The ingathering of the exiles will be accompanied by the *shofar* — as it is written *(Isaiah 27:13): And it will be on that day, He will blow on a great shofar, and they will come — those who were lost in the land of Assyria, and those cast out in the land of Egypt — and they will bow to HASHEM on the holy mountain, in Jerusalem.*
> Thus it is written *(Isaiah 58:1): Call out from the throat, do not withhold, like the shofar raise your voice ...*

Lofty Intentions

🎗️ 'Why do we blow [the *shofar*] on Rosh Hashanah?' the Talmud asks. In answer, the Talmud exclaims indignantly, 'Why do we blow? — the Torah has told us to blow!' *(Rosh Hashanah 16a).*

What better reason, what further rationale do we need? The Torah clearly states *(Numbers 29:1): In the seventh month, on* [day] *one of the month ...* יוֹם תְּרוּעָה יִהְיֶה לָכֶם, *a day of* [shofar] *blowing shall it be unto you.* Indeed, according to R' Elimelech of Lizhensk the primary intent upon which one should concentrate during the sounding of the *shofar* is to fulfill the will of the Creator.

☐ R' Shlomo HaKohen of Radomsk in his *Tiferes Shlomo* finds an allusion to this point in the verses *(Psalms 81:4-5): Blow the shofar* [on

Rosh Hashanah] ... *because it is a decree for Israel, a judgment for the God of Jacob.* The Hebrew word for decree, חֹק, usually alludes to a Torah law the reason for which is not revealed in Scripture. The word מִשְׁפָּט, *judgment*, on the other hand, alludes to a law which has a readily understood rationale. Thus the *mitzvah* of *shofar* is a חֹק to Israel, for God has not revealed His reasons for this commandment. Nevertheless, we are certain that to Him, in His infinite wisdom, it is a מִשְׁפָּט with a clear and logical base.

☐ That Israel needs no rationale other than, 'The Torah has told us to blow,' is illustrated with a story told about the renowned chassidic *tzaddik* R' Levi Yitzchak of Berditchev:

One year R' Levi Yitzchak spent a long time in search of a man who would be worthy of blowing the *shofar* in his synagogue. Rosh Hashanah was fast approaching, and though many righteous folk sought the privilege, vying with each other in demonstrating their expertise in the mystical kabbalistic secrets associated with the *shofar,* none of them were to his taste.

One day a new applicant came along, and R' Levi Yitzchak asked him on what deep mysteries he meditated while he was performing the awesome *mitzvah.*

'Rebbe,' said the newcomer, 'I'm only a simple Jew; I don't understand too much about the hidden things of the Torah. But I have four daughters of marriageable age, and when I blow the *shofar,* this is what I have in mind: "Master of the universe! Right now I am carrying out Your will. I'm doing Your *mitzvah* and blowing the *shofar.* Now supposing You, too, do what *I* want, and help me marry off my daughters!"'

My friend,' said R' Levi Yitzchak, 'you will blow the *shofar* in my synagogue!' (Retold by R' S.Y. Zevin in *A Treasury of Chassidic Tales.*)

Awake, O Sleepers

◆§ Nevertheless, many of the earlier commentaries and codifiers have sought a deeper understanding of the purposes underlying the *mitzvah* of *shofar* blowing. *Rambam (Hilchos Teshuvah* 3:4) writes:

Although the blowing of the *shofar* on Rosh Hashanah is a Scriptural decree [and must therefore be observed whether or not one knows the reason behind it], there is an allusion in it. Namely: 'Awake, O sleepers, from your sleep! Arouse yourselves, O slumberers, from your slumber! Scrutinize your deeds! Return with contrition! Remember your Creator! Those of you who forget the truth in the futilities of the times and let all your years elapse in futility and emptiness ... peer into your souls, improve your ways and your deeds. Each of you should abandon his evil way and his bad thoughts.'

External Stimulus

☙ *Chinuch (mitzvah 405)* follows another line of reasoning. As a physical being man is not always capable of girding himself for the task at hand but most rely upon external stimulants to arouse him to action. This is the reason for the trumpet blasts and war shouts that lead an army into battle. Similarly on Rosh Hashanah when each person stands before the Heavenly Tribunal, he must prepare himself with repentance and contrition. But his heart will rarely initiate this remorse; it must be prodded externally. When one hears the *shofar* call, particularly the broken-note *teruah*, he is reminded to break the evil inclination of his heart and to abandon his lust after This-Worldly desires. When one sees the curved shape of the *shofar,* he is inspired to bend his intransigence and submit to the will of his Creator.

Redemption from Egypt

☙ Still another reason offered for the sounding of the *shofar* on Rosh Hashanah is related to the Exodus from Egypt. According to the Talmud *(Rosh Hashanah* 11a), the Israelites in Egypt ceased working as slaves on the day of Rosh Hashanah [six and a half months before they actually left the land]. But it is with the sound of the *shofar* that slaves are set free (see *Leviticus* 25:9-10). Thus the *shofar* is another in a long series of *mitzvos,* each of which is זֵכֶר לִיצִיאַת מִצְרַיִם, *a memorial of the Exodus from Egypt (Radak* to *Psalms* 81:4).

Ten Symbolisms

☙ R' Saadiah Gaon enumerates ten symbolic meanings alluded to by the *mitzvah* of the *shofar:*

☐ 1. Rosh Hashanah marks the anniversary of the world's creation. As such it is also the day on which God's sovereignty over Creation began. Since it is customary to sound the trumpets at the coronation of a new king, we likewise proclaim His sovereignty over us on this day with the sounding of the *shofar.* This is in accord with the verse *(Psalms* 98:6): *With trumpets and shofar sound call out before the King, HASHEM.*

☐ 2. Rosh Hashanah initiates the Ten Days of Repentance. Just as a king will proclaim a period during which amends can be made before a decree is to be enforced, so does the *shofar* blast proclaim, 'Whosoever wishes to repent — let him repent now. If not, let him not complain later.'

☐ 3. At Mount Sinai the Jews shouted, *'We will do and we will listen' (Exodus* 24:7), when they accepted the Torah. At that time, *the sound of* the *shofar* continually increased and was very great (ibid. 19:19). On Rosh Hashanah the *shofar* reminds us to renew our commitment to 'do' and to 'listen.'

☐ 4. The *shofar* reminds us of the admonitions of the prophets and their calls to repentance — as it is stated *(Ezekiel 33:2-9)*:
Ben Adam [i.e., Ezekiel], speak to the children of your people and say to them: 'When I bring a sword upon a land, and the people of the land take one man from among them and set him as their sentinel; and he sees the sword coming upon the land, he blows the *shofar* and warns the people. If a listener heard the sound of the *shofar* but did not heed the warning and the sword came and took him; his blood shall be upon his own head. He heard the sound of the *shofar* but did not heed the warning; his blood shall be upon himself. Had he heeded the warning, he would have saved his life' ... Now you, Ben Adam — I have made you a sentry for the family of Israel, and when you hear a matter from My mouth, warn them for Me. When I say of the wicked one, 'Wicked one, you shall surely die,' and you did ... warn the wicked one concerning his way that he should repent of it, and he did not repent of his way, he shall die for his sin.

☐ 5. The *shofar* reminds us to pray for the rebuilding of the destroyed Holy Temple, of which the prophet *(Jeremiah 4:19-20)* lamented: *I shall not be silent, for the sound of the shofar have you heard, O my soul, the shout of war. Destruction upon destruction has been proclaimed ...*

☐ 6. The *shofar,* a ram's horn, reminds us of *Akeidas Yitzchak,* the Binding of Isaac *(Genesis 22)*, when Abraham sacrificed a ram in lieu of his son. We similarly offer to sacrifice our lives in Sanctification of the Holy Name. Thus, may our remembrances ascend before Him for the good. [According to one opinion *(Pesikta Rabbasi 40:6)*, the *Akeidas Yitzchak* took place on Rosh Hashanah.]

☐ 7. The sound of the *shofar* inspires fear and trembling in the hearts of all who hear it — as the prophet *(Amos 3:6)* asks: *Can a shofar be blown in a city, and the people not tremble?*

☐ 8. The *shofar* reminds us of the great and awesome Judgment Day of the future — which *Zephaniah* (1:14-16) describes: *Near is the great day of HASHEM ... a day of wrath is that day; a day of trouble and oppressiveness; a day of utter desolation; a day of darkness and blackness; a day of clouds and thick fog; a day of shofar and shouting ...*

☐ 9. The *shofar* reminds us of the long anticipated day of the ingathering of the exiles and arouses an inner yearning in our hearts for that time. *And it will be on that day, He will blow on a great shofar, and they will come — those who were lost in the land of Assyria, and those* cast out in the land of Egypt — and they will bow to HASHEM on the holy mountain, in Jerusalem (Isaiah 27:13).

☐ 10. The *shofar* reminds us of the resurrection of the dead and awakens our belief and yearning for that day. For then: *All inhabitants of the world and dwellers of the earth, when he raises a banner upon the mountains, you shall see, and when he blows the shofar, you shall hear* (ibid. 18:3).

To Confound Satan

◆§ The Talmud *(Rosh Hashanah* 16a-b) explains the reason for blowing the *shofar* both before and during the *Amidah* of *Mussaf:*
Rabbi Yitzchak asked ... Why do they blow *tekiah* and *teruah* when they are seated [i.e., before the *Amidah* when it is permissible to sit] and again blow *tekiah* and *teruah* when they are standing [i.e., during the *Amidah* which must be recited while standing]? — In order to confound Satan [i.e., the Accuser].
Rabbi Yitzchak further stated: Any year in which they do not blow the *shofar* at its onset [this does not apply when Rosh Hashanah falls on a Sabbath and *shofar* blowing is prohibited *(Tosafos)*], they will cry at its conclusion. Why is this so? — Because they did not confound Satan.

☐ It is the repetition of the *shofar* blasts that confounds the Accuser. Similarly we find that the repeated shaking of the *lulav* on Succos is done 'to shake the power of the Accuser' *(Rosh* to *Succos* 3:26 citing *Ravyah).*

☐ *Rashi* explains that when the accusing angel sees Israel's love and devotion to the performance of *mitzvos,* his words get caught in his throat.

☐ *Tosafos* cites an alternative interpretation offered by R' Nassan of Rome in his *Aruch.* The prophet *Isaiah* (25:8) proclaimed that with the advent of the Messiah, *He will consume death forever.* Moreover: *On that day He will blow on a great shofar ...* (ibid. 27:13). When Satan hears the first series of *shofar* blasts he hastens in confusion [to prepare his accusations]. But when he hears the second series, he says, 'This must certainly be the blast of the great *shofar.* The time has come to be consumed.' Thus he becomes confounded and [when he finally realizes his mistake] does not have sufficient time to properly arrange his accusations.

☐ The views cited above all assume, with *Rosh,* that the primary fulfillment of the *mitzvah* of *shofar* blowing is accomplished with the initial series of blasts. The subsequent series serves merely to confound

Satan. According to these views the purpose of confounding Satan is to prevent him from carrying out his accusations against Israel, whether collectively or individually. Satan, however, plays other roles — as the Talmud *(Bava Basra* 16a) states: He is שָׂטָן, *Satan;* he is יֵצֶר הָרָע, *the Evil Inclination;* he is מַלְאַךְ הַמָּוֶת, *the Angel of Death.* First, as the Evil Inclination, he tempts man and entices him to sin. Then, as Satan, he becomes the Accuser before the Heavenly Tribunal and demands that retribution be meted out. Finally, as the Angel of Death, he is charged with carrying out the sentence.

☐ According to *Ran,* confounding Satan refers to him in the guise of the Evil Inclination. Moreover, the *mitzvah* of *shofar* is primarily fulfilled with the second series of blasts blown during the *Amidah.* The first series is blown to confound the Evil Inclination, to prevent him from hampering the penitent in his attempt to return to God. According to this opinion the primary series of blasts follows, rather than precedes, the secondary series, due to the apprehension that people, realizing that the *mitzvah* has already been fulfilled with the first blasts, will be unwilling to remain for the 'less important' series, blown to confound Satan.

☐ *Yalkut Yitzchak* cites another view, based upon the mishnaic teaching: The order of the *shofar* blasts is three sets of three blasts each *(Rosh Hashanah* 4:9). The convergence of threes symbolizes the three successive roles played by Satan: Evil Inclination, Accuser, Angel of Death; first he incites people to sin, then accuses them before God, and finally carries out the Heavenly judgment against the sinner. These three roles are also represented by the three letters of Satan's name, שָׂטָן, a name alluded to in the passage of *Isaiah* read as the *haftarah* of Yom Kippur (chs. 57-58). *The wicked* [who refuse to repent] *are pursued like the* [waves of the] *sea* [just as each wave sees the one before it being broken against the shore yet does not abandon its destruction-destined path and return to the sea, so do the evil ones follow each other blindly along the road to self-destruction] *which cannot be still; its waters throw out* רֶפֶשׁ וָטִיט, *mud and mire.* אֵין שָׁלוֹם, *there can be no peace, says my God, for the wicked* (57:20-21; bracketed comments from *Rashi).* The final letters of the words רֶפֶשׁ וָטִיט אֵין שָׁלוֹם spell the name שָׂטָן, *Satan.* But the very next verse (58:1) tells how to pull oneself out of the quagmire of sinfulness and confound Satan: *Call out from the throat, do not withhold, like the shofar raise your voice and tell My people of their iniquity, and the House of Jacob their sins.* [That is, prayer, the shofar, and confession will merge to confound Satan and put an end to his accusations.]

☐ An additional allusion to the *shofar's* power to confound Satan is found in the initial letters of the words *(I Kings* 5:18): אֵין שָׂטָן וְאֵין פֶּגַע רָע,

there is neither Satan nor evil occurrence, which spell שׁוֹפָר, shofar (Yalkut Yitzchak). That this verse alludes to the shofar of Rosh Hashanah is hinted at by its gematria (numeric value) — 910 — which is the same as the gematria for תִּשְׁרֵי, Tishrei, the month of Rosh Hashanah (Metzareif Dahava).

The Shofar — A Cure for the Sick Soul

⋄§ Just as a person's body can be healthy, sick or dead — so it is regarding his soul. R' Yeshayah HaLevi Hurwitz, author of Sh'lah, explains:

Healthiness of the soul is directly dependent upon one's fulfillment of Torah and mitzvos, and his righteousness of character. To the extent that Torah and mitzvos are missing, or even worse, that their opposites are present, the soul is sick. The remedy for this spiritual malady is repentance, remorse, a total commitment to self-improvement in matters of the soul. And just as unchecked sickness can cause physical death, so it is that when a person continuously sins and thereby abuses his spiritual health, his soul will be cut off from its nation [the punishment of כָּרֵת, kares, spiritual excision]. For this reason evil-doers, even while they are physically alive, are considered as dead (Berachos 18b).

Each of the three shofar notes (see p. 66) denotes the soul in a different stage of spiritual well-being. The unbroken, unwavering sound of the tekiah indicates that the soul was created pure and straight. Any impurities, crookedness, or spiritual malady was introduced by the sufferer himself. The broken groan of the shevarim calls to mind the moaning of the sick, while the staccato sobbing of the teruah represents uncontrolled crying over the death of a dear one. Nevertheless, at the very end, the tekiah is repeated to teach that God is always ready to receive the penitent who sincerely attempts to return to his original state of spiritual purity.

□ The Talmudic statement (cited above p. 62) — Any year in which they do not blow the shofar at its onset, they will cry at its conclusion ... because they did not confound Satan — can be understood in terms of the curative powers of the shofar. R' Meir Simchah HaKohen in his work Meshech Chachmah (Emor) explains that sounding the shofar is different from other mitzvos. Regarding other mitzvos, one's lack of performance does not incur a penalty if the omission was the result of circumstances beyond his control. Sounding the shofar, however, is analogous to medication prescribed for a sick person. If the proper dosage is not taken — no matter how good the excuse — the patient will not recover. Similarly, shofar is a medicament prescribed for the ailing soul. Just as a medicine fights the germs that underlie the disease, so does the shofar confound and silence the Accuser standing before the Heavenly Tribunal. But when the shofar is not blown, when its call to repentance is missing, there is nothing to prevent the Accuser from having his say and winning his case.

Ignoring the Call

◈§ The prophet *(Amos 3:6)* proclaims: *Can a shofar be blown in a city, and the people not tremble? Can evil befall a city, and HASHEM did not cause it?* Nevertheless, we find people who are completely unmoved by the sounding of the *shofar*. Even as they stand in the synagogue and hear the blasts, their minds — and sometimes even their conversations — are miles away. The *shofar* affects them no more than a whispered call from a great distance. They are totally oblivious to its presence.

Pardes Yosef explains that this phenomenon is due to a general lack of belief on the part of these people. They deny Divine intervention in the affairs of man; they attribute every occurrence, be it good or bad, to accidents of coincidence; they are blind to the hand of God that guides the events of the world in general and of every individual in particular. An allusion to this is found in the verse cited above which can also be translated: *If a shofar shall be blown in a city and the people shall not tremble,* [it is because] *if evil shall befall a city* [they will say], *'HASHEM did not cause it.'*

Order of the Shofar Blasts

The Types of Blasts

◈§ There are three different types of blasts blown on the shofar: (a) תְּקִיעָה, *tekiah* — a simple extended unwavering blast; (b) שְׁבָרִים, *shevarim*, literally, *broken* — a blast broken in three so that it sounds like meaning; (c) תְּרוּעָה, *teruah,* literally *crying* — a staccato or wavering blast that is reminiscent of sobbing.

At what points in the prayer service the *shofar* is blown, in what combination of notes, and how often each combination is repeated are all dependent upon both halachic consideration and local customs, as is described below.

The Number of Blasts

◈§ The number and the nature of the required *shofar* blasts is referred to in the Mishnah: The order of *shofar* blasts is three [sets] of three [blasts] each — [that is, three soundings, each sounding consisting of three blasts] *(Rosh Hashanah 4:9).*

❑ The Scriptural requirement consists of nine blasts: three of what the Torah calls *teruah* [which, as will be explained, may or may not be the same as what we now call *teruah*], each of these *teruos* preceded and followed by an 'extended' blast — the type called *tekiah*. The Talmud (ibid. 34a) explains that the nine blasts are derived from the combination of three separate verses dealing with the *shofar* (Leviticus 25:9; 23:24; Numbers 29:1). Taking all three verses together, we find the word *teruah* mentioned three times; this accounts for the three *teruos*. The *tekiah* before each *teruah* is derived from the verse: וְהַעֲבַרְתָּ שׁוֹפַר תְּרוּעָה, *And you shall sound the shofar, a teruah ... (Leviticus 25:9)*. Here we see that preceding the *teruah* there is a simple sounding of the *shofar*, i.e., extended and unvaried, for it is referred to simply by the word *shofar*. After the *teruah* we again find that there is to be a simple sounding of the *shofar*, for the verse continues: תַּעֲבִירוּ שׁוֹפָר, *You shall sound the shofar*. Thus there are nine blasts in all — *tekiah, teruah, tekiah*, sounded three times. These, then, are the blasts of the Scriptural order.

❑ On the Rabbinic level, there are more shofar blasts — the extra ones necessitated by doubt as to the nature of the Biblical *teruah*. One possibility is that when the Torah calls for *teruah*, it means a sound similar to גְּנוּחֵי גָנַח, *the sound of groaning*, the type of blast now called שְׁבָרִים, *shevarim*, literally *broken*. Another possibility is that the Biblical *teruah* is יְלוּלֵי יָלִיל, *the sound of whimpering*, the intermittent quavering blast that we refer to as *teruah*. A third possibility is that what the Torah meant by *teruah* is a combination of both these sounds. In order to fulfill all the possible meanings, R' Abahu in Caesarea enacted a Rabbinic decree that the blowing should consist of three groups of the type which today we call *tashrat* [תַּשְׁרָ"תְ] — an acronym for **t**ekiah, **sh**evarim, **t**eruah, **t**ekiah]; three of the type called *tashat* [תַּשַׁ"תְ] — **t**ekiah, **sh**evarim, **t**ekiah]; and three of the type called *tarat* [תַּרָ"תְ] — **t**ekiah, **t**eruah, **t**ekiah]. Since each *tashrat* consists of four notes, while *tashat* and *tarat* each consist of three, the Rabbinic order contains a total of thirty blasts.

❑ R' Hai Gaon was asked, how is it possible that doubt could arise as to the nature of a *mitzvah* (the Biblical *teruah*) which is performed every year? The gist of his reply is: From earliest times there were two customs in Israel. Some blew light short blasts (those called *teruah* today), and others blew heavy short blasts, that is, *shevarim*. Either manner of blowing was sufficient to fulfill the obligation. R' Abahu decreed that all Israel should follow a single practice so that there should not be among them anything that might be misconstrued as a division.

Seated and Standing

☙ The Talmud *(Rosh Hashanah* 16a-b) speaks of blowing *shofar* 'when they are seated,' i.e., before the *Amidah* when it is permissible to sit, and 'when they are standing,' i.e., during the *Amidah* which must be recited while standing. As early as the days of the *Geonim* and the *Rishonim* there were different customs as to the order of the *shofar* soundings during the *Amidah* prayer of *Mussaf,* that is, the soundings 'while standing':

Rif and *Rambam* write that after the blessing of *Malchuyos, tashrat* is sounded once; after *Zichronos, tashat;* and after *Shofaros, tarat.*

Rabbeinu Tam, followed by *Rama,* rules that *tashrat* is sounded after each of the three blessings.

Shulchan Aruch rules that after *Malchuyos, tashrat* is sounded three times; after *Zichronos, tashat* three times; and after *Shofaros, tarat* three times.

Sh'lah writes that the 'preferred way' is to sound *tashrat, tashat, tarat* for each of the blessings.

☐ Another question on which customs diverge is whether the *shofar* should be sounded during the silent recitation of the *Amidah.* Most chassidic groups sound the *shofar* during the silent *Amidah* too (in accordance with the 'preferred way' recommended by *Sh'lah*). Communities that follow the Ashkenaz version of the prayer service generally do not sound the *shofar* during the silent *Amidah.*

The Shofar: Its Composition and Its Shape

⇛ The Mishnah states: All *shofars* are valid, except that of the cow (*Rosh Hashanah* 3:2). The Talmud offers three explanations: (a) The horn of the cow does not come within the category of *shofar*, but is called merely a 'horn' (קֶרֶן): (b) the cow recalls the sin of the Golden Calf, and its horn is invalid according to the dictum, אֵין קַטֵגוֹר נַעֲשֶׂה סַנֵּגוֹר, a *prosecutor cannot become a defender,* i.e., the object used in committing a sin should not be used to effect forgiveness; (c) since a cow's horn is composed of layers, it appears like two or three *shofaros* [within one another] — and the Torah says *shofar* [in the singular], not *shofars* (ibid. 26a).

☐ As to the first choice for the *Shofar,* the Sages disagree whether this should be the horn of the *ya'el* or of the ram. *Rashi* identifies the *ya'el* as an animal called steinbok, i.e., the ibex. The Talmud (ibid. 16a) rules in favor of the horn of the ram, because it calls to mind *Akeidas Yitzchak,* the Binding of Isaac [in whose place a ram was sacrificed].

All agree that the horns of most types of wild animals are disqualified, for they consist of one solid bone and therefore are not classified as *shofar,* a term that alludes to a hollow horn, for the word שׁוֹפָר, *shofar,* is derived from שְׁפוֹפֶרֶת, *shefoferes,* tube.

☐ Concerning the proper shape of the *shofar*, the Talmud (ibid. 26b) records two opposing opinions — straight or curved — and decides that [one should perform the] *mitzvah* of Rosh Hashanah with a curved *shofar* to symbolize that the more a man bends his will, the better. Here we find a connection between the required *shofar* and the required shape. The horn of the ram is normally curved, while that of the *ya'el* is usually straight.

The Persons Obligated

⊷§ Every man of Israel is obligated in the *mitzvah* of *shofar*. Women are exempt since this is a positive *mitzvah* which must be performed at a specified time — מִצְוַת עֲשֵׂה שֶׁהַזְּמַן גְּרָמָא — and women are exempt from all such *mitzvos*. Although women are exempt on both the Scriptural and Rabbinical levels from hearing the *shofar*, there is a virtually universal custom that they also fulfill this *mitzvah* (see p. 87 §47).

☐ Exempt for other reasons are a *cheresh* (deaf-mute), a *shoteh* (mentally incompetent), and a *kattan* (minor). Though *cheresh* usually refers to a deaf-mute, for this *mitzvah* even a deaf person who can speak is exempt from the obligation; nor can the sound of a *shofar* blown by such a person be used by others to fulfill their obligation. Since he cannot — and therefore is not obligated to — hear the *shofar*, he is also unacceptable to perform the *mitzvah* for others, on the principle that one cannot do for others what one cannot do, or is not obligated to do, for oneself.

Some Aspects of The Prayer Service

Hallel is not Recited

⊷§ The ministering angels asked the Holy One, Blessed is He, 'Master of the universe, why does Israel not recite *Hallel* (psalms of joyous praise) before You on Rosh Hashanah and Yom Kippur?'

He answered them, 'Is it proper that when the King is sitting on the throne of judgment — with the Books of the Living and the Books of the Dead open before Him — that Israel should sing *Hallel*?' (*Rosh Hashanah* 32b; *Arachin* 10b).

☐ *Rambam* (Hil. Chanukah 3:6) explains that since Rosh Hashanah and Yom Kippur are days of repentance, awe and trembling, and not days of excessive joy, *Hallel* is not said on these days.

Avinu Malkeinu

◆§ Once, during a drought, R' Eliezer decreed a series of thirteen fasts upon the community, yet no rains fell. At the end of the final fast day, when the congregation began leaving the synagogue, he asked them, 'Have you prepared graves for yourselves?' Upon hearing his words they all burst out in tears; and the rains began falling.

Another time, also during a drought, R' Eliezer led the prayers and recited the twenty-four blessings [ordained for a public fast day (see *Taanis* 15a)] but was not answered. R' Akiva approached the *chazzan's* lectern after him and said, 'אָבִינוּ מַלְכֵּנוּ אֵין לָנוּ מֶלֶךְ אֶלָּא אָתָּה, *Our Father, our King, we have no King other than You.* אָבִינוּ מַלְכֵּנוּ לְמַעֲנָךְ רַחֵם עָלֵינוּ *Our Father, our King, for Your sake be merciful with us.*' And the rains fell. Those present began to doubt [R' Eliezer's righteousness] when a Heavenly voice proclaimed, 'Not because this one [R' Akiva] is greater than that one [R' Eliezer], but because this one is patient and uncomplaining while the other is not' *(Taanis* 25b).

□ When the Rabbis of that generation saw the efficacy of R' Akiva's prayer, they added various entreaties to it and ordained that it be recited during the Ten Days of Repentance *(Beis Yosef* 584 citing *Kol Bo).*

□ *Beis Yosef* adds that since Rosh Hashanah is a festival day, we omit such confessional passages as, אָבִינוּ מַלְכֵּנוּ חָטָאנוּ לְפָנֶיךָ, *Our Father, our King, we have sinned before You.* Additionally, *Mishnah Berurah* points out, the passages should not be recited on Rosh Hashanah because they open the door for the Accuser and give him material with which to substantiate his accusations.

□ Nevertheless, *Rama* writes that the *Avinu Malkeinu* prayers should be recited in full. *Ba'er Heiteiv* defends this ruling by citing a traditional interpretation of this prayer which explains the words 'we have sinned before You' in conjunction with the next two sentences, in a non-confessional manner: ... *we* [i.e., our ancestors who were idolaters] *have sinned before You* ... [but as for us, their children] *we have no King other than You* ... [therefore] *treat us for Your Name's sake.*

The Torah Reading and the Haftarah

◆§ On the first day of Rosh Hashanah, the Torah reading is the portion beginning, *HASHEM remembered Sarah ... (Genesis* chap. 21). The *haftarah* is from the beginning of *I Samuel* (1:1-2:10). Both of these selections — the first relating how the barren Sarah was 'remembered' by God and bore Isaac; the second telling how the childless Hannah was blessed with a son, Samuel — are based on the Talmudic dictum *(Rosh Hashanah* 10b): On Rosh Hashanah, Sarah, Rachel and Hannah were 'remembered' *(Megillah* 31a; *Ran).*

☐ On the second day, the Torah reading is from *Genesis,* dealing with the *Akeidas Yitzchak,* the binding of Isaac *(Megillah* 31a). *Rashi* explains that this passage was selected to recall the merits that accrued to Israel as a result of the devotion to God shown by the Patriarchs Abraham and Isaac during this episode. *Ran* adds that one of the reasons for blowing the *shofar* on Rosh Hashanah is to recall the *Akeidas Yitzchak* at which a ram was sacrificed in place of Isaac (see p. 61). [Additionally, there is a view *(Pesikta Rabbasi* 40:6) that the *Akeidah* took place on Rosh Hashanah.]

☐ The *haftarah (Jeremiah* 31:1-19) of the second day includes a verse that alludes to the role of Jeroboam, the Ephraimite, who led the secession of the Ten Tribes from the Davidic monarchy. Jeroboam was directly responsible for the proliferation of idolatry among the Ten Tribes, which resulted in their eventual corruption, conquest, and exile. The *haftarah* concludes: *'Is Ephraim* [i.e., Jeroboam] *My precious son? Is he a beloved child that whenever I speak of him, remember do I remember* [*My love for him*] *again? Therefore My innards pine for him; merciful shall I be merciful with him,'* says HASHEM. The phrases זָכֹר אֶזְכְּרֶנּוּ, *remember do I remember,* and רַחֵם אֲרַחֲמֶנּוּ, *merciful shall I be merciful,* are quite appropriate to the theme of the day *(Megillah* 31a; *Rashi).*

☐ Additionally, this *haftarah* speaks of Rachel and her children: *A voice is heard on high — moaning, crying bitterness. Rachel is crying for her children; she refuses to be assuaged for her children, for they are gone. Thus says HASHEM, 'Restrain your voice from crying, and your eyes from tears. For there is reward for your labors ... there is hope in your future ... [your] children will return to their borders'* (vs. 14-15). And as we have seen above, Rachel, in her barrenness, was 'remembered' on Rosh Hashanah.

Unesanah Tokef

◈§ One of the most stirring compositions in all of the liturgy of the Days of Awe is the prayer *Unesanah Tokef,* which begins: וּנְתַנֶּה תּוֹקֶף קְדֻשַּׁת הַיּוֹם, *We shall express the might of this day's sanctity.* Written by R' Amnon of Mainz, Germany, about one thousand years ago, it has become one of the highlights of the *chazzan's* repetition of the *Mussaf Amidah* on both Rosh Hashanah and Yom Kippur.

☐ R' Amnon composed *Unesanah Tokef* as the result of a spiritual ordeal from which his soul emerged unscathed, although it cost him his life in This World. The bishop of Mainz insisted that his friend and advisor, R' Amnon, convert to Christianity. In order to buy time, R' Amnon asked for three days of grace to meditate upon the question. Upon returning home he was distraught at having given the impression that he even considered betraying his God.

R' Amnon spent the three days in solitude, fasting and praying to be forgiven for his sin. At the end of the allotted time, the bishop demanded an answer. R' Amnon replied that his tongue, which had sinned by saying he would consider the matter, should be cut out. Furious, the bishop ordered his hands and feet cut off as well, and R' Amnon was transported home.

When Rosh Hashanah arrived a few days later, R' Amnon asked to be carried to the Ark. Before the congregation recited *Kedushah*, R' Amnon asked to be allowed to hallow God's name. He recited *Unesaneh Tokef* and then died.

Three days later, R' Amnon appeared in a dream to R' Klonimos ben Meshullam, taught him the text to *Unesanah Tokef,* and asked him to send it to all parts of Jewry to be entered in their liturgy. R' Amnon's wish was carried out, and the prayer became an integral part of the Rosh Hashanah and Yom Kippur services.

☐ In this *piyut* (liturgical poem) R' Ammon describes the Heavenly Tribunal's awesome process of judgment:

וְיִכּוֹן בְּחֶסֶד כִּסְאֶךָ וְתֵשֵׁב עָלָיו בֶּאֱמֶת — *Your throne is set up in mercy and You sit upon it in truth.*

R' Levi Yitzchak of Berditchev explained: When God judges His world with strict justice, His decision may be repealed by the repentance, prayer and charity of Israel. Such reversible judgment cannot be spoken of as being 'in truth.' But when He renders His decisions from the Throne of Mercy, then they are everlasting and 'in truth.'

☐ וּבְשׁוֹפָר גָּדוֹל יִתָּקַע, וְקוֹל דְּמָמָה דַקָּה יִשָּׁמַע, וּמַלְאָכִים יֵחָפֵזוּן — *Then the great shofar is blown, and a soft, thin sound is heard; and the angels hasten as fear and trembling seize them ...*

Upon hearing the weak, barely audible sounds issuing from the *shofar* blown by R' Chaim of Zanz, one of the chassidim present thought of a novel interpretation of this passage: 'When the *shofar* is blown by a great man, even if only a soft, thin sound is heard, nevertheless, the angels are seized with fear and trembling.'

☐ Additionally, this *piyut* offers the formula with which man can cause the severity of the decision to be repealed — וּתְשׁוּבָה וּתְפִלָּה וּצְדָקָה מַעֲבִירִין אֶת רֹעַ הַגְּזֵרָה, *Teshuvah* (repentance), *tefillah* (prayer), and *tzedakah* (charity) cast aside the harshness of the decree.

☐ In almost all editions of the Rosh Hashanah and Yom Kippur *machzor,* the words וּתְשׁוּבָה וּתְפִלָּה וּצְדָקָה, *repentance, prayer, and charity,* are crowned in smaller type with the words צוֹם קוֹל מָמוֹן, *fasting, voice, money.* These superscripts are meant to indicate that sincere repentance consists of fasting, prayer recited in a loud voice, and donations to charity.

Additional allusions are to be found in the *gematria* of these three small words, each of which equals 136, while the combined *gematria* is 3x136=408. This *gematria* alludes to the Yom Kippur service of the *Kohen Gadol* [High Priest], who entered the Temple's most sanctified part only one day each year — Yom Kippur — to perform the incense service *(Leviticus* ch. 16). This service is introduced with the words: בְּזֹאת, with *"this"* [i.e., the following instructions] *shall Aaron* [the High Priest] *enter the Holy* (v. 3). The word זאת has a *gematria* of 408, indicating that even the *Kohen Gadol* must resort to repentance, prayer and charity, if he is to effect atonement for the nation *(Nachal Kedumim; Tzemach Tzaddik).*

☐ **Teshuvah** — One year, the day before Rosh Hashanah, R' Moshe Teitelbaum of Ujhely retold a dream he had had the previous night:

'In my dream I saw people running en masse to the *shul.* There they sat with tear-streaked faces and fervently recited *Psalms,* as they poured out their hearts in remorse for the sins they had committed during the past year. "But," I thought, "this does not apply to me. After all, what sins have I done? My entire year was spent fulfilling *mitzvos,* studying Torah, giving charity. What is there for me to repent?" Suddenly I saw all of my *mitzvos* and good deeds wallowing in the mud. Nobody paid them any heed; nobody thought them worthy enough to be pulled out of the mire. Then I awoke with a start. "It seems," I told myself, "that it is high time for me to do *teshuvah* also." '

☐ **Tefillah** — R' Aharon HaGadol of Karlin was once praying with particular fervor during the Days of Awe. Upon reaching the word הַמֶּלֶךְ, *the King,* which refers to God, the King of the universe, he suddenly fell in a swoon. After the services someone asked him what brought on this sudden weakness that caused him to faint. R' Aharon explained that when he addressed God with the word הַמֶּלֶךְ, he was reminded of an incident that took place during the siege of Jerusalem just prior to the Destruction of the Second Temple. The story is told in the Talmud *(Gittin* 56b):

Rabban Yochanan ben Zakkai, the leading sage of Jerusalem, wished to negotiate with the general of the Roman army surrounding the Holy City but was prevented from doing so by a militant band known as the *biryonim.* Finally, after three years of siege, Rabban Yochanan ben Zakkai succeeded in leaving the city and approached the general, Vespasian. Upon meeting Vespasian, Rabban Yochanan greeted the Roman with the words, 'Peace upon you, O King! Peace upon you, O King!' Vespasian replied, 'You are guilty of a capital offense, for if I am the king, why did you tarry so long before coming to greet me?'

R' Aharon concluded, 'When I addressed the Holy One, Blessed is He, as King, I remembered Vespasian's rebuke and I thought, why have I waited until now to repent to God, my King.'

☐ **Tzedakah** — At a gathering to raise money for the benefit of the

Vaad HaYeshivos (a united fund for the support of yeshivos in Eastern Europe), R' Yisrael Meir of Radin, known as the *Chofetz Chaim*, received substantial donations from all the wealthy people of the city of Bialistock, with one exception. Although this lone dissenter listened respectfully to the rabbi's warm words and impassioned description of the fiscal problems faced by the *yeshivos* and their students, he had one rebuttal that he kept repeating, 'I have done my share; I have fulfilled my obligation! Look at this stack of receipts!'

Finally, the *Chofetz Chaim* told him, 'You claim to have fulfilled your obligation, but are you aware that there are many ways in which this may be accomplished? Permit me to cite some examples.

'Every person must have food, shelter and clothing. One is obligated to eat and protect himself from the elements if he is to remain alive. There are millions of people in the world who eat a bare minimum, some potatoes, cabbage and perhaps a small portion of chicken once or twice a week. Yet they fulfill their obligation to eat. They too, are alive, aren't they?

'And regarding shelter, there are people with large families, say ten or twelve children, who live in one-room hovels. They also fulfilled their obligation of providing shelter for the family. This is proven by the fact that the family survives.

'Let us turn to the topic of clothing. There are poor villagers who wear the same suit of clothing day in and day out, year after year. Patch upon patch covers the original material, yet these people clearly fulfill their obligations to wear clothing. They do stay dry in the rain, and warm in the winter.

'Nevertheless, my good man,' the *Chofetz Chaim* said, bringing his point home to the wealthy man, 'When it comes to your shelter, clothing, and nourishment, you have chosen not to merely "fulfill your obligation" with the bare minimum. Instead you maintain a standard of living that befits your wealth. And so it is with *tzedakah*. One may do his share, fulfill his obligation, with a bare minimum. On the other hand, he may seek to carry out this *mitzvah* in a way befitting his station. Should a man with your wealth give only as much charity as someone much less well-to-do?

'Look at it way. When you stand before the Heavenly Tribunal, they will ask you, "Have you given *tzedakah?*" and you will reply, "Certainly, I have a stack of receipts to prove that I have fulfilled my obligation!" There is no doubt that you will receive a share in *Gan Eden* (Paradise) in return for your charity. But when you arrive at your appointed place, in some out-of-the-way corner of *Gan Eden*, you will complain, "Is this just? Is this all I receive?" And they will answer, "You gave *tzedakah* just to fulfill your obligation with a bare minimum. We have rewarded you in kind, with a minimal share in *Gan Eden*."'

❒ אָדָם יְסוֹדוֹ מֵעָפָר וְסוֹפוֹ לֶעָפָר — *Man's origin is from dust and his end is in dust.* These words are often accompanied by much weeping. R' Yitzchak Meir of Ger, known as the *Chiddushei HaRim,* wondered about this. Certainly, had man been formed of gold and later faded into dust, that would be something about which to cry. But since man arises from dust, why is his return to dust an occasion for tears?

Man — explained the *Chiddushei HaRim* — was endowed with the potential of elevating the dust of which he was created from its mundane physical existence to an extremely high spiritual plateau. However, if at life's end he has not reached (or even reached for) the heights he could have scaled, then there is certainly much over which to cry.

Some Talmudic Teachings about Rosh Hashanah

Creation, the Patriarchs, Redemption

R' Eliezer says: In Tishrei the world was created (see p. 43); in Tishrei the Patriarchs [Abraham and Jacob] were born; in Tishrei the Patriarchs died; on Pesach Isaac was born; on Rosh Hashanah Sarah, Rachel and Hannah were remembered (see p. 69); on Rosh Hashanah Joseph was released from prison; on Rosh Hashanah [before the Exodus] the slavery of our ancestors in Egypt was ended (see p. 60); in Nissan they were redeemed and in Tishrei they are destined to be redeemed.

R' Yehoshua says: In Nissan the world was created; in Nissan the Patriarchs were born; in Nissan the Patriarchs died; on Pesach Isaac was born; on Rosh Hashanah Sarah, Rachel and Hannah were remembered; on Rosh Hashanah [before the Exodus] the bondage of our ancestors in Egypt was ended; in Nissan they were redeemed and in Nissan they are destined to be redeemed.

☐ R' Eliezer said [in substantiation of his view]: How do we know that the world was created in Tishrei? — Because Scripture states: *God said, 'Let the earth sprout vegetation: herbage yielding seed, fruit trees ...'* (Genesis 1:11). Which is the month in which the earth sprouts vegetation and the tree is full of fruit? — One must say this is Tishrei, and that period is the season of rainfall. The rains came and caused the plants to sprout, as Scripture states: *A mist ascended from the earth* (ibid. 2:6).

R' Yehoshua said: How do we know that the world was created in Nissan? — Because Scripture states: *And the earth brought forth vegetation: herbage yielding seed after its kind, and trees yielding fruit* (ibid. 1:12). Which is the month in which the earth brings forth vegetation and the tree brings forth fruit? — One must say this is Nissan.

As for the other [i.e., R' Eliezer], how does he explain the words *'trees yielding fruit'?* — That is written as a blessing for future generations.

And as for the other [i.e., R' Yehoshua], how does he explain the words *'fruit trees'?* — That is in accordance with R' Yehoshua ben Levi's dictum — for R' Yehoshua ben Levi said: All objects of the Creation were created in their full stature, with their consent, and in their full beauty, as Scripture states: *Thus the heaven and the earth were completed and all their array [צְבָאָם] (Genesis 2:1).* Read not צְבָאָם, their array, but צִבְיוֹנָם, their character.

R' Eliezer says: How do we know that the Patriarchs were born in Tishrei? — Because Scripture states: *And they gathered unto King Solomon, all the men of Israel, in the month of the Eisanim, on the festival (I Kings 8:2)* — that is, the month in which the *Eisanim* [literally, *the powerful ones,* i.e., the Patriarchs of powerful faith] of the world were born ...

R' Yehoshua said: How do we know that the Patriarchs were born in Nissan? — Because Scripture states: *And it was in the four hundred and eightieth year after the Children of Israel's Exodus from the land of Egypt, in the fourth year, in the month of Ziv* [lit. *shine*] (ibid. 6:1) — that is, the month in which the brilliant ones of the world were born. But it is written: *the month of the Eisanim?* — That refers to [the month] which is powerful in *mitzvos* [*shofar,* Yom Kippur, *succah, lulav,* etc.].

And as for the other [i.e., R' Eliezer], how does he explain the words *the month of Ziv?* — That means when there is splendor for the trees, for R' Yehudah has said: He who goes forth in the springtime and sees that the trees are blossoming should say, 'Blessed is He ... Who has not left His world deficient of anything, and He has created in it good creatures and good trees for mankind to find pleasure in them' *(Rosh Hashanah* 10b-11a; the Talmudic discussion continues with each *Tanna,* R' Eliezer and R' Yehoshua, adducing Scriptural verses to support his opinion regarding each disputed point).

Three Books are Opened

≈§ R' Kruspedai said in the name of R' Yochanan: Three books are opened [before the Heavenly Tribunal] on Rosh Hashanah — one for the unquestionably wicked; one for the unquestionably righteous; and one for those between [these extremes]. The unquestionably righteous are immediately inscribed and sealed for life; the unquestionably wicked are immediately inscribed and sealed for death. [But the judgment of] those between stands in abeyance from Rosh Hashanah until Yom Kippur. If they are found worthy, they are inscribed for life; if they are not found worthy, they are inscribed for death *(Rosh Hashanah* 6b).

Rains, Abundant or Scarce

≈§ *The eyes of HASHEM, your God, are perpetually upon it* [the Land of

Israel] *(Deuteronomy* 11:12). At times [He looks upon it] for good; at times for evil.

'At times for good' — when is that? If Israel was [classified among] the unquestionably wicked on Rosh Hashanah, and minimal rainfall was decreed for them, [but] afterwards they repented. [For God] to increase [rainfall] is impossible, because the decision has been made. The Holy One, Blessed is He, therefore sends down the [minimal] rains in their [most propitious] season on the land that requires them [most], all depending upon the area.

'At times for evil' — when is that? If Israel was [classified among] the unquestionably righteous on Rosh Hashanah, and abundant rainfall was decreed for them, [but] afterwards they reverted [to sin]. To diminish the rainfall is impossible, because the decision has been made. The Holy One, Blessed is He, therefore sends down [the rains] not in their [propitious] season and on land that does not require them *(Rosh Hashanah* 17b).

Days of Judgment

Mishnah: At four junctures [of the year] the world is judged: on Pesach for the grain; on Shavuos for the fruit of the tree; on Rosh Hashanah all who walk the earth pass before Him like *bnei maron* [see below], as Scripture states *(Psalms* 33:15): *He Who fashions all their hearts together, Who comprehends all their deeds;* and on the Festival [of Succos] for the water *(Rosh Hashanah* 1:2).

☐ **Gemara:** 'On Rosh Hashanah all who walk the earth pass before Him like *bnei maron.*' What is the meaning of *bnei maron?* — Here [in the study halls of Babylon] it was translated, *like young sheep.* [Rashi explains that when newly born sheep are counted for tithing, they are assembled in a corral and are released through a narrow gate so that only one at a time can pass through to be counted.]

Resh Lakish said: Like the ascent of Beis Maron [a very narrow mountain trail on which people could walk only in single file *(Rashi)*].

R' Yehudah said in the name of Samuel: Like the troops of the House of David [*maron* is derived from מָר, master, i.e., the king *(Rashi)*].

Rabbah bar Chanah said in the name of R' Yochanan: [All the same] they are all seen with one glance.

R' Nachman bar Yitzchak said: We also have learned the same idea: *He Who fashions their hearts all together, Who comprehends all their deeds (Psalms* 33:15). What does this mean? Shall I say it means that He has created all [the creatures of] the world and unites all their hearts together? But we see that this is not so! Rather this is what it means: *The Creator sees their hearts together and comprehends all their deeds (Rosh Hashanah* 18a).

Insights [76]

ஃ Observance / Selected Laws and Customs

    The Month of Elul
    Selichos
    Erev Rosh Hashanah
    Night of Rosh Hashanah
    Day of Rosh Hashanah
    Sounding the Shofar
    Second Day of Rosh Hashanah

—Rabbi Hersh Goldwurm

✥ Selected Laws and Customs

The following laws and customs are culled, in the main, from the authorities having the widest acceptance, the *Shulchan Aruch Orach Chaim* [here abbreviated OC], *Mishnah Berurah* [MB], and R' Ephraim Zalman Margulies' classic work *Matteh Ephraim*, on the laws and customs of the period from Rosh Chodesh Elul through Succos. This halachic summary concentrates on those laws which relate to the individual. We have not included most details concerning the *shofar* and the prayers as these *mitzvos* generally are performed in public where a rabbi or other knowledgeable person is likely to be present to resolve halachic questions.

✥ The month of Elul

1. Rosh Chodesh Elul marks the beginning of a forty-day period of repentance that ends on Yom Kippur. This span corresponds with Moses' third and last forty-day stay on Mount Sinai, at the conclusion of which God proclaimed His forgiveness to Israel (see *Rashi* to *Exodus* 33:11 and *Deuteronomy* 9:18). Therefore these forty days have been set aside as a period of repentance and introspection. The mood of contrition and supplication is heralded on the day before Rosh Chodesh with the observation of *Yom Kippur Kattan* (the minor Yom Kippur). The custom of *Yom Kippur Kattan* (attributed to the great scholar and kabbalist R' Moshe Cordovero) designates the day preceding every Rosh Chodesh as a day of repentance, fasting and the recital of penitential prayers (*selichos*). This practice was widely accepted in past generations when people were more sensitive to their spiritual well-being. Nowadays it is observed by relatively few people. However, the *Yom Kippur Kattan* preceding Rosh Chodesh Elul is still widely observed. Many people fast at least until the afternoon (see *Matteh Ephraim* 581:3), and recite the *Yom Kippur Kattan* liturgy at the *Minchah* prayer service. When Rosh Chodesh falls on a Sunday, *Yom Kippur Kattan* is observed on the preceding Thursday, (ibid.).

2. In most communities לְדָוִד ה' אוֹרִי (Psalm 27) — which the Midrash interprets as referring to the Days of Awe (יָמִים נוֹרָאִים) — is recited twice a day from Rosh Chodesh Elul until Shemini Atzeres, once in the morning after *Shacharis* and once after either *Minchah* or *Maariv* depending on local custom (see *Matteh Ephraim* 581:6). Most communities begin this recitation on the second day of Rosh Chodesh, while a few begin on the first day.

3. Every day of Elul, the *shofar* is blown after *Shacharis*. Here, too, there are two customs. Most communities begin on the second day of Rosh Chodesh (*Rama* 581:1), while in some the *shofar* is sounded even on the first day.

4. Another feature of the month of Elul is the increased recital of psalms. Many customs exist in this regard, among them the following one cited by *Matteh Ephraim* (581:8; see also *MB* 581:3): On every weekday [at least] ten psalms are said so that the en-

tire *Tehillim* (comprising 150 psalms) is completed twice before Rosh Hashanah — the total number of psalms included in this double recitation of *Tehillim* is three hundred, which is the numerical equivalent of כַּפֵּר, *forgive*. During the Ten Days of Repentance, *Tehillim* is said in its entirety another time.

5. When writing a letter during Elul, it is customary to include wishes for the recipient's well-being in the coming year and to his attaining a good judgment on Rosh Hashanah, the Day of Judgment *(Matteh Ephraim 581:9).*

6. One should utilize the month of Elul to repent for one's sins. Therefore a person should set aside time each day for introspection and examination of his deeds. During Elul one should be more diligent and careful than usual with regard to the fulfillment of the *mitzvos*. Some have their *mezuzos* and *tefillin* inspected by a qualified scribe at this time *(Matteh Ephraim 581:10).*

◆§ Selichos

7. The custom of saying *selichos* (penitential prayers) dates back to the times of the *Geonim* and has been accepted by all Jewish communities (see *Tur OC 581).* Customs differ regarding the date on which the recitation of *selichos* is started. Sephardic communities begin *selichos* as early as Rosh Chodesh Elul *(OC 581:1).* The custom prevalent in Ashkenazic communities is to say *selichos* for at least four days before Rosh Hashanah, but always to begin the recitation on the night following the Sabbath *(Rama, OC 581:1).* Therefore, if Rosh Hashanah is on Thursday or on the Sabbath (it cannot fall on Wednesday or Friday), *selichos* are begun on the Sunday immediately preceding Rosh Hashanah. If the first day of Rosh Hashanah falls on Monday or Tuesday (it cannot occur on Sunday), *selichos* must be begun on the Sunday preceding the last Sunday before Rosh Hashanah, in order to allow for four days of *selichos* recitation.

8. Sunday is always chosen to be the first day of *selichos* in order to avoid the confusion that would be caused if every year a different day was chosen to begin *selichos (Levush, Turei Zahav OC 581:2).*[1]

9. Owo reasons are given for the four-day minimum: There was a widespread custom to fast a total of ten days during the general period of the Ten Days of Repentance (beginning with the first day of Rosh Hashanah and ending with Yom Kippur). But on four of these days fasting is not permitted (the two days of Rosh Hashanah, one Sabbath, and the day preceding Yom Kippur on which it is a *mitzvah* to feast). To complete the series of ten fasts, a four day period of fasting, accompanied by *selichos*, is designated before Rosh Hashanah *(Levush 581:8).*

Alternatively: On Rosh Hashanah a person should view himself as a sacrifice to God. An allusion to this concept is found in the language the Torah uses to introduce the *Mussaf* offerings of Rosh Hashanah, *And you shall make*

---

1. The *Belzer Rebbe* offered a different explanation based on a Talmudic teaching. The *Gemara* states: One who prays on the Sabbath eve and recites וַיְכֻלּוּ [the Torah portion in Genesis 2:1-3 which speaks about the first Sabbath of Creation and which is recited three times on the Sabbath eve] is considered by Scripture as a partner to the Holy One, Blessed is He, in Creation *(Shabbos* 119b). Now one's relationship to his partner is radically different from his relationship to any other person; one cannot dismiss a partner offhandedly or close the door on him. Therefore we start reciting *selichos* right after the Sabbath, and stress our 'partnership' status by reciting the *selichah* that begins: בְּמוֹצָאֵי מְנוּחָה, *At the departure of [the day of] rest we began to approach You.*

(וַעֲשִׂיתֶם) *a burnt offering ... (Numbers 29:2)* instead of the usual וְהִקְרַבְתֶּם, *you shall offer.* The unusual phraseology is understood as an allusion that on Rosh Hashanah you *shall make yourself* into an offering. Just as an offering is inspected for disqualifying blemishes for four days prior to its sacrifice, so should a person inspect his defects and repent of his sins so that he be a fit offering on the Day of Judgment *(Eliyah Rabbah 581:8).* [1]

10. The *selichos* should ideally be said during the last third (אַשְׁמוּרָה) of the night *(OC 581:1 with Magen Avraham)*, close to daybreak *(Pri Megadim)*, or at midnight (see *Magen Avraham 1:4)* because these times are periods of Divine compassion. Most communities accept the ruling of those authorities who forbid the recitation of the *selichos* in the first half of the night *(Sha'arei Teshuvah 581:1)*. Although nowadays many congregations are not careful to say *selichos* before daybreak, they should make every effort to do so for the first *selichos*, because the *selichos* of that day refer specifically to our rising early to supplicate before God.

11. Prior to the recital of *selichos* in the morning, one should recite the *berachos*: אֲשֶׁר and עַל נְטִילַת יָדַיִם, upon relieving oneself and washing one's hands; and אֱלֹקַי, thanking God for restoring us to full consciousness. Since the *selichos* prayers contain Scriptural verses, one should also recite the *berachos* for the Torah. If one had arisen before daybreak to say *selichos*,

he should wash his hands again at the completion of *selichos* after dawn has broken *(Matteh Ephraim 581:12).*

12. The recitation of the 'Thirteen Attributes of Mercy' — a cardinal facet of the *selichos* — is based upon God's promise to Moses not to ignore a prayer accompanied by its recitation. A *minyan* [a quorum of ten adult males] must be present when the 'Thirteen Attributes' is recited. If for whatever reason one is unable to participate in the public *selichos* services, one must [either] omit all mention of the 'Thirteen Attributes' [or chant them in the manner one chants verses of Torah; not in the manner of prayer]. Additionally, he should omit the Aramaic passages found at the end of the *selichos* prayers *(MB 581:4).*

13. Every *selichah* is prefaced with the words אֱלֹקֵינוּ וֵאלֹקֵי אֲבוֹתֵינוּ, *Our God, God of our ancestors,* except those *selichos* that begin with any of the Names of God (ibid.).

◆§ Erev Rosh Hashanah

14. On the day before Rosh Hashanah a greater number of *selichos* is recited than in previous or subsequent days.

15. Many people fast on this day because it is a propitious time for atonement (see *Tur* and *Shulchan Aruch OC 581:2).* Some people are accustomed to taste some food before dawn prior to the recital of *selichos.* This custom is based on the Biblical in-

---

1. *Vilna Gaon (Beur HaGra OC 581)* cites *Ran's (Comm. to Rif, Rosh Hashanah 16a)* explanation for a custom similar to the four-day recitation of *selichos.* In *Pesikta (D'Rav Kahana* ch. 23) we find that Adam was created, on the sixth day of Creation, on the first of Tishrei. It is because of this that Rosh Hashanah is designated the Day of Judgment. It follows therefore that the first day of Creation occurred on the twenty-fifth of Elul. The custom providing for four days of *selichos* ensures that the twenty-fifth of Elul falls within the *selichos* period. [When Rosh Hashanah falls on a Thursday and *selichos* is said on only four days, the twenty-fifth of Elul occurs on the Sabbath when *selichos* are not permitted to be recited.]

junction against adopting the ways of the gentiles, and there was a period when gentiles would fast on the day before their festivals *(Rama* there).

Although a voluntary fast can usually be accepted upon oneself only with a declaration made during the preceding day's *Minchah* prayer (see *OC* 562:5), no such declaration is needed for the Erev Rosh Hashanah fast or for the other fast days of this period. Nor must one fast until nightfall. It is preferable to fast at least until an hour and a quarter before night, but it is sufficient to end the fast half an hour after noon *(Matteh Ephraim* 581:35).

16. *Tachanun* is not said during *Shacharis* on Erev Rosh Hashanah, but it is said after *selichos* even if the recitation ended after daybreak. However customs differ regarding the recital of לַמְנַצֵּחַ *(Psalm* 20) before וּבָא לְצִיּוֹן, during the latter part of the service *(Matteh Ephraim* 581:49).

17. The shofar is not sounded after *Shacharis* on Erev Rosh Hashanah *(Rama OC* 581:3).

18. It is customary to establish an ad hoc *beis din* (court of law) for the dissolution of vows that one may have undertaken during the year, and to declare that future vows that one may make precipitously during the year be voided retroactively *(Matteh Ephraim* 581:49; *Sh'lah,* beginning of *Maseches Yoma).*

A *beis din* for this purpose consists of three people. The formula for this dissolution is printed in many *siddurim* and *selichos.*

19. On Erev Rosh Hashanah it is also customary, wherever practicable, to visit the cemetery and to pray there *(Rama* 581:4). Because the graveyard is the resting place for the *tzaddikim* (righteous people) who are buried there, it is a 'holy place' and prayers are more apt to be heard there. However one should not pray to the *tzaddikim* themselves, but should beseech Hashem to have compassion in the merit of the *tzaddikim (Maharil* cited in *MB* 581:27). One should distribute charity while at the graveyard *(Rama* 581:4 with *Ba'er Heitev).*

20. One should take a haircut and launder his clothing to honor Rosh Hashanah *(OC* 581:4) and to show one's confidence that God will have compassion on him and render his judgment favorably *(Yerushalmi* cited by *Tur).* However, overly costly and ornate clothing should not be worn for it is incumbent to be in awe of the judgment to be pronounced. One's attire should express this mood. In some communities it is customary for all the congregants to wear the *kittel* (white robe) even on Rosh Hashanah *(MB* 581:25).

21. There is a widely practiced custom to immerse oneself in a *mikveh* prior to Rosh Hashanah *(Rama OC* 581:4). If one is not well enough to go to a *mikveh* he may have nine *kav* (opinions regarding present-day equivalents range from 432 to 864 fl. oz.) of water spilled over himself (see *MB* 88:4 on particulars pertaining to this). Some authorities permit one to stand under a shower until this amount of water has fallen on him.

⋄§ **Night of Rosh Hashanah**

22. It is customary for (most) women to recite the blessing שֶׁהֶחֱיָנוּ prior to lighting the *Yom Tov* candles (see *Shaarei Teshuvah* 263:4). In a situation where the same person who lights the candles recites the *Kiddush,* e.g., a man or woman living alone, the שֶׁהֶחֱיָנוּ may be said only once, preferably after *Kiddush.*

23. Several passages are interpolated into each *Amidah* from the first night of Rosh Hashanah until the end of Yom Kippur. In the first blessing the formula, זָכְרֵנוּ, *Remember us*, is added; in the second, מִי כָמוֹךָ, *Who is like to You*; in the second to last, וּכְתוֹב, *And inscribe*; and in the last blessing, בְּסֵפֶר, *In the book*. If one forgot to say any of these additions he should not recite the *Shemoneh Esrei* again. However, if he became aware of the omission prior to saying the word HASHEM in the conclusion of the respective blessing, he may return to the place where the passage should have been interpolated and continue from there (*OC* 582:5 with *MB*).

24. The ending of the third blessing of the *Amidah* — הָאֵל הַקָּדוֹשׁ, *the holy God*, — is changed to הַמֶּלֶךְ הַקָּדוֹשׁ, *the holy King*. This emendation is made to accentuate God's role as Ruler and Judge of the world.

If one recited the usual ending, he may correct himself immediately by saying הַמֶּלֶךְ הַקָּדוֹשׁ. ['Immediately' in this regard is defined as the span of time it takes to say שָׁלוֹם עָלֶיךָ מוֹרִי (see *MB* 582:7, 206:2, and 487:4 with *Shaar HaTziyun*).]

If, however, he did not correct himself in time, he must begin the *Amidah* anew (*OC* 582:1).

If one had already begun the next blessing before realizing his mistake (even if the above time span has not elapsed), he must begin the *Amidah* anew (*Shaarei Teshuvah* to *OC* 582:2, *Daas Torah* there, *Matteh Ephraim* 582:9, *Beur Halachah* to 487:1 s.v. תוך).

If one had merely said the word הָאֵל but had not yet ended the blessing with the word הַקָּדוֹשׁ, then he may correct himself even if he had waited longer than the allotted time (*Daas Torah* and *Eishel Avraham* to *OC* 582).

If one is in doubt whether he said the correct version, he must assume that he said the version he is accustomed to recite every day. Consequently, he must begin the *Amidah* anew (*MB* 352:3).

25. In the prayers of Rosh Hashanah and Yom Kippur (but not on the intervening days) a lengthy interpolation of special prayers, beginning וּבְכֵן תֵּן פַּחְדְּךָ, is inserted in the third blessing. However, if someone forgot to recite the insertion, but recited the regular formula and ended it with הַמֶּלֶךְ הַקָּדוֹשׁ, he need not correct his oversight. *Derech HaChayim* rules that if one merely concluded the third blessing (with the formula הַמֶּלֶךְ הַקָּדוֹשׁ), even if he did not yet begin the following one, he should not say the omitted prayers. *R' Tzvi Pesach Frank* (*Mikraei Kodesh* p. 212) demonstrates that according to *Eishel Avraham* it is permissible, though not obligatory, to recite the omitted prayers between the third and fourth blessings.

Conversely, if one interpolated the prescribed prayers but is in doubt whether he ended the blessing correctly, he may assume that he recited the correct formula. In this case, logic dictates that since he was reciting the special holiday formula he must have concluded it with the holiday ending (*MB* 582:4).

26. Many *siddurim* that follow the liturgy known as *Nusach Ashkenaz* emend the ending of the last blessing in the *Amidah* from הַמְבָרֵךְ אֶת עַמּוֹ יִשְׂרָאֵל בַּשָּׁלוֹם, *Who blesses His people Israel with peace*, to עוֹשֵׂה הַשָּׁלוֹם, *Who makes peace* (see *Levush* 582:5). *R' Seligman Baer* in his siddur (*Avodas Yisrael* p. 113) demonstrates that this version is rooted in traditions of great antiquity.

Many of the later authorities, however, object to the change and maintain that the ending of this blessing not be changed (see *Sh'lah* and *R' Yaakov Emden* in their siddurim; *Tosefes*

ROSH HASHANAH / Its Significance, Laws, and Prayers

Maaseh Rav citing R' Chaim Volozhiner, Minhagei Chasam Sofer, et al.). Matteh Ephraim rules that the ending should be the same as year-round but that in the formula עוֹשֶׂה שָׁלוֹם בִּמְרוֹמָיו which is said at the conclusions of both the Amidah and Kaddish, one should say עוֹשֶׂה הַשָּׁלוֹם (see also Kaf HaChayim 582:15 in the name of Pri Eitz Chayim). However, he cautions that a chazzan or one reciting the mourner's Kaddish should not deviate from the version in use in the community (582:22).

27. It is customary to recite a prayer beginning with יְהִי רָצוֹן [yehi ratzon], May it be Your will ..., when eating the foods which serve as good omens (see pp. 55-58; 104-109). One of these foods is an apple dipped in honey. Before eating the apple one must first recite the usual blessing over fruit. Since one may not talk unnecessarily in the interval between the recital of the blessing and partaking of the food, the yehi ratzon should be recited after one has eaten a bit of apple (MB 583:4). The same applies to the yehi ratzon said after eating the challah dipped in honey. However the custom practiced in the Chabad-Lubavitch community is to recite the blessing, immediately followed by the yehi ratzon, after which the apple is eaten (see the justification of this custom in an excerpt from a letter by the Lubavitcher Rebbe printed in the Siddur Baal HaTanya, p. 739). Even those who customarily taste the apple before reciting yehi ratzon need not repeat the blessing if they erred and recited the yehi ratzon before eating (Matteh Ephraim 358:1).

28. Some people avoid eating nuts during this period because the Hebrew word for nut — אֱגוֹז, egoz — has the same numerical value as (חֵטְא), sin. Additionally, nuts have a tendency to elicit an excessive flow of saliva and mucus to the mouth and may disturb a person's concentration on his prayers (Rama OC 583:2). Many people abstain from nuts until Shemini Atzeres (see Ketzei HaMatteh 583:16).

29. It is customary not to eat sour or bitter things, e.g., sour pickles (Matteh Ephraim 583:3).

30. Some have a custom to study the four chapters of the Mishnah Rosh Hashanah at the end of the meal (Matteh Ephraim 583:4), while others study one chapter after each of the four meals of the festival (Ketzei HaMatteh).

31. Before reciting Bircas HaMazon (Grace after Meals) one should wash his hands or tips of his fingers [מַיִם אַחֲרוֹנִים] even if he does not follow this practice during the rest of the year (Matteh Ephraim 583:4).

32. In Bircas HaMazon one must recite יַעֲלֶה וְיָבֹא, Yaaleh VeYavo, (the passage added on each festival) and interpolate בְּיוֹם הַזִּכָּרוֹן הַזֶּה, on this Day of Remembrance (Matteh Ephraim 583:4).

33. If one omitted Yaaleh VeYavo but did not realize his oversight until he had already concluded the blessing בּוֹנֶה בְרַחֲמָיו יְרוּשָׁלַיִם אָמֵן, he must interpolate the following compensatory blessing:

בָּרוּךְ אַתָּה ה' אֱלֹהֵינוּ מֶלֶךְ הָעוֹלָם אֲשֶׁר נָתַן יָמִים טוֹבִים לְעַמּוֹ יִשְׂרָאֵל אֶת יוֹם הַזִּכָּרוֹן הַזֶּה. בָּרוּךְ אַתָּה ה', מְקַדֵּשׁ יִשְׂרָאֵל וְיוֹם הַזִּכָּרוֹן.

If Rosh Hashanah falls on the Sabbath and he forgot both רְצֵה and יַעֲלֶה וְיָבֹא, he recites the following:

בָּרוּךְ אַתָּה ה' אֱלֹהֵינוּ מֶלֶךְ הָעוֹלָם אֲשֶׁר נָתַן שַׁבָּתוֹת לִמְנוּחָה לְעַמּוֹ יִשְׂרָאֵל בְּאַהֲבָה לְאוֹת וְלִבְרִית וְיָמִים טוֹבִים לְעַמּוֹ יִשְׂרָאֵל אֶת יוֹם הַזִּכָּרוֹן הַזֶּה. בָּרוּךְ אַתָּה ה', מְקַדֵּשׁ הַשַּׁבָּת וְיִשְׂרָאֵל וְיוֹם הַזִּכָּרוֹן.

Laws and Customs [84]

If one does not remember this formula he must begin *Bircas HaMazon* anew *(MB* 188:17,19; see *Shaar HaTziyun* 15 there).

If he had not finished the blessing he may recite *Yaaleh VeYavo* as long as he did not say HASHEM in the ending of the blessing. Even if he had already uttered HASHEM but did not yet say the next word, he may, in accord with *Mishnah Berurah's* novel ruling, interpolate the words לַמְּדֵנִי חֻקֶּיךָ, thus converting the blessing into the recital of a verse from *Psalms* (119:12), then return to *Yaaleh VeYavo (MB* 188:22 see *Shaar HaTziyun* there and *Beur Halachah* to 114:6 s.v. בלא).

If he did not realize his omission until he began the fourth and last blessing, he must begin *Bircas HaMazon* anew *(Matteh Ephraim* 583:4; *MB* 188:19 does not make a final ruling on this question). The *Baal HaTanya (Siddur;* cf. *Shulchan Aruch HaRav* 188:10) draws a distinction between *Bircas HaMazon* of the night, which must be repeated when one omits *Yaaleh VeYavo*, and that of the daytime meal where such an omission does not necessitate a repetition. This distinction is based on the consideration that all authorities agree that it is obligatory to have a meal on the night of Rosh Hashanah, but according to some authorities it is permissible to fast on the day of Rosh Hashanah, so that the meal (with its recitation of *Bircas HaMazon)* has a voluntary character (see *OC* 597:1,2; *MB* there §4).

If one is in doubt whether he has said *Yaaleh VeYavo* he should assume that he has omitted it and conduct himself in accord with the laws outlined earlier *(MB* 188:15).

34. The entire discussion in §33 pertains to men only. If a woman forgot to recite *Yaaleh VeYavo* she should not repeat *Bircas HaMazon* because the requirement to eat on Rosh Hashanah was not extended to women *(Teshuvos R' Akiva Eiger* 1; *Daas Torah* to *OC* 188:6). She may, however, recite the compensatory blessing if applicable (see §33; see R' A.Y. Silber, *Birur Halachah, OC* 188).

35. After finishing the recital of *Birkas HaMazon* one should study Torah for a while before saying *Shema* and retiring for the night. If the *Shema* during the *Maariv* service was recited before it was definitely night, one must recite all three sections of the *Shema* and have in mind that he wishes to fulfill the Scriptural *mitzvah* of *Shema* with this recital *(Matteh Ephraim* 583:5). In this context night is the time one would be permitted to work if it were the conclusion of the Sabbath (see *OC* 235:1).

◆§ The Day of Rosh Hashanah

36. One should be sure to recite *Shema* within the first quarter of the day. If one is not sure that the *Shema* in the *Shacharis* prayer will be said within this period, he should say the three passages of *Shema* before the synagogue service begins.

37. In many communities *Psalm* 130 (שִׁיר הַמַּעֲלוֹת מִמַּעֲמַקִּים) is recited after יִשְׁתַּבַּח, *Yishtabach*. If an individual lags behind the congregation and has not reached *Yishtabach* when they begin this psalm, he may nevertheless recite it together with the congregation. If he so wishes, he may recite it again immediately after he says *Yishtabach (Elef LaMatteh* 584:2).

38. After the *Amidah* the entire prayer אָבִינוּ מַלְכֵּנוּ [*Avinu Malkeinu*], Our Father, our King, is recited *(Rama OC* 584). Some authorities cite the instruction of the *Zohar* not to confess one's sins on Rosh Hashanah (see *Magen Avraham* 584:2) and therefore omit the first stich, which is couched in the form of a confession. Others, however, permit its recitation (see *MB* 584:3). In the siddur used in *Chabad* communities the first stich and all those that mention sin are deleted; others omit the first stich only *(Matteh Ephraim* 584:10). In most communities the entire prayer is said without any deletions (see p. 69). *Avinu Malkeinu* may be said by an individual praying without a *minyan* (op. cit. 584:14).

39. In many synagogues it is customary to have a short recess before the sounding of the *shofar*. One should not spend the intervening time in idle chatter but try to utilize every precious minute of the Day of Judgment. Some people use this time to recite *Tehillim*, study the laws and intentions of the *shofar* service and so on.

Because there has been a recess, one should wash his hands again before returning to his prayers *(Mateh Ephraim* 585:16).

In many communities it is customary for people to make *Kiddush* and eat something during this recess. Strictly speaking, however, it is forbidden to eat before hearing the *shofar* except for those who are too ill or weak to go without food until after *Mussaf*. The communities that make *Kiddush* at this point do so because they finish *Mussaf* well into the afternoon and it would impose an extreme hardship on many people not to eat before then. Certainly a full meal should not be eaten at this time, just enough light refreshment to enable one to concentrate on his prayers (see *Matteh Ephraim* 588:2 and *Ketzei HaMatteh* 588:4,5).

➳§ Sounding the Shofar

40. Two blessings are recited by the *tokea* [the person appointed to sound the *shofar*]; the congregation fulfills its obligation to recite the blessings by listening and responding אָמֵן, Amen. Therefore, it is of utmost importance to listen to every word and to intend to fulfill one's obligation thereby. One should not say the customary formula בָּרוּךְ הוּא וּבָרוּךְ שְׁמוֹ, *Blessed is He, and Blessed is His Name*, for this would be an unnecessary interruption (הֶפְסֵק) in the blessing.

41. The *tokea* should stand erect during the recital of the blessing and the sounding of the *shofar*. However, even if one performed the *mitzvah* while sitting, he has nevertheless fulfilled his obligation. Nowadays it is customary for the entire congregation to stand when the *shofar* is blown *(OC* 585:1 with *MB* §2).

42. During the sounding of the *shofar* it is absolutely essential that one listen intently in order to hear every single *shofar* blast. It is helpful to follow the notes in one's *machzor* (holiday prayer book) or *siddur* so that one is always aware of which note is being sounded.

43. The laws of the *shofar* are complex and many complications can arise. Care should be taken that the *makrei* [the person appointed to verbally direct the *tokea* as to what type of blast to sound] be a competent Torah scholar since he is responsible to decide if a particular blast was improper and must be repeated *(Matteh Ephraim* 585:2).

44. In many *machzorim* there are prayers to be said between the various sets of blasts. Many authorities have raised questions about both the propriety of saying prayers during the blasts and the contents of these prayers (see *Ketzeh HaMatteh* 590:23). Those who do say these prayers should not pronounce the names of angels mentioned in them *(Matteh Ephraim*

590:36). If one is accustomed to say these prayers but is in a congregation where they are omitted, it is advisable to omit them lest he miss the next set of blasts. The authorities insist that one should refrain from making any noise whatsoever during the sounding of the *shofar* (e.g., yawning, etc.) for it is absolutely essential to hear every *shofar* sound from beginning to end. Even if the *tokea* prolongs a note unnecessarily, one must hear it from beginning to end *(Rama, OC 587:3 MB 592:9).*

45. From the recitation of the blessings until the last blasts have been completed at the end of *Mussaf*, one may not speak about matters not concerning the blasts or prayers. If one did speak after he had heard the first *tekiah* blast, he need not recite the blessing again. However, if he spoke between *shevarim* and *teruah* — even concerning something relevant to the *mitzvah* — he should repeat that set of sounds [*tekiah, shevarim-teruah, tekiah*] later on *(OC 592:3 with MB* §13).

Some authorities draw a distinction between interrupting before the conclusion of the blasts before the *Amidah* and those blown during and after the *Amidah*. In the former case one may not talk unless it is essential for the *mitzvah* of the *shofar*, therefore, even prayers should not be inserted then. After these blasts have been concluded one may recite prayers but should not talk about extraneous matters *(MB 592:12).*

46. The interval between the blessing and the first blast is even more stringent in this regard. One may not say any prayer; if one did so he must recite the blessing anew. If it was necessary to speak about matters essential to the mitzvah of *shofar* (e.g., to bring a *shofar*), one may do so and need not repeat the blessing. This applies not only to the *tokea*, but also to the congregants *(MB 582:14).*

47. Women are not obligated by either Scriptural or Rabbinic law to fulfill the *mitzvah* of *shofar (OC 589:3).* However, it is a universally observed custom for them to observe the performance of this *mitzvah*. If a woman could not hear the *shofar* blasts in the synagogue she may blow the *shofar* herself *(OC 589:6).* In regard to the recitation of the blessing there is a difference of opinion between *R' Yosef Caro*, who forbids it, and *Rama*, who allows it (ibid.). In general it can be assumed that Sephardic Jews follow R' Yosef Karo's view while the Ashkenazim follow *Rama.* However, *Birkei Yosef (OC 654; Kaf HaChaim OC 589:6)* relates that even some Sephardic communities follow *Rama's* ruling in this regard.

48. A man who has already fulfilled the *mitzvah* and sounds the *shofar* for a woman should not recite the blessings for her; rather the woman should say them for herself *(Rama 589:6).* However, if he blows the *shofar* for her before he himself has fulfilled his obligation, he may opt to fulfill the *mitzvah* with the blasts he blows for her, in which case he should recite the blessings. However, he should not sound the *shofar* in the first three hours of the day *(MB 589:11).*

49. In many communities *tekios* are sounded even during the silent *Amidah*. At the conclusion of each set of *shofar* blasts the prayer הַיּוֹם הֲרַת עוֹלָם is said, but the prayer אֲרֶשֶׁת שְׂפָתֵינוּ is said only after the *shofar* blasts of the *Amidah* recitation by the *chazzan (Matteh Ephraim 591:13).* However, the author of the *Tanya* instituted the practice not to recite even הַיּוֹם הֲרַת עוֹלָם during the silent *Amidah*

(*Shaar HaKollel*), and this is the practice in *Chabad*-Lubavitch communities.

50. If an individual is still in the middle of his silent *Amidah* when the *shofar* is about to be sounded, he may pause in the middle of his prayer and listen to the *shofar* blasts. However, he may not recite הַיוֹם הֲרַת עוֹלָם for this would be an unauthorized interpolation in the prayer. Rather, he should continue his *Amidah* and recite הַיוֹם הֲרַת עוֹלָם when he reaches that point in the *machzor (Matteh Ephraim* 591:13).

51. It is customary not to sleep at all during the daytime of Rosh Hashanah *(Rama OC* 583:2). However, one who idles his time is considered as though he were sleeping. *Chayei Adam* says one should learn Torah after the meal, while it is customary in many communities to recite the entire book of *Psalms (MB* 583:9). In some communities the entire *Tehillim* (comprising 150 psalms) is recited on both days so that a total of 300 psalms — the numerical equivalent of בַּפֵּר, *forgive* — is said on Rosh Hashanah *(Matteh Ephraim* 598:1).

52. In the afternoon of the first day of Rosh Hashanah the *Tashlich* prayer is said at a body of water, preferably containing live fish *(OC* 583:2). If the first day is on the Sabbath, *Tashlich* is postponed until the second day *(MB* 583:8). In cases where it is difficult or far to go to a body of water, some communities go to *Tashlich* during the Ten Days of Repentance *(Ketzei HaMatteh* 598:12). It is forbidden to throw bits of food into the water for the fish to eat for it is forbidden on *Yom Tov* to feed animals or fish not dependent on oneself (see *OC* 497:2; *Matteh Ephraim* 598:5; *Machatzis HaShekel* 583:5; *Maharil*; *Eliyah Zuta* on *Levush* 597).

◈§ **The Second Day of Rosh Hashanah**

53. Although the two-day celebration of Rosh Hashanah is halachically viewed as a single *Yom Tov* consisting of two days (יוֹמָא אֲרִיכְתָּא; see §56), this is so only on a Rabbinical level. On a Scriptural level only the first day has *Yom Tov* status, and the second day is regarded as a weekday. This has the result that the 'single *Yom Tov'* status applies only to situations where such a classification will cause a stringent ruling; where the weekday status of the second day has a stringency aspect, that status is adopted as the halachic criterion. Therefore it is forbidden to cook on the first day of Rosh Hashanah for the second day, or to make any kind of preparations from one day to the other *(OC* 503:1 with *MB).* Even in the twilight period between the two days (בֵּין הַשְּׁמָשׁוֹת) it is forbidden to make any preparations for the night; one must wait until it is definitely night *(Pri Megadim* cited in *Beur Halachah* to 503:1).

54. It is customary to postpone the *Maariv* service until it is definitely night because, as a matter of course, the preparations for the evening *Yom Tov* meal are begun immediately upon commencement of the service *(Matteh Ephraim* 599:2).

55. One may light candles at the end of the afternoon of the first day if their light is needed at the time they are lit, even though their main use will be at night *(Matteh Ephraim* 598:8). However, the *Yom Tov* candles which are lit with the recitation of a blessing should be lit only after it is definitely night (preface of *Prishah* to *Yoreh Deah*; see *Eleph LaMatteh* 625:51 and *Ketzei HaMatteh* there).

56. The two-day celebration of Rosh Hashanah differs from the

Laws and Customs [88]

two-day celebrations of other festivals in the Diaspora in that the former is regarded as a single period of holiness (קְדוּשָׁה אַחַת), while the latter is viewed as two separate, consecutive, periods of holiness (שְׁתֵּי קְדוּשׁוֹת). This distinction is at the root of a disagreement among the early authorities as to whether the שֶׁהֶחֱיָנוּ benediction should be recited on the second day of Rosh Hashanah as it is on other second days of Yom Tov (see Tur OC 600). In order to avoid the problem of reciting an unnecessary blessing, one should wear a new garment or place a new fruit which one has not yet eaten this season on the table during Kiddush (OC 200:2). If one does not have a new garment or fruit, שֶׁהֶחֱיָנוּ should be recited anyhow (ibid.).

57. It is customary for (most) women to recite the שֶׁהֶחֱיָנוּ prior to lighting the Yom Tov candles (see Shaarei Teshuvah 263:4). In order to avoid the problem of whether or not to say the benediction on the second day of Rosh Hashanah, it is preferable that a woman put on a new garment just prior to lighting the candles. If this is not possible she should defer the candle lighting until immediately before Kiddush and intend the blessing to refer to the new fruit which will be consumed after Kiddush, as indicated in the previous paragraph (Matteh Ephraim 599:9).

58. If a new fruit is used to circumvent the problem of the שֶׁהֶחֱיָנוּ, it should be eaten by the person reciting the Kiddush immediately after drinking of the Kiddush wine; it is not necessary for all of the participants in the meal to do so. Nevertheless it is customary for all of those present to partake of the fruit as a good omen (Matteh Ephraim 600:6).

59. Some people eat the species which are considered a good omen even on the second night of Rosh Hashanah (Sha'arei Teshuvah 583; Matteh Ephraim 583:2, 22:14; see Ketzei Hamatteh) while others do this only on the first night (Bnei Yisaschar, Chodesh Tishrei 4:11).

60. There is a widespread custom to dip the challah in honey at this meal as well as during all of the meals of Shabbos and Yom Tov until Shemini Atzeres (cf. Matteh Ephraim 597:4).

61. One should not begin to eat a meal in the three-hour period preceding the Sabbath (OC 249:2).[1] If the second day of Rosh Hashanah occurred on Friday and one began the meal within the three-hour period, he should eat less than he normally would during the meal so that he will have an appetite to eat the Sabbath meal at night (Matteh Ephraim 601:5).

---

1. The 'hours' referred to here are not clock hours of sixty minutes each. Rather, these 'hours' are each measured as one-twelfth of the day (MB 249:17). However, since Rosh Hashanah is in the part of the year when the day is approximately twelve hours long, this distinction will not result in any great variation from the usual three-hour period.

❧ Observance / Prayers and Ritual

    Eruv Tavshilin
    Kindling of Yom Tov Lights
    LeShanah Tovah
    Kiddush
    Significant Omens
    Sounding the Shofar
    Kiddusha Rabba

—Rabbi Avie Gold

עירוב תבשילין

When Yom Tov falls on a Friday, an eruv tavshilin must be made on the day before Yom Tov [see commentary].
The eruv-foods are held while the blessing and the declaration are said.

בָּרוּךְ אַתָּה יהוה אֱלֹהֵינוּ מֶלֶךְ הָעוֹלָם, אֲשֶׁר קִדְּשָׁנוּ בְּמִצְוֹתָיו, וְצִוָּנוּ עַל מִצְוַת עֵרוּב.

בְּהָדֵין עֵרוּבָא יְהֵא שָׁרֵא לָנָא לַאֲפוּיֵי וּלְבַשּׁוּלֵי וּלְאַצְלוּיֵי וּלְאַטְמוּנֵי וּלְאַדְלוּקֵי שְׁרָגָא וּלְתַקָּנָא וּלְמֶעְבַּד כָּל צָרְכָּנָא מִיּוֹמָא טָבָא לְשַׁבַּתָּא — לָנוּ וּלְכָל יִשְׂרָאֵל הַדָּרִים בָּעִיר הַזֹּאת.

הדלקת הנר

The candles are lit and the following blessings are recited:

בָּרוּךְ אַתָּה יהוה אֱלֹהֵינוּ מֶלֶךְ הָעוֹלָם, אֲשֶׁר קִדְּשָׁנוּ בְּמִצְוֹתָיו, וְצִוָּנוּ לְהַדְלִיק נֵר שֶׁל (*on the Sabbath, insert* שַׁבָּת וְשֶׁל) יוֹם טוֹב.

בָּרוּךְ אַתָּה יהוה אֱלֹהֵינוּ מֶלֶךְ הָעוֹלָם, שֶׁהֶחֱיָנוּ וְקִיְּמָנוּ וְהִגִּיעָנוּ לַזְּמַן הַזֶּה.

◆§ Eruv Tavshilin

The Biblical prohibition against the performance of labor on *Yom Tov* specifically excludes preparation of food: *No work shall be done on them, except that which is to be eaten by any person, that alone may be done by you* (Exodus 12:16). Thus, the Mishnah teaches that there is no difference between the categories of work forbidden on *Yom Tov* and those forbidden on the Sabbath except that certain work necessary in the preparation of food is permitted on *Yom Tov* (Megillah 1:5). Although it is forbidden to prepare food on *Yom Tov* for use on a weekday, when *Yom Tov* falls on Friday it is permitted to prepare food needed for the Sabbath (Pesachim 46b).

Nevertheless, the Rabbis prohibited such preparations unless they were begun before *Yom Tov* (ibid.). In other words, if *Yom Tov* falls on Friday, preparations for the Sabbath meal must begin on Thursday (Wednesday, if *Yom Tov* is on Thursday and Friday). This Rabbinical enactment is called עֵרוּב תַּבְשִׁילִין [*eruv tavshilin*], literally, *mingling of cooked foods*, and consists of a *challah*, *matzah* or loaf of bread, along with any other cooked food (such as fish, meat or an egg). These are set aside on the day before *Yom Tov* to be

The Prayers [92]

✥ Eruv Tavshilin

When Yom Tov falls on a Friday, an eruv tavshilin must be made on the day before Yom Tov [see commentary].
The eruv-foods are held while the blessing and the declaration are said.

Blessed are You, HASHEM, our God, King of the universe, Who has sanctified us with His commandments and has commanded us concerning the mitzvah of Eruv.

Through this Eruv may we be permitted to bake, cook, fry, insulate, kindle flame, prepare for, and do anything necessary on the festival for the sake of the Sabbath — for ourselves and for all Jews who live in this city.

✥ Kindling of Yom Tov Lights

The candles are lit and the following blessings are recited:

Blessed are You, HASHEM, our God, King of the universe, Who has sanctified us with His commandments, and commanded us to kindle the lamp of the (on the Sabbath, insert: **Sabbath and of the**) festival.

Blessed are You, HASHEM, our God, King of the universe, Who has kept us alive, sustained us, and brought us to this season.

---

eaten on the Sabbath. The *eruv*-foods are held in the hand *(Orach Chaim 527:2)* and a blessing is recited. Additionally, the rationale [see below] for the enactment of *eruv tavshilin* requires that the person setting the *eruv* must understand its purpose. For this reason, the accompanying declaration must be said in a language understood by that person.

Two reasons are given in the Talmud for the enactment of *eruv tavshilin*. According to Rava, the purpose of the *eruv* is to remind one that, in his celebration of *Yom Tov*, he should not forget to reserve a fine portion for the approaching Sabbath. Rav Ashi says that the *eruv* was instituted to prevent the impression that if one could cook on a *Yom Tov* Friday for the Sabbath, then one could cook on any *Yom Tov* for the next day, weekdays as well. It is assumed that if one is prohibited even from making Sabbath preparations on *Yom Tov* unless he set an *eruv* before *Yom Tov*, then he will realize that weekday preparation may not be made on *Yom Tov* (Beitzah 15b as explained by *Rashi*).

✥ Kindling Lights

Since women are found in the home more often than their husbands, and since women generally look after household matters, the mitzvah of kindling the lights has devolved upon the mistress of the house *(Rambam, Hil. Shabbos 5:1,3)*. Nevertheless, a man living alone, or with other men, or one whose wife is too ill to light, is required

לְשָׁנָה טוֹבָה

After the evening Maariv services are completed it is customary to greet one another with a short blessing (Rama 582:9).

לְשָׁנָה טוֹבָה תִּכָּתֵב וְתֵחָתֵם *(to a man)*
לְאַלְתַּר לְחַיִּים טוֹבִים וּלְשָׁלוֹם.

לְשָׁנָה טוֹבָה תִּכָּתֵבִי וְתֵחָתֵמִי *(to a woman)*
לְאַלְתַּר לְחַיִּים טוֹבִים וּלְשָׁלוֹם.

לְשָׁנָה טוֹבָה תִּכָּתֵבוּ וְתֵחָתֵמוּ *(to men)*
לְאַלְתַּר לְחַיִּים טוֹבִים וּלְשָׁלוֹם.

לְשָׁנָה טוֹבָה תִּכָּתַבְנָה וְתֵחָתַתְמְנָה *(to women)*
לְאַלְתַּר לְחַיִּים טוֹבִים וּלְשָׁלוֹם.

to kindle the lights and recite the proper blessing *(Magen Avraham 263:6).*

There should be light in every room that will be used, and indeed this is a halachic requirement. Nevertheless, the blessing is recited upon the lamps or candles that are kindled in the dining room *(Mishnah Berurah 263:2).*

The lights honor the Sabbath and Yom Tov by brightening the festive meal and thereby lending it an air of formality and importance *(Rashi, Shabbos 25b).* Alternatively, one's delight in a festive meal is enhanced in a well-lit dining room *(Tosafos).*

נֵר — *The lamp.* The prevalent custom calls for at least two candles to be lit on the Sabbath and Yom Tov. According to *Eliyah Rabbah (263:2),* the two candles symbolize man and wife. Nevertheless, since one can fulfill the *mitzvah* with a single candle [indeed, *Mishnah Berurah (263:3)* advises one whose means are extremely limited to purchase one candle of good quality rather than two inferior ones] the blessing is couched in the singular form, נֵר, *lamp,* and not נֵרוֹת, *lamps.*

שֶׁל (שַׁבָּת וְשֶׁל) יוֹם טוֹב — *Of the (Sabbath and of the) festival.* Sabbath is mentioned first, following the Talmudic rule that a more frequently performed *mitzvah* takes precedence over a less frequent one *(Berachos 51b).* This same principle applies to the blessing of *Kiddush:* 'Who sanctifies (the Sabbath and) Israel and the Day of Remembrance.'

↞§ LeShanah Tovah

More than with any other festival, halachah requires that each Jew greet his fellow on the night of Rosh Hashanah with a heartfelt blessing. Friendship and brotherhood are prerequisites for the absorption into one's soul of the unique holiness of this day. The root of the word תְּרוּעָה, *shofar blast,* is the same as that of רֵעוּת, *friendship* [see *Rashi* to *Numbers 23:21*], for only when combined with רֵעוּת can the תְּרוּעָה have its cleansing affect and evoke Divine mercy *(R' Aharon of Karlin* in *Beis Aharon).*

The greeting is based on the Talmud *(Rosh Hashanah 16b)* which relates that

✣ LeShanah Tovah

After the evening Maariv services are completed it is customary to greet one another with a short blessing (Rama 582:9). Hebrew grammar requires that the wording vary with the number and gender being addressed. Nevertheless, the English translation is the same for all the forms of this blessing.

For a good year may you be inscribed and sealed, immediately, for a good life and for peace.

three books are opened [before the Heavenly Tribunal] on Rosh Hashanah: One for the unquestionably wicked; one for the unquestionably righteous; and one for those between these extremes.

The unquestionably righteous [i.e., those whose merits exceed their sins (Rashi)], נִכְתָּבִין וְנֶחְתָּמִין לְאַלְתַּר לְחַיִּים, are immediately inscribed and sealed for life; the unquestionably wicked [i.e., those whose sins exceed their merits (Rashi)] are immediately inscribed and sealed for death. [But the judgment of] those between [i.e., whose merits and sins counterbalance each other (Rashi)] stands in abeyance from Rosh Hashanah until Yom Kippur. If they are found worthy [during this period], they are inscribed for life; if they are not found worthy, they are inscribed for death (ibid.).

Tosafos points out that the expressions "for life" and "for death" do not refer to physical existence in This World, for experience teaches that even the righteous die, while evildoers often survive to a ripe old age. Rather the allusion is to everlasting life in the World to Come.

[On the evening of Rosh Hashanah we greet each other by expressing the wish that the Heavenly Tribunal find us unquestionably righteous and immediately inscribe us for "a good year" in This World, and "for life" in the World to Come.]

The text of the greeting presented here follows *Matteh Ephraim*. Various shorter versions are also recorded:

☐ לְשָׁנָה טוֹבָה תִּכָּתֵב, *For a good year may you be inscribed* (Rama, Vilna Gaon);[1]

☐ לְשָׁנָה טוֹבָה תִּכָּתֵב וְתֵחָתֵם, *For a good year may you be inscribed and sealed* (Magen Avraham; Baer Hetev);[2]

☐ תִּכָּתֵב וְתֵחָתֵם לְאַלְתַּר לְחַיִּים טוֹבִים, *May you be inscribed and sealed immediately for a good life* (Chayei Adam 139:5);

☐ תִּכָּתֵב בְּשָׁנָה טוֹבָה, *May you be inscribed for* [literally, in] *a good year* (Tur). In this version the prefix ב *(in)* appears in place of ל *(to)*. This substitution is made to avoid the initials תלט which suggests the word תְּלוֹט, Aramaic for תְּאַר, *you shall curse* (Perishah; see Onkelos to Exodus 22:27).

---

1. This is the version adopted by the Kahal Adas Yeshurun community of Frankfurt am Main, Germany. These customs were transplanted to America in 1939 when that community relocated in the Washington Heights section of Manhattan under the guidance of HaGaon HaRav Yosef Breuer, זצ"ל. I am grateful to HaGaon HaRav Shimon Schwab, שליט"א, rav of that distinguished community, for acquainting me with its unique customs, a number of which are described in this book.

2. This is the version adopted by the Chabad-Lubavitch community, with two variations: The final word is vowelized וְתֵחָתֵם; and only the singular form is used (Siddur Baal HaTanya).

קידוש

On Friday night begin here:

וַיְהִי עֶרֶב וַיְהִי בֹקֶר

יוֹם הַשִּׁשִּׁי: וַיְכֻלּוּ הַשָּׁמַיִם וְהָאָרֶץ וְכָל צְבָאָם. וַיְכַל אֱלֹהִים בַּיּוֹם הַשְּׁבִיעִי מְלַאכְתּוֹ אֲשֶׁר עָשָׂה, וַיִּשְׁבֹּת בַּיּוֹם הַשְּׁבִיעִי מִכָּל מְלַאכְתּוֹ אֲשֶׁר עָשָׂה. וַיְבָרֶךְ אֱלֹהִים אֶת יוֹם הַשְּׁבִיעִי וַיְקַדֵּשׁ אֹתוֹ, כִּי בוֹ שָׁבַת מִכָּל מְלַאכְתּוֹ אֲשֶׁר בָּרָא אֱלֹהִים לַעֲשׂוֹת.

On all nights other than Friday begin here; on Friday night include all passages in parentheses.

סַבְרִי מָרָנָן וְרַבָּנָן וְרַבּוֹתַי:

בָּרוּךְ אַתָּה יהוה אֱלֹהֵינוּ מֶלֶךְ הָעוֹלָם, בּוֹרֵא פְּרִי הַגָּפֶן.

◆§ Kiddush

Every Sabbath and *Yom Tov* is ushered in by *Kiddush*, a declaration of the day's sanctity. Even though we have already proclaimed the holiness of the day in our evening prayers, its proper celebration belongs in the home where we usually pursue our weekday activities. As we gather for our festive meal, therefore, we begin by dedicating ourselves to the special message of the day. [Parts of the commentary here are culled from other ArtScroll volumes: *Zemiroth, The Haggadah* and *Succos*. The parts pertaining specifically to Rosh Hashanah, however, appear here for the first time.]

וַיְהִי עֶרֶב — *And there was evening.* When *Yom Tov* falls on the Sabbath, we preface the *Kiddush* with the same verses that we recite every Friday night, and which describe the Sabbath of the week of Creation, to remind us of the profound purpose of the Sabbath.

For a full explanation of the plain meaning of, and the classical commentaries to, the first paragraph of the Sabbath *Kiddush*, see ArtScroll *Bereishis* 2:1-3. The comments below are primarily homiletical.

יוֹם הַשִּׁשִּׁי — *The sixth day.* Strictly speaking, these two words *(Genesis 1:31)* are not part of *Kiddush* because they do not relate to the testimony of the Sabbath's holiness. However, they are attached to *Kiddush* because their initials together with the initials of וַיְכֻלּוּ הַשָּׁמַיִם form the Four-Letter Name of God. Because these two isolated words have no logical meaning standing alone, the Sages incorporated the preceding words: וַיְהִי עֶרֶב וַיְהִי בֹקֶר, and *there was evening and there was morning*, to form a complete thought. Those words, however, are said quietly. Technically, all of *Genesis 1:31* should have been said in introduction to *Kiddush* (rather than only the verse's final phrase), because it is improper to recite fragments of verses. The Sages did not

The Prayers [96]

∾§ Kiddush

> *On Friday night begin here:*
> *(And there was evening and there was morning)*
>
> The sixth day. Thus the heavens and the earth were finished, and all their array. On the seventh day God finished His work which He had done, and He abstained on the seventh day from all His work which He had done. God blessed the seventh day and hallowed it, because on it He abstained from all His work which God created to make (Genesis 1:31-2:3).

On all nights other than Friday begin here; on Friday night include all passages in parentheses.

By your leave, my masters and teachers:

Blessed are You, HASHEM, our God, King of the universe, Who creates the fruit of the vine.

---

follow that course because, *Midrashically*, the earlier part of the verse alludes to the creation of death, an unpleasant concept which the Sages preferred not to make part of the *Kiddush (Responsa Chasam Sofer; Orach Chaim* 10).

וְכָל צְבָאָם — *And all their array.* R' Bunam of P'shis'cha notes that the word צָבָא is frequently used in Scripture to refer to the heavenly host, i.e., the organized array of the heavenly bodies. However, only in this verse do we find earthly creation described as צְבָא, an *array* or *host*. What, then, is the *earthly* צְבָא? R' Bunam comments that the word denotes a disciplined force, as in a military unit which is also called a צְבָא. Such organization is visible in the heavens, which function in accord with the will of God, their Master, but not in the often confusing, conflicting deeds and aspirations that characterize the inhabitants of earth, who often deny the authority of God. The emergence of the Jewish nation changed that. Only people who acknowledge the sovereignty of the Creator and their responsibility to obey His will are worthy of the name צְבָא.

וַיְכַל אֱלֹהִים בַּיּוֹם הַשְּׁבִיעִי — *On the seventh day God finished.* This phrase presents a difficulty, for God completed His work not on the seventh day, but on the sixth! *Rashi* explains that with the close of the sixth day only one phase of Creation was missing — the world lacked rest, but בָּאת שַׁבָּת בָּאת מְנוּחָה, *when the Sabbath came, rest came,* and thus Creation was completed [i.e., the work ended with the onset of the rest on the seventh day *(Maharal)*].

R' Simcha Zisel Ziev notes that constant striving is the source of all woes, because when man rushes from goal to goal — never satisfied, never contemplating — he cannot evaluate his actions and change his directions. With the Sabbath comes blessed, holy rest — the opportunity to take stock and assess the spiritual content of life.

בָּרוּךְ אַתָּה ... בּוֹרֵא — *Blessed are You ... (He) Who creates.* The blessing begins by addressing God directly in second person — אַתָּה, *You;* it then reverts to third person — בּוֹרֵא, *He Who creates.* This is true of all blessings. They begin by addressing God in second person because prayer is so exalted that it

בָּרוּךְ אַתָּה יהוה אֱלֹהֵינוּ מֶלֶךְ הָעוֹלָם, אֲשֶׁר בָּחַר בָּנוּ מִכָּל עָם, וְרוֹמְמָנוּ מִכָּל לָשׁוֹן, וְקִדְּשָׁנוּ בְּמִצְוֹתָיו. וַתִּתֶּן לָנוּ יהוה אֱלֹהֵינוּ בְּאַהֲבָה אֶת יוֹם (הַשַּׁבָּת הַזֶּה וְאֶת יוֹם) הַזִּכָּרוֹן הַזֶּה, יוֹם (זִכְרוֹן) תְּרוּעָה (בְּאַהֲבָה) מִקְרָא קֹדֶשׁ, זֵכֶר לִיצִיאַת מִצְרָיִם. כִּי בָנוּ בָחַרְתָּ וְאוֹתָנוּ קִדַּשְׁתָּ מִכָּל הָעַמִּים, וּדְבָרְךָ אֱמֶת וְקַיָּם לָעַד. בָּרוּךְ אַתָּה יהוה, מֶלֶךְ עַל כָּל הָאָרֶץ, מְקַדֵּשׁ (הַשַּׁבָּת וְ) יִשְׂרָאֵל וְיוֹם הַזִּכָּרוֹן.

enables mortal man to turn directly to God, so to speak. Then the blessings change to third person because the balance of the blessing speaks of His outward manifestations as He guides and controls the universe. Of that aspect of God, we have no direct understanding — only an imperfect perception of outward appearances (*Michtav MeEliyahu*).

אֲשֶׁר בָּחַר בָּנוּ ... וְקִדְּשָׁנוּ בְּמִצְוֹתָיו — *Who has chosen us ... and sanctified us with His commandments.* The Sabbath *Kiddush* begins with reference to God's commandments and only later refers to His designation of Israel as His people [*Who has sanctified us with his commandments, took pleasure in us, ...*]. The festival *Kiddush*, however, has the opposite order — it begins with reference to Israel's chosen status and only later mentions the commandment of the festival. This is because the Sabbath commandment was given to Israel in Marah, before it was designated as God's chosen people at Sinai. The designation of Israel *did* precede the commandments of the various festivals, however (*Abudraham*).

אֲשֶׁר בָּחַר בָּנוּ מִכָּל עָם — *Who has chosen us from every nation ...* The wording here is reminiscent of the *Shemoneh Esrei* (*Amidah*) of Yom Tov. There the central blessing begins with the words, 'You have chosen us from all nations; You have loved us and favored us; You have exalted us above all tongues; and You have sanctified us with Your commandments.'

וְרוֹמְמָנוּ מִכָּל לָשׁוֹן — *(And) exalted us above every tongue.* This will be made manifest in Messianic times, for, as *Pesikta Rabbasi* (36) teaches, at that time all the tongues [i.e., the nations] will prostrate themselves before the Messiah and before Israel and proclaim, 'Let us be servants to you and to Israel.'

R' Bunam of P'shis'cha explained this phrase homiletically: You have exalted us to a degree that no tongue is capable of describing.

יוֹם הַזִּכָּרוֹן הַזֶּה יוֹם (זִכְרוֹן) תְּרוּעָה ... — *This Day of Remembrance, a day of (remembrance of) [shofar] blowing ...* The terms 'a day of *shofar* blowing' and 'a remembrance of *shofar* blowing' as appellations for Rosh Hashanah are based upon the verse (*Leviticus* 23:24) which refers to the day as זִכְרוֹן תְּרוּעָה מִקְרָא קֹדֶשׁ, *a remembrance of [shofar] blowing, a convocation of holiness* (*Rashi, Eruvin* 40a), and the verse (*Numbers* 29:1): יוֹם תְּרוּעָה יִהְיֶה לָכֶם, *It shall be a day of [shofar] blowing unto you.* When Rosh Hashanah falls on a weekday the *shofar* is blown during the *Mussaf* service. Therefore in both *Kiddush* and *Shemoneh Esrei* the expression יוֹם תְּרוּעָה, *a day of shofar blowing,* is used. However, on the Sabbath when the *shofar* is not sounded, this phrase is emended to read [as in *Leviticus*], יוֹם

Blessed are You, HASHEM, our God, King of the universe, Who has chosen us from every nation, exalted us above every tongue, and sanctified us with His commandments. And You, HASHEM, our God, have lovingly given us (this Sabbath day and) this Day of Remembrance, a day of (remembrance of) shofar blowing (in love), a convocation of holiness, a memorial of the Exodus from Egypt. For You have chosen us and You have sanctified us above all the nations, and Your word is true and established forever. Blessed are You, HASHEM, King over the entire earth, Who sanctifies (the Sabbath and) Israel and the Day of Remembrance.

זִכְרוֹן תְּרוּעָה, *a day of remembrance of shofar blowing*, to indicate that the shofar is only mentioned but not used (*Tur* 582 citing *R' Sar Shalom*).

מִקְרָא קֹדֶשׁ — *A convocation of holiness*, i.e., a day on which the entire nation gathers to declare the sanctity of the day with prayer and praise of the Almighty; a day celebrated by donning fresh *Yom Tov* clothing and by partaking of festive meals. *Nehemiah* (8:10) describes the festivities of the day: *Eat rich foods, drink sweet beverages, and send portions to whomever has none prepared for himself, for today is holy unto our Lord; be not sad, for the rejoicing of HASHEM is your strength* (*Ramban, Leviticus* 23:2).

זֵכֶר לִיצִיאַת מִצְרָיִם — *A memorial of the Exodus from Egypt*. This phrase occurs in every *Kiddush*, not only that of Pesach which specifically celebrates the Exodus. The other festivals, and the Sabbath, too, serve as reminders of the departure from Egypt, for their observance began with the birth of the Jewish people at the time of the Exodus (*Abudraham*). Moreover, a memorial of the Exodus' is particularly apt for Rosh Hashanah because it was on the Rosh Hashanah before the Exodus that the slavery of our ancestors in Egypt ended, six and a half months before the actual Exodus (*Radak* to *Psalms* 81:4).

There is also a deeper connection between the holy days and the Exodus. Every year and every day we are called upon to renew our service of God. The key to doing so is our awareness that God, King of the universe, revealed Himself to the world at the Exodus and made us His people. That He did so, and in the process demonstrated His mastery over the universe, was vivid proof to our ancestors that He is the Creator Who existed before there was anything else. Our daily prayers recall that God freed us from our slave labors in Egypt, a basic element of our belief in Him as Creator and Master of the universe *(Ramban, Or HaChaim* to *Deut.* 5:15).

וְאוֹתָנוּ קִדַּשְׁתָּ מִכָּל הָעַמִּים — *And You have sanctified us above all the nations*. This phrase is based upon *Deuteronomy* 26:19: וְלִהְיוֹתְךָ עַם קָדֹשׁ, *and that you be a holy nation*. The context of that verse is that God chose Israel from among all the nations and imposed upon it the commandments of the Torah so that it would be elevated and become a holy nation *(Etz Yosef).*

Iyun Tefillah infers from our phrase that holiness can be present among all nations; God has given Israel more sanctity than any others, but they, too, can hallow themselves should they wish to do so. He cites *Eliyah Rabbah* (9): 'I [God] call heaven and earth to bear witness that whether Jew or gentile,

[99] **ROSH HASHANAH** / Its Significance, Laws, and Prayers

> On Saturday night add the following two Havdalah blessings. Two candles should be held before the person reciting the Havdalah.

בָּרוּךְ אַתָּה יהוה אֱלֹהֵינוּ מֶלֶךְ הָעוֹלָם, בּוֹרֵא מְאוֹרֵי הָאֵשׁ.

> Hold the fingers up to the flames to see the reflected light.

slave or maidservant — everyone, according to the deeds he does, can have the Holy Spirit rest on him.' Thus, a degree of holiness comes upon every human being who performs a good deed of his own free will. This, in turn, enables him to go on to further good deeds. The eminence of Israel is in the degree of holiness, not its exclusivity.

וּדְבָרְךָ אֱמֶת וְקַיָּם לָעַד — *And Your word is true and established forever.* This phrase is borrowed from the Rosh Hashanah *Amidah*, and is based upon King David's declaration *(Psalms 119:89): Forever, HASHEM, Your word stands firm in heaven.* This refers to a promise God had made to Adam on the first Rosh Hashanah — as the Midrash relates:[1]

Adam was created on Rosh Hashanah. During the first hour [of that day] He [i.e., God] contemplated [creating Adam]; in the second He took counsel with the ministering angels [see *Genesis* 1:26]; in the third He gathered his dust; in the fourth He kneaded it; in the fifth He gave [the kneaded dust] a rough shape; in the sixth He articulated [human] features; in the seventh He blew a soul into him (ibid. 2:7); in the eighth He stood him on his feet and led him into the Garden of Eden (ibid. v. 8); in the ninth He commanded him [not to eat from the Tree of Knowledge (ibid. v. 17)]; in the tenth he [Adam] sinned (ibid. 3:6); in the eleventh he was judged; and in the twelfth he was sentenced mercifully[2] by the Holy One, Blessed is He. Then God assured Adam, 'You shall be a sign unto your children. Just as you have stood before Me in judgment on this day, and have been released with mercy, so shall your offspring stand before Me in judgment on this day, and they will be released with mercy.' To what day does this refer? — to the first of Tishrei — Rosh Hashanah *(Vayikra Rabbah* 29:1; *Pesikta* 23; cf. *Midrash Tehillim* 92:3).

1. *Kol Bo* cites an alternative Midrash which explains why the phrase 'and Your word is true and established forever' is also said on Yom Kippur:

R' Siman said: The day on which Adam's iniquity was forgiven was a Sabbath day and Yom Kippur. The Holy One, Blessed is He, promised him that on that day, in the future, He would forgive the sins of Israel.

Others said: It was a Sabbath and Rosh Hashanah.

In deference to the two views stated in this Midrash we allude to this promise on both Rosh Hashanah and Yom Kippur.

2. God had told Adam regarding the Tree of Knowledge, *'You must not eat thereof; for on the day you eat of it you shall surely die' (Genesis* 2:17). Yet when Adam ate of its fruit, God did not kill Adam immediately, but allowed him to remain alive for nine hundred and thirty years ... The angel complained, 'Master of the world ... have You not decreed *"on the day you eat of it you shall surely die"*?'

The Holy One, Blessed is He, replied, 'Did I specify to him whether I meant one of My days or one of his days? I shall allow him one of My days [i.e., one thousand years — as the Psalmist (90:4) states: *For a thousand years in Your eyes are like a day* ...]. I shall grant him nine hundred and thirty years, and his descendants seventy years each *(Pesikta Rabbasi* 41).

Thus, Adam was judged mercifully and allowed to live nine hundred and thirty years (see *Genesis* 5:5) before his death sentence was carried out.

> On Saturday night add the following two Havdalah blessings.
> Two candles should be held before the person reciting the Havdalah.
>
> **B**lessed are You, HASHEM, our God, King of the universe,
> Who creates the illuminations of the fire.
>
> Hold the fingers up to the flames to see the reflected light.

Thus, we say, 'Your word is true and established forever,' as we pray that God will fulfill His promise to Adam and judge us mercifully on this day *(Kol Bo)*.

מֶלֶךְ עַל כָּל הָאָרֶץ — *King over the entire world.* The *Amidah* of the *Mussaf* service of each festival consists of seven blessings — the first three and last three of the regular *Shemoneh Esrei* and one middle blessing that describes the Sanctification of the day, specifically with regard to the additional *(Mussaf)* Temple Altar offerings. This blessing concludes with the sanctity of the day: 'Blessed are You, HASHEM, Who sanctifies Israel and the seasons.'

On Rosh Hashanah the *Mussaf Amidah* is enlarged by the addition of three long blessings containing מַלְכִיּוֹת זִכְרוֹנוֹת שׁוֹפָרוֹת, verses regarding *Kingship, Remembrance* and *Shofar.* That is, ten Biblical verses which mention kingship are recited to allude to God's domination as King of the universe. These verses are followed by the blessing, 'King over the entire world.' Similarly, ten verses regarding remembrance and ten that speak of the *shofar* are followed respectively by the blessings, 'He Who remembers the covenant,' and 'He Who hearkens to the *shofar* blasts of Israel, His nation with mercy.'

Accordingly, the *Mussaf Amidah* of *Rosh Hashanah* should contain ten blessings — the seven of every *Mussaf Amidah*, plus the three added blessings. In actual practice, however, there are only nine blessings, for the first of the three added blessings, that of Kingship, is merged with the Sanctification blessing of the regular *Amidah*, while the remaining two are inserted as separate blessings. The Sanctification blessing, having been enhanced by the Kingship blessing, must now conclude with both themes: 'King over the entire earth, Who sanctifies Israel and the Day of Remembrance.' In order not to cause confusion by ending the Sanctification blessing one way in the *Mussaf Amidah* and a different way elsewhere, the Sages ordained that this concluding passage be used commonly for all the prayers of the day, i.e., the *Amidah, Kiddush* and *Haftarah* blessings *(Aroch HaShulchan 582:13).*

מְקַדֵּשׁ (הַשַּׁבָּת וְ) יִשְׂרָאֵל וְיוֹם הַזִּכָּרוֹן — *Who sanctifies (the Sabbath and) Israel and the Day of Remembrance.* The *Kiddush* recited on Rosh Hashanah closes by blessing God Who *sanctifies the people of Israel and the Day of Remembrance* — we mention the Sabbath before Israel. The seventh day of the week was sanctified at the creation of the world, long before the Jewish people was created. In the case of the festivals, however, although the Torah ordains the date on which they are to be celebrated, this date depends on the Jewish people — represented by the Rabbinic Court — which, according to the Torah, regulates and fixes the calendar. We therefore mention the festival only *after* first proclaiming the sanctity of the Jewish people itself *(Beitzah 17a).*

◈§ Havdalah

If *Yom Tov* falls on Sunday, it is insufficient to sanctify its beginning by reciting *Kiddush* — we must also mark the end of the Sabbath with הַבְדָּלָה, *Havdalah,* the ceremony by which we separate the Sabbath with its greater holiness from the rest of the week.

בָּרוּךְ אַתָּה יהוה אֱלֹהֵינוּ מֶלֶךְ הָעוֹלָם, הַמַּבְדִּיל בֵּין קֹדֶשׁ לְחוֹל, בֵּין אוֹר לְחֹשֶׁךְ, בֵּין יִשְׂרָאֵל לָעַמִּים, בֵּין יוֹם הַשְּׁבִיעִי לְשֵׁשֶׁת יְמֵי הַמַּעֲשֶׂה. בֵּין קְדֻשַּׁת שַׁבָּת לִקְדֻשַּׁת יוֹם טוֹב הִבְדַּלְתָּ, וְאֶת יוֹם הַשְּׁבִיעִי מִשֵּׁשֶׁת יְמֵי הַמַּעֲשֶׂה קִדַּשְׁתָּ. הִבְדַּלְתָּ וְקִדַּשְׁתָּ אֶת עַמְּךָ יִשְׂרָאֵל בִּקְדֻשָּׁתֶךָ. בָּרוּךְ אַתָּה יהוה, הַמַּבְדִּיל בֵּין קֹדֶשׁ לְקֹדֶשׁ.

On all nights conclude here.

בָּרוּךְ אַתָּה יהוה אֱלֹהֵינוּ מֶלֶךְ הָעוֹלָם, שֶׁהֶחֱיָנוּ וְקִיְּמָנוּ וְהִגִּיעָנוּ לַזְּמַן הַזֶּה.

We are permitted certain activities on *Yom Tov*, such as baking or cooking, that are forbidden on the Sabbath; therefore it is necessary to declare the Sabbath as ended. For this purpose, we pronounce the blessing, 'Who creates the illuminations of the fire,' over the *Yom Tov* lights, and also the blessing of *Havdalah* which distinguishes between the Sabbath and *Yom Tov*. This latter blessing alludes to seven distinctions that we should take to heart: between the sacred and the profane, between light and darkness, between Israel and the nations, between the Sabbath and weekdays, between the holiness of Sabbath and that of *Yom Tov*; and — within the Jewish people — between *Kohanim* and Levites, and between Levites and Israelites.

When *Yom Tov* falls on Saturday night, the *Kiddush/Havdalah* comprises five blessings: the blessing over wine (יַיִן); the *Kiddush* blessing (קִידוּשׁ); the blessing over the candles (נֵר); the *Havdalah* blessing (הַבְדָּלָה); and the *Shehecheyanu* blessing (זְמַן). To remember the order of the blessings, many people refer to them as יַקְנְהַז, an acronym formed by the Hebrew names for the blessings and used by the Talmud *(Pesachim* 102b) for this purpose.

The ordering of the five blessings is explained by *Rashbam* (ad loc.). There is a general rule regarding the precedence of one *mitzvah* over another: תָּדִיר וְשֶׁאֵינוֹ תָּדִיר תָּדִיר קוֹדֵם, *a more frequently performed mitzvah takes precedence over a less frequently performed mitzvah* (Berachos 51b). Thus the blessing over wine is recited first. *Kiddush* (which marks the beginning of *Yom Tov*) comes before *Havdalah* (which designates the departure of the Sabbath) to avoid the impression that we are anxious to 'unburden' ourselves of the Sabbath. On the contrary, we delay its departure as long as possible. The blessing over the candle precedes *Havdalah* as it does every other week of the year. And *Shehecheyanu* is recited last because it is not inherently bound to either *Kiddush* or *Havdalah*. In fact, the obligation to recite the *Shehecheyanu* at the end of *Yom Tov* could be fulfilled at a different time, e.g., when kindling the *Yom Tov* lights (see pg. 83 §26); at the *Maariv* service (as is the custom on Yom Kippur when *Kiddush* obviously cannot be recited); or even while walking in the street.

> Blessed are You, HASHEM, our God, King of the universe, Who distinguishes between sacred and secular, between light and darkness, between Israel and the nations, between the seventh day and the six days of activity. You have distinguished between the holiness of the Sabbath and the holiness of a festival, and have sanctified the seventh day above the six days of activity. You distinguished and sanctified Your nation, Israel, with Your holiness. Blessed are You, HASHEM, Who distinguishes between holiness and holiness.

On all nights conclude here.

> Blessed are You, HASHEM, our God, King of the universe, Who has kept us alive, sustained us, and brought us to this season.

Havdalah at the close of the Sabbath usually includes a blessing over the scent of sweet-smelling spices. R' David Abudraham explains that this custom is based on a Talmudic dictum: God presents a person with נְשָׁמָה יְתֵרָה, an *additional soul,* upon the arrival of the Sabbath, and takes it from him at the departure of the Sabbath *(Beitzah* 16a). When the additional soul of the Sabbath leaves, then one's own soul pines for its lost companion. To ease this spiritual longing, one smells sweet-scented spices.

However, since *Yom Tov* also brings with it an additional soul, the spices are omitted from the *Havdalah* service when Sunday is *Yom Tov (Rashbam).* Alternatively, the enhanced spirituality of the *Yom Tov* itself, along with the sumptuous festival meals, serves to alleviate the soul's longing *(Tosafos).*

✌§ Shehecheyanu

שֶׁהֶחֱיָנוּ — *Who has kept us alive.* This blessing is called בִּרְכַּת הַזְּמַן, *the blessing of the time,* or simply זְמַן, *time.* It is recited: on the festivals; over fruits of a new season, provided they ripen at recurring intervals and are not always available; upon *mitzvos* that are performed at seasonal intervals such as *shofar, lulav* and others connected with the annual festivals; upon seeing a friend whom one has not seen for a significant interval; upon purchasing a new garment of significance; and upon benefiting from a significant event [see *Orach Chaim* 225].

This blessing is technically in the category of בִּרְכוֹת הוֹדָאָה, *blessings of thanksgiving.* It expresses our gratitude to God for having granted us the life and sustenance to celebrate another festive season.

שֶׁהֶחֱיָנוּ וְקִיְּמָנוּ וְהִגִּיעָנוּ — *Who has kept us alive, sustained us, and brought us to this season.* The threefold expression with which we thank God for allowing us to live to celebrate this festival is based upon the Psalmist's trebled praise *(Psalms* 146:1-2) in gratitude for his life: *Praise HASHEM, O my soul; I shall praise HASHEM while I live; I shall sing [praises] to my God while I endure (Rokeach* 351 cited by *Anaf Yosef).*

סִימָנָא מִילְתָא

Various symbolic foods are eaten at the festive meal on the first night of Rosh Hashanah (in some communities they are also eaten on the second night), and a short prayer alluding to the symbolism is recited for each food. Although customs vary from community to community, many of the foods have been eaten since Biblical and Talmudic times. There is also an almost universally accepted custom of dipping the first piece of challah into honey. After the challah has been eaten, a piece of apple sweetened with honey is given to each participant and the blessing is recited:

בָּרוּךְ אַתָּה יהוה אֱלֹהֵינוּ מֶלֶךְ הָעוֹלָם, בּוֹרֵא פְּרִי הָעֵץ.

A small piece of the apple is eaten and the following prayer is said before the apple is finished.

יְהִי רָצוֹן מִלְּפָנֶיךָ, יהוה אֱלֹהֵינוּ וֵאלֹהֵי אֲבוֹתֵינוּ, שֶׁתְּחַדֵּשׁ עָלֵינוּ שָׁנָה טוֹבָה וּמְתוּקָה.

◆§ Significant Omens

The custom of eating symbolic foods on Rosh Hashanah is based on a Talmudic teaching: Abaye taught, Now that you have said that an omen is significant, each person should habituate himself to eat, at the beginning of the year, gourds, fenugreek, leeks, beets and dates *(Horayos* 12a; *Kerisus* 6a).

The symbolism of the different foods falls into various groupings. Some are sweet tasting and indicate a sweet year, while others grow rapidly and in abundance and indicate an abundance of merits *(Rashi)*. The names of some of these foods allude to abundance and symbolize an increase of Israel's *mitzvah* performance; others allude to destruction and eradication and are applied to Israel's sins and enemies *(Mordechai; Or Zarua)*. For further discussion on the rationale of the significant omens, see pp. 13-17.

Dipping the challah into honey. The obvious intention here, as stated in the short prayer recited over the apple dipped in honey (see below), is an allusion to a sweet year. Indeed, among the Jews of Baghdad, the *challah* is not dipped into honey but into sugar.

A deeper allusion to the custom of dipping the *challah* into honey may be found in the verse *(Psalms 81:17): But He would feed him with the cream of the wheat, and from a rock sate you with honey.* This verse comes at the end of the psalm which the Talmud *(Rosh Hashanah* 30b) identifies as the song sung by the Levite chorus of the *Beis HaMikdash* to accompany the Temple sacrifices on Rosh Hashanah. *Imrei Noam* cites this verse as the source of the custom of using honey at the festival Rosh Hashanah meals: *the cream of the wheat* — i.e., the *challah* — is eaten *with honey.*

[Another basis for the custom of dipping the *challah* into honey may be the Talmudic passage *(Beitzah* 16a): *All of man's provisions are determined for him from Rosh Hashanah to Rosh Hashanah.* As *Rashi* explains, all that man will earn for his sustenance during the year is determined on Rosh Hashanah, therefore one should not overspend because he will not be allotted additional funds. (The Talmud enumerates certain exceptions for which he is provided in excess of the predetermined amount; see p. 126.) Stated in other words, man must beseech God on

The Prayers [104]

~§ Significant Omens

Various symbolic foods are eaten at the festive meal on the first night of Rosh Hashanah (in some communities they are also eaten on the second night), and a short prayer alluding to the symbolism is recited for each food. Although customs vary from community to community, many of the foods have been eaten since Biblical and Talmudic times. There is also an almost universally accepted custom of dipping the first piece of challah into honey. After the challah has been eaten, a piece of apple sweetened with honey is given to each participant and the blessing is recited:

Blessed are You, HASHEM, our God, King of the universe, Who creates the fruit of the tree.

A small piece of the apple is eaten and the following prayer is said before the apple is finished.

May it be Your will, HASHEM, our God and the God of our ancestors, that You renew for us a good and a sweet year.

Rosh Hashanah to apportion him an abundant share for the coming year; and he must rely wholeheartedly on God's beneficence for his sustenance.

The period during which reliance upon Divine mercy for one's daily requirements was most evident was the forty-year sojourn of the Israelites in a desert described *(Jeremiah 2:6)* as: *A wilderness, a wasteland of pits, a land of desolation and the shadow of death.* Nothing grew there; if left to their own designs they would have perished from hunger (see *Exodus 16:3*). Yet God supplied them with a daily portion of manna. For forty years, each day's meals fell from heaven and were there for the taking. Reliance on God's beneficence was total. And what was the taste of the manna? *Its taste was that of dough fried with honey* (ibid. v. 31). So on Rosh Hashanah, when our annual provisions are determined, we recall the manna and our total dependence on God's beneficence by eating our dough, i.e., challah, dipped in honey.]

Bnei Yisaschar notes that דְּבַשׁ, *honey,* has the same *gematria* — 306 — as אָב הָרַחֲמִים, *Father of Mercy,* and thus evokes Divine comparison and mercy.

תַּפּוּחַ — Apple. The selection of the apple above other fruits for this symbolic purpose is based upon the verse *(Genesis 27:27)* which describes the sightless Patriarch Isaac attempting to identify his son: *See, the fragrance of my son is like the fragrance of a field which HASHEM has blessed ...* The Talmud *(Taanis 29b)* identifies this fragrance as that of a field of apple trees *(Biyur HaGra; Maharil,* cited in *Darkei Moshe).*[1] Moreover there is a view *(Zohar Chadash)* that the blessing of Jacob which is prefaced by this verse took place on Rosh Hashanah *(Biyur HaGra).* From this verse we see that Israel is compared to the apple. A

---

1. The apple represents not only Israel, it also is used to symbolize both God and Torah — and as *Zohar (Vayikra 73)* teaches: קוּדְשָׁא בְּרִיךְ הוּא אוֹרַיְיתָא וְיִשְׂרָאֵל חַד, *God, Torah and Israel are one.* Israel says of God *(Song of Songs 2:3): Like the apple among the trees of the forest ... His fruit is sweet to my palate ...* According to *Vilna Gaon* this is an additional allusion to the apple dipped in honey *(sweet to my palate).* [In kabbalistic literature the apple also is used as a simile to allude to God. The term חֲקַל תַּפּוּחִין קַדִּישִׁין, *Field of Sacred Apples,* is a frequently found expression used to describe the שְׁכִינָה, *manifestation of the Divine Presence.*] Two verses further (ibid. v. 5) Israel asks God: *Sustain me with dainties, spread apples about me.* The Talmud *(Soferim 16:4)* allegorically interprets the dainties as the halachic portion of the Torah and the apples as the Aggadic teachings

Other foods which are symbolic and should be eaten at this meal are mentioned in the Talmud, Shulchan Aruch and by other authorities. The list below follows no particular order. However, the blessing already recited on the apple exempts the other fruits. If the vegetables are eaten without challah, the blessing בּוֹרֵא פְּרִי הָאֲדָמָה, Who creates the fruit of the earth, should be recited before the first vegetable is eaten.

(רוּבְיָא — fenugreek)

יְהִי רָצוֹן מִלְּפָנֶיךָ, יהוה אֱלֹהֵינוּ וֵאלֹהֵי אֲבוֹתֵינוּ, שֶׁיִּרְבּוּ זְכִיּוֹתֵינוּ.

(כָּרְתֵי — leek)

יְהִי רָצוֹן מִלְּפָנֶיךָ, יהוה אֱלֹהֵינוּ וֵאלֹהֵי אֲבוֹתֵינוּ, שֶׁיִּכָּרְתוּ שׂוֹנְאֵינוּ.

(סִילְקָא — beet)

יְהִי רָצוֹן מִלְּפָנֶיךָ, יהוה אֱלֹהֵינוּ וֵאלֹהֵי אֲבוֹתֵינוּ, שֶׁיִּסְתַּלְּקוּ אוֹיְבֵינוּ (alternatively — חַטֹּאתֵינוּ).

(תַּמְרֵי — dates)

יְהִי רָצוֹן מִלְּפָנֶיךָ, יהוה אֱלֹהֵינוּ וֵאלֹהֵי אֲבוֹתֵינוּ, שֶׁיִּתַּמּוּ שׂוֹנְאֵינוּ.

(קְרָא — gourd)

יְהִי רָצוֹן מִלְּפָנֶיךָ, יהוה אֱלֹהֵינוּ וֵאלֹהֵי אֲבוֹתֵינוּ, שֶׁיִּקָּרַע גְּזַר דִּינֵנוּ וְיִקָּרְאוּ לְפָנֶיךָ זְכִיּוֹתֵינוּ.

similar comparison appears in God's statement to Israel *(Song of Songs* 7:9): *And the scent of your breath is like apples.*

בּוֹרֵא פְּרִי הָעֵץ — *Who creates the fruit of the tree.* Since the apple is not really part of the meal, the blessing over the challah, which generally covers the entire meal, does not exempt the apple from a separate blessing *(Maharil,* cited in *Darkei Moshe).* Additionally, since when two foods are eaten in combination the blessing over the primary food exempts the other one, no blessing need be recited over the honey which is only secondary to the apple *(Magen Avraham).* Nevertheless, some authorities feel that since the purpose of eating the apple and honey is to symbolize sweetness, the honey may perhaps be considered the more important of the two. To avoid any problems these authorities eat the apple and honey with a slice of *challah,* in which case both become secondary to the *challah* and no additional blessing is required *(Baer Hetev* citing *Responsa Shevus Yaakov).*

The prayer should not interpose between the blessing and eating the apple. For this reason, a bit of the apple should be eaten before the prayer is recited *(Magen Avraham),* or the prayer should precede the blessing *(Aroch HaShulchan).* According to the custom of *Chabad*-Lubavitch, however, see p.

Other foods which are symbolic and should be eaten at this meal are mentioned in the Talmud, Shulchan Aruch and by other authorities. The list below follows no particular order. However, the blessing already recited on the apple exempts the other fruits. If the vegetables are eaten without challah, the blessing בּוֹרֵא פְּרִי הָאֲדָמָה, *Who creates the fruit of the earth*, should be recited before the first vegetable is eaten.

(fenugreek)
May it be Your will, HASHEM, our God and the God of our ancestors, that our merits increase.

(leek)
May it be Your will, HASHEM, our God and the God of our ancestors, that our enemies be decimated.

(beet)
May it be Your will, HASHEM, our God and the God of our ancestors, that our adversaries (alternatively — sins) be removed.

(dates)
May it be Your will, HASHEM, our God and the God of our ancestors, that our adversaries be consumed.

(gourd)
May it be Your will, HASHEM, our God and the God of our ancestors, that the decree of our sentence be torn asunder; and may our merits be proclaimed before You.

---

84 §27, the blessing and prayers are recited together before the apple is eaten.

וּמְתוּקָה — *And sweet.* Although the custom of dipping a raw apple into honey is almost universal, the Jews of Baghdad eat apple cooked in sugar *(Ben Ish Chai).*

רוּבְיָא — *Fenugreek* is an herb, indigenous to western Asia, whose seeds are used in cookery and medicine.

Magen Avraham writes that רוּבְיָא — derived from רבה, *to increase* — is not limited to the specific species mentioned in the Talmud. In reality, any food the name of which implies increase and abundance may be used in its place. This applies not only to the Hebrew name for the food, but even to its name in another language used locally for that particular food. Based on this view it has become customary in many communities to eat carrots. The Yiddish word for carrots is *mehren,* a word which can also mean 'increase.' Similarly, the German word for carrots, *Mohrrube,* calls to mind both *mehr,* more, and רוּבְיָא (based on *Aroch HaShulchan* and *Chayei Adam).*

Another custom based on this view is that of the Jews of Baghdad. Since the Arabic word for רוּבְיָא is *lubia,* the Jews of that community add the word וּתְלַבְּבֵינוּ, *and treat us in a heartfelt manner (Ben Ishi Chai).*

Many communities have developed interesting customs based upon the names of foods. Thus *Bircas Chaim* records that Ukranian Jews would give their children chicken livers on Rosh Hashanah. The Yiddish word for livers, *leberlach,* is homophonous with *leb ehrlich,* or 'live honestly.'

סִילְקָא — *Beets.* Sour borscht, however, should not be served on Rosh Hashanah, for only sweet foods should be eaten *(Pri Megadim).*

[107]   **ROSH HASHANAH** / Its Significance, Laws, and Prayers

(רמון — pomegranate)

יְהִי רָצוֹן מִלְּפָנֶיךָ, יהוה אֱלֹהֵינוּ וֵאלֹהֵי אֲבוֹתֵינוּ, שֶׁנִּרְבֶּה זְכִיּוֹת כְּרִמּוֹן.
(alternatively — שֶׁיִּרְבּוּ זְכִיּוֹתֵינוּ כְּגַרְעִינֵי רִמּוֹן.)

(דָּג — fish)

יְהִי רָצוֹן מִלְּפָנֶיךָ, יהוה אֱלֹהֵינוּ וֵאלֹהֵי אֲבוֹתֵינוּ, שֶׁיִּפְרוּ וְיִרְבּוּ כְּדָגִים.

(רֹאשׁ כֶּבֶשׂ — head of a sheep)

יְהִי רָצוֹן מִלְּפָנֶיךָ, יהוה אֱלֹהֵינוּ וֵאלֹהֵי אֲבוֹתֵינוּ, שֶׁנִּהְיֶה לְרֹאשׁ וְלֹא לְזָנָב.
(some add — וִיהִי רָצוֹן שֶׁיִּזְכּוֹר לָנוּ זְכוּתָא דְיִצְחָק אָבִינוּ.)

דָּגִים — *Fish*. The custom of eating fish and reciting the associated prayer is mentioned by *Abudraham* and *Pri Etz Chaim*. An additional reason for this custom is based on the Talmudic dictum (*Berachos* 20a): The Evil Eye has no power over that which is hidden from the eye; since fish are hidden under the water, the Evil Eye cannot affect them. Thus eating fish is a symbolic request that we be protected from the Evil Eye (*Pri Megadim*).

Maharshal generally enjoyed eating fish. On Rosh Hashanah, however, he would refrain from eating fish as an excercise in self-control (*Magen Avraham*). This abstention from fish, however, does not apply to the average person. Nevertheless, the fish should not be prepared in brine or vinegar, for only sweet foods should be eaten (*Pri Megadim*).

Avodas HaKodesh cites a view (based on a teaching of *Zohar*) that fish should not be eaten on Rosh Hashanah. *Bircas Chaim* reports that Moroccan Jews refrain from fish (דָּג) on Rosh Hashanah because the name evokes the word דְּאָגָה, *worry*. However, the overwhelming majority of authorities do not accept this view.

לְרֹאשׁ וְלֹא לְזָנָב — *As the head and not as the tail*. This prayer is based on the verse (*Deuteronomy* 28:13): *And HASHEM shall place you as a head and not as a tail ... because you have listened to the commandments of HASHEM, your God ...* In *Targum Onkelos* these words are paraphrased: *As a mighty one and not as a weakling.* According to *Targum Yonasan* the phrase means: *As royalty and not as commonfolk.*

The wording of the verse seems to be redundant. If one is at the head, he is surely not at the tail! Why does Scripture repeat the obvious? *Ramban* explains: *HASHEM shall place you as a head* over many nations. But lest you think that you will nevertheless be subservient to some other power, God

The Prayers [108]

(pomegranate)
May it be Your will, HASHEM, our God and the God of our ancestors, that our merits increase as [the seeds of] a pomegranate.

(fish)
May it be Your will, HASHEM, our God and the God of our ancestors, that we be fruitful and multiply like fish.

(head of a sheep)
May it be Your will, HASHEM, our God and the God of our ancestors, that we be as the head and not as the tail. (some add — And may it be Your will that the merit of our Patriarch Isaac be remembered for us.)

---

adds: *And not as a tail,* i.e., you will lead all and follow none.[1]

A sheep's head is used for this symbolic food because it serves as an additional reminder of the merits of the *Akeidah,* the Binding of Isaac (see above p. 61), at which a ram replaced Isaac on the Altar. According to one view *(Pesikta Rabbasi* 40:6) the *Akeidah* took place on Rosh Hashanah. As a further allusion to the *Akeidah,* Maharam of Rothenburg preferred using a ram's head to that of a ewe (cited in *Tur).*

After offering the ram in lieu of Isaac, Abraham prayed, 'May it be the will of he who saw the ram that I offered in place of my son, that it be considered as if I had indeed offered my son, him and all his future descendants. May the name of this place be יִרְאֶה, *He shall see;* and may the prayer of everyone who will ever recite His Name be included in my prayer today.'

The Spirit of Holiness replied, 'That which is said by Abraham today will be seen ...' *(Midrash Tehillim).*

Nevertheless, if a sheep's head is not available, any other head may be substituted. Although the allusion to the *Akeidah* would not be present, the other symbol — *that we be as the head and not as the tail* — would remain *(Magen Avraham). Hagahos Ashri* notes that the head should be dipped in honey.

שֶׁיִזָּכוֹר לָנוּ זְכוּתָא דְיִצְחָק אָבִינוּ — *That the merit of our Patriarch Isaac be remembered for us.* This prayer is added by *Siddur Tefillah Yesharah Berditchev.* According to *Ben Ish Chai,* the following phrase is added: וְתִזְכּוֹר לָנוּ עֲקֵידָתוֹ וְאֵילוֹ שֶׁל יִצְחָק אָבִינוּ בֶּן אַבְרָהָם אָבִינוּ עֲלֵיהֶם הַשָּׁלוֹם, *And remember for us the Akeidah and the ram of our Patriarch Isaac, son of our Patriarch Abraham, peace upon them.*

---

1. R' Eliezer of Dzikov offered another interpretation of the term לְרֹאשׁ, *as a head.* The word לְרֹאשׁ is an acronym for the phrase, לַעֲשׂוֹת רְצוֹן אָבִינוּ שֶׁבַּשָּׁמַיִם, *to fulfill the will of our Father in heaven.*

◆§ תקיעת שופר

The congregation recites psalm 47 seven times.

א לַמְנַצֵּחַ, לִבְנֵי קֹרַח מִזְמוֹר. ב כָּל הָעַמִּים תִּקְעוּ כָף, הָרִיעוּ לֵאלֹהִים בְּקוֹל רִנָּה. ג כִּי יהוה עֶלְיוֹן נוֹרָא, מֶלֶךְ גָּדוֹל עַל כָּל הָאָרֶץ. ד יַדְבֵּר עַמִּים תַּחְתֵּינוּ, וּלְאֻמִּים תַּחַת

◆§ Psalm 47

In most communities,[1] psalm 47 is recited seven times prior to the blowing of the *shofar* on Rosh Hashanah. Much of the commentary appearing here has been culled from the ArtScroll *Tehillim* where a more complete commentary appears.

The theme woven into the fabric of the text is the ability of the *shofar* blast to inspire mankind and to arouse God's mercy. The *shofar* described here refers to the horn of redemption which the Messiah is destined to blow. However, the Rabbis teach us that it also alludes to the *shofar* blown every Rosh Hashanah, which symbolizes the individual soul's redemption from its sins.

Although the Torah gives no reason for sounding the *shofar* on Rosh Hashanah, many authorities have sought allusions in this *mitzvah*. Notable among these is R' Saadiah Gaon who finds ten such allusions, many of which are hinted at in psalm 47, as the commentary below indicates. (For the complete list, and for the opinions of other authorities, see above, pp. 16-20).

The Name אֱלֹהִים, *ELOHIM*, which refers to God's manifestation as the Dispenser of Strict Justice, appears here seven times. Thus in the sevenfold repetition this Divine Name is recited a total of forty-nine times.

The Sages teach that there are forty-nine levels of spiritual impurity before the lowest depth from which no redemption is possible. Correspondingly, there are forty-nine ascending levels of sanctity which man can attain. The forty-nine times which the Name is recited allude to the power of these verses to transform the forty-nine possible levels of spiritual uncleanliness into forty-nine corresponding levels of sanctity and purity. When Israel is inspired to purify and perfect itself with such intensity, surely God's strict justice will be changed to His Attribute of Mercy (*Matteh Ephraim, Elef HaMagen* 585:5).

Although this psalm was first composed by Korach's sons, David adopted it as his own and endowed it with universal dimensions. The *Yalkut* asserts that David's harp was related to the Messianic *shofar* and the future redemption. R' Chanina taught that every part of the ram which Abraham sacrificed instead of his son Isaac on Mount Moriah was assigned a special purpose. Its sinews were fashioned into harpstrings for David. Its hide became the belt which girded Elijah's loins. Its left horn was sounded on Mount Sinai. Its right horn will be sounded at the time of the future redemption.

---

1. A notable exception is the *Kahal Adas Yeshurun* community of Frankfurt am Main which omits all the verses and prayers that precede the blessing over sounding the *shofar*. In this community, as in many others, the rabbi addresses the congregation before *shofar* blowing. After the sermon, the rabbi and the *tokea* [shofar blower] stand at the *bimah* in the center of the synagogue. The *tokea* recites a silent prefatory prayer and then announces aloud, שְׁתִיקָה יָפָה בִּשְׁעַת תְּקִיעַת שׁוֹפָר וּבְרִכּוּתֶיהָ,' *Silence is proper at the time of sounding the shofar and its blessings.*

◆§ Sounding the Shofar

The congregation recites psalm 47 seven times.

¹ **F**or *the Conductor, by the sons of Korach, a song.* **²** *All you nations, join hands! Sound the shofar to God with a cry of joy.* **³** *For HASHEM is Most High, awesome, a great King over all of the earth.* **⁴** *He shall lead nations under us, and kingdoms beneath our feet.* **⁵** *He will choose*

2. תִּקְעוּ כָף — *Join hands.* This is a call to all nations to join hands in an alliance to collectively call out and praise God (*Rashi*).

Chazeh Tzion notes that the numerical value of the word כָף is one hundred. On Rosh Hashanah, all of the nations pass before God in judgment (*Rosh Hashanah* 16a), and at that time we are commanded: תִּקְעוּ, *Blow* [on the shofar] כָף, *one hundred blasts.*

הָרִיעוּ לֵאלֹהִים — *Sound the shofar to God.* Malbim observes that it is customary to sound the trumpets during a royal coronation ceremony. This is what the nations will do when they appoint God as their sovereign.

Similarly, the first of *R' Saadiah Gaon's* ten reasons for blowing the shofar on Rosh Hashanah is that since Rosh Hashanah corresponds to the first day of man's (Adam's) creation, humanity is obligated to coronate God as King with fanfare on this day, as King David says (*Psalms* 98:6): *With trumpets and shofar sound call out before the King, HASHEM* (*R' Avrohom Chaim Feuer*).

Specifically הָרִיעוּ refers to the *teruah*, or broken note, of the *shofar* (see p. 66). *Chazeh Tzion* thus explains that with the sound of the broken *teruah*-blast of Rosh Hashanah, the heart of the sinner is broken with fear and trembling, and likewise does God's wrath dissipate and turn into Divine mercy. [This corresponds to *R' Saadiah Gaon's* seventh reason for blowing the *shofar.*]

3. כִּי ה' עֶלְיוֹן נוֹרָא — *For HASHEM is Most High, awesome.* This is the cry of joy which the nations are urged to shout

(*Ibn Ezra*). He is *Most High* because He controls everyone; He is *awesome* because He performs wonders that cause the nations to fear Him (*Radak*).

מֶלֶךְ גָּדוֹל עַל כָּל הָאָרֶץ — *A great King over all of the earth.* This alludes to *R' Saadiah Gaon's* second reason for sounding the *shofar.* Before a king punishes his subjects for neglecting his decrees, he gives them a final warning. Rosh Hashanah initiates the Ten Days of Repentance, culminating in the final judgment of Yom Kippur. The *shofar* blast represents God's final warning to His people (*R' Feuer*).

4. יַדְבֵּר עַמִּים תַּחְתֵּינוּ — *He shall lead nations under us.* God will lead the nations from the ends of the earth to Jerusalem, to bring them under Israel's rule.

וּלְאֻמִּים תַּחַת רַגְלֵינוּ — *And kingdoms beneath our feet.* The translation of לְאֻמִּים as *kingdoms* follows *Tehillos Hashem*, who emphasizes that the wicked nobles who control the hierarchy of *kingdoms* will suffer much more than the simple peasants who are described above as עַמִּים, *nations,* meaning *followers.* Because the nobles conspired to tyrannize and oppress Israel, they are condemned to be crushed *beneath our feet.* The common folk, who did not initiate any persecutions but merely followed their cruel leaders, will now be led under the guidance and rule of Israel.

Sforno believes that this Jewish domination will be entirely beneficial to the nations. They will be under our intelligent guidance and will follow the path of our feet, as the prophet

[111]   **ROSH HASHANAH** / Its Significance, Laws, and Prayers

רַגְלֵינוּ. ה יִבְחַר לָנוּ אֶת נַחֲלָתֵנוּ, אֶת גְּאוֹן יַעֲקֹב אֲשֶׁר אָהֵב סֶלָה. ו עָלָה אֱלֹהִים בִּתְרוּעָה, יהוה בְּקוֹל שׁוֹפָר. ז זַמְּרוּ אֱלֹהִים זַמֵּרוּ, זַמְּרוּ לְמַלְכֵּנוּ זַמֵּרוּ. ח כִּי מֶלֶךְ כָּל הָאָרֶץ אֱלֹהִים, זַמְּרוּ מַשְׂכִּיל. ט מָלַךְ אֱלֹהִים עַל גּוֹיִם, אֱלֹהִים יָשַׁב עַל כִּסֵּא

foretells: *You will be named the priests of HASHEM, men shall call you the ministers of our God (Isaiah 61:6).*

5. אֶת גְּאוֹן יַעֲקֹב — *The pride of Jacob.* This is the *Beis HaMikdash,* or Holy Temple, where God's spirit resides in splendor. The Jewish nation views the fact that God dwells in its midst with great גָּאוֹן, *pride,* and sees the Divine Presence as its most remarkable advantage over other nations *(Radak).*

Why does the Psalmist here refer to all of Israel as *Jacob? Alshich* comments that the first two Temples, which were temporary, were identified with Abraham and Isaac. However, the third and final *Beis HaMikdash,* which will endure eternally, is ascribed to the merit of Jacob, who also lives forever — as the Talmud teaches: Our forefather Jacob never (really) died *(Taanis 5b; see Ramban, Genesis 49:33* and ArtScroll comm. to that verse).

R' Saadiah Gaon's fifth reason for sounding the *shofar* is to remind us of the *Beis HaMikdash,* which lies in ruins. The gentile marauders blew their horns and trumpets in battle as they vanquished Israel and destroyed the Temple. The sound of the *shofar* should arouse us to beseech God to rebuild the *Beis HaMikdash,* which is our pride *(R' Feuer).*

6. עָלָה אֱלֹהִים בִּתְרוּעָה — *God has ascended with the blast.* According to *Pirkei d'Rabbi Eliezer* (chapter 46), these words allude to the transmission of the Second Tablets at Sinai. The original Tablets were destroyed because of the Golden Calf, which was made as a result of confusion concerning the precise time of Moses' ascent and descent from the mountain. When Moses went up the second time, the days were clearly marked off and recorded by the daily blast of the *shofar.* At that time, the faith of the people rose high above the threat of idolatry; therefore, *God ascended with the blast.*

For this reason, the custom is to sound the *shofar* publicly from the first of Elul, the day of Moses' third ascent *(Tur Orach Chaim 581;* but see p. 79). R' Saadiah Gaon's third reason for sounding the *shofar* on Rosh Hashanah is to recall the blasts sounded at Sinai *(R' Feuer).*

Many *Midrashim* suggest that the Psalmist alludes to the blast of the *shofar* on Rosh Hashanah. Specifically the תְּרוּעָה, *teruah,* is the broken blast which symbolizes the harsh, shattering punishments of אֱלֹהִים, *the Dispenser of strict justice.* When the Jew hears the sound of the *teruah,* he realizes that he deserves shattering punishment for his sins and is inspired to repent. Having felt remorse for his sins, he is forgiven, and God arises from His Throne of Strict Judgment and sits down on His Throne of Mercy where He converts harsh justice to compassion *(Midrash Vayikra Rabbah 29).*

בְּקוֹל שׁוֹפָר 'ה — *HASHEM, with the sound of the shofar. Sforno* observes that this is the long awaited blast that will signal the ingathering of the exiles: *And it will be on that day, He will blow on a great shofar, and they will come — those who were lost in the land of Assyria, and those who were cast out in the land of Egypt — and they will bow to HASHEM on the holy mountain, in Jerusalem (Isaiah 27:13).*

The ninth reason offered by R' Saadiah Gaon for the sounding of the *shofar* reflects this verse. He stresses that when one hears the *shofar* on Rosh

The Prayers [112]

for us our heritage, the pride of Jacob which He loved, Selah. ⁶ *God has ascended with the blast, HASHEM, with the sound of the shofar.* ⁷ *Make music for God, make music! Make music for our King, make music!* ⁸ *For God is King of all the earth, make music, O enlightened one!* ⁹ *God reigns over the peoples, God sits upon His holy*

Hashanah, he should pray for the day of the Ingathering of the Exiles *(R' Feuer).*

Alshich, pursuing the theme of Rosh Hashanah, explains that after the broken *teruah* blast, אֱלֹהִים, signifying strict justice, is tempered with 'ה, the Name that represents Divine mercy.

Ramban relates the word שׁוֹפָר to שֶׁפֶר, *beauty.* The blast of the *shofar* arouses Israel to repent and beautify its ways so that it may serve as an example of rectitude for all nations.

7. זַמְּרוּ אֱלֹהִים זַמֵּרוּ — *Make music for God, make music.* The word מִזְמוֹר is usually translated as *a song* or *a psalm;* however, the root word זמר is more accurately translated as *the instrumental accompaniment* to lyrics, which are called שִׁירָה. Since the previous verse speaks of a musical instrument, the *shofar,* the word זַמְּרוּ is best rendered *make music.*

R' Samson Raphael Hirsch notes that זֶמֶר is related to זְמוֹרָה, *vine, branch.* Inside the branch, the sap gathers long before the fruit emerges. When a sufficient amount of this nutritious liquid accumulates, the tree is ready to burst forth with fruit.

So, too, with song. All feelings and emotions are gathered into the strains of the wordless melody. When these feelings reach a crescendo, they overflow into original words of praise. The well-chosen, inspired words of song are thus the fruits of the זֶמֶר.

זַמְּרוּ לְמַלְכֵּנוּ זַמֵּרוּ — *Make music for our King, make music!* This repetition indicates that one melody inspires the next *(Divrei Shlomo).*

8. כִּי מֶלֶךְ כָּל הָאָרֶץ אֱלֹהִים — *For God is King of all the earth.* The prophet Zechariah (14:9) teaches: *HASHEM will be acknowledged as King over the entire earth.* At that time the *shofar* blast will herald universal peace. But today the *shofar* is used as an instrument of war — as Joshua (6:17) said to the people: *'Blow (the shofar) for HASHEM has given you the city.'*

זַמְּרוּ מַשְׂכִּיל — *Make music, O enlightened one.* Even the ordinary people are exhorted to *join hands and sound the shofar to God with a cry of joy* (v. 2), for this simple form of merriment is within their ability. However, the composition of music is a complex art reserved for the enlightened one of superior intelligence *(Radak).*

Otzar Nechmad draws attention to a grammatical inconsistency. The singular form מַשְׂכִּיל, *enlightened one,* follows the plural verb זַמְּרוּ. This implies that although many intelligent men are urged to compose, each should pursue the task individually, for each man's comprehension of God's glory is unique.

According to *R' Yosef Kimchi* (quoted by his son, *Radak*) and *Meiri,* 'enlightened' is not a description of the composer but of the composition [thus: *make enlightened music*]. Do not compose a mere folk tune, but a work of the highest excellence, one that wins its listener's attention and stimulates him to use his mental facilities to recognize the dominion of God.

9. מָלַךְ אֱלֹהִים עַל גּוֹיִם — *God reigns over the peoples.* Until now, God has only ruled over Israel; henceforth, he shall reign over all peoples [see *Zechariah* 14:9] *(Radak).*

אֱלֹהִים יָשַׁב עַל כִּסֵּא קָדְשׁוֹ — *God sits upon His holy throne* [lit. *the throne of His*

קָדְשׁוֹ. ּ נְדִיבֵי עַמִּים נֶאֱסָפוּ, עַם אֱלֹהֵי אַבְרָהָם, כִּי לֵאלֹהִים מָגִנֵּי אֶרֶץ, מְאֹד נַעֲלָה:

Before the blessings of the shofar are recited, the tokea [shofar-blower] or chazzan recites the following seven verses responsively with the congregation:

תהלים קיח:ה — מִן הַמֵּצַר קָרָאתִי יָּהּ, עָנָנִי בַמֶּרְחָב יָהּ.

The initial letters of the next six verses spell the phrase קְרַע שָׂטָן, *Tear up Satan.*

איכה ג:נו — **ק**וֹלִי שָׁמָעְתָּ, אַל תַּעְלֵם אָזְנְךָ לְרַוְחָתִי, לְשַׁוְעָתִי.

תהלים קיט:קס — **ר**ֹאשׁ דְּבָרְךָ אֱמֶת, וּלְעוֹלָם כָּל מִשְׁפַּט צִדְקֶךָ.

שם קכב — **ע**ֲרֹב עַבְדְּךָ לְטוֹב, אַל יַעַשְׁקוּנִי זֵדִים.

שם קסב — **שָׂ**שׂ אָנֹכִי עַל אִמְרָתֶךָ, כְּמוֹצֵא שָׁלָל רָב.

שם סו — **ט**וּב טַעַם וָדַעַת לַמְּדֵנִי, כִּי בְמִצְוֹתֶיךָ הֶאֱמָנְתִּי.

שם קח — **נ**ִדְבוֹת פִּי רְצֵה נָא יהוה, וּמִשְׁפָּטֶיךָ לַמְּדֵנִי.

---

holiness]. *Shevet MiYisrael* views this as an allusion to the *Midrash (Bereishis Rabbah* 82:9) which states: When God judges Israel He does so hastily, while standing [as it were], so that their examination will be brief and superficial and their verdict lenient. When judging the nations, however, He sits, in order to conduct a lengthy and exacting investigation of their deeds. Then He adopts the role of a prosecutor and accuses them.

Thus, the Psalmist foretells that when God rules the gentiles He will sit upon His holy throne [of judgment].

R' Saadiah Gaon's eighth reason for the sounding of the *shofar* is to bring to mind the awesomeness of the Final Judgment, as the prophet says *(Zephaniah* 1:14, 16): *Near is the great day of HASHEM, it is near and swiftly draws close ... A day of shofar and shouting* (R' Feuer).

10. נְדִיבֵי עַמִּים — *The nobles of the nations. Radak* and *Ibn Ezra* identify these as the great nobles of the gentile nations. According to *Rashi*, the נְדִיבִים are the non-Jews who nobly submitted to slaughter and martyrdom in order to sanctify God's Name.

Abraham is considered the paragon of נְדִיבוּת, *nobility* and *self-sacrifice*. Israel, more than any other nation, is called בַּת נָדִיב, *daughter of nobility* (*Songs* 7:2). This designation applies especially when Israel is prepared to sacrifice the comforts of home in order to make the arduous festival pilgrimage to Jerusalem *(Chagigah* 3a). At these times the Jews resemble Abraham, who gave up everything in order to follow God to the land of Canaan. The noble gentiles who gather in Israel are following in the footsteps of Abraham and deserve to be called נְדִיבִים.

R' Saadiah Gaon's sixth reason for the sounding of the *shofar* is to remind us of *Akeidas Yitzchak*, when Abraham's son Isaac was prepared to give up his life for God. So should every Jew be ready to sacrifice himself for God (R' Feuer).

עַם אֱלֹהֵי אַבְרָהָם — *The nations of the God of Abraham.* These martyrs are identified as the nation of *Abraham's God* because Abraham was the first man to sacrifice his entire being for the sake of God, by becoming the first convert [for Abraham incurred the wrath of Nimrod, who threw him into a blazing

The Prayers [114]

throne. ¹⁰ *The nobles of the nations gathered, the nation of the God of Abraham, for God's are the shields of the earth — He is exceedingly exalted.*

Before the blessings of the shofar are recited, the tokea [shofar-blower] or chazzan recites the following seven verses responsively with the congregation:

From the straits I called upon YAH;
   YAH answered me with expansiveness.

The initial letters of the next six verses spell the phrase קְרַע שָׂטָן, *Tear up Satan.*

קוֹלִי **You have heard my voice;**
   do not shut Your ear to my relief, to my cry.

רֹאשׁ **Your very first utterance is truth,**
   and eternal is Your righteous judgment.

עֲרֹב **Be Your servant's guarantor for good;**
   let not willful sinners exploit me.

שָׂשׂ **I rejoice over Your word,**
   like one who finds abundant spoils.

טוּב **Good reasoning and wisdom teach me,**
   for in Your commandments do I believe.

נְדָבוֹת **My mouth's offerings please accept favorably,**
   HASHEM, and Your judgments teach me.

---

furnace for his belief; see ArtScroll *Bereishis* p. 348] *(Rashi).*

מְאֹד נַעֲלָה — *He is exceedingly exalted.* According to *Rashi, Radak* and *Ibn Ezra,* this describes God, who is no longer degraded as impotent but recognized as the Omnipotent Protector of His faithful.

Sforno interprets this as praise for Abraham, who fathered a nation which faithfully adheres to his actions and beliefs. This feat has never been duplicated by any other man.

מִן הַמֵּצַר ... בַּמֶּרְחָב — *From the straits ... with expansiveness.* God taught His prophet *(Isaiah* 58:1) how to admonish the nation: *Call out from the throat, do not withhold, like the shofar raise your voice ...* The *shofar,* explains *Ramasayim Tzofim,* has a narrow mouthpiece at the end where the sound originates and widens at its bell where the sound issues and radiates in all directions. So it is with the prophet. His words should originate from deep down in his throat, that is, from the depths of his heart. When they reach the throat and beyond they increase in intensity; they issue forth loudly and clearly; the words reverberate far and wide and they penetrate hearts, urging the people to repentance.

[Perhaps this interpretation also explains the reason for reciting the verse, *From the straits* [i.e., from deep in my heart like the narrow opening of the *shofar*] *I called upon YAH; YAH answered me with expansiveness* — like the wide bell end of the *shofar.*

קְרַע שָׂטָן — *Tear up Satan.* [As we have seen above (p. 20) the *shofar* is particularly efficacious in confounding the Accuser and voiding his accusations. But the expression here is more than just a fanciful acrostic. It is the second of seven six-letter sets that, according to kabbalistic teachings, form the forty-two-letter Divine Name alluded to in the Talmud *(Kiddushin* 71a; see below).

[115]   **ROSH HASHANAH** / Its Significance, Laws, and Prayers

Some add the following prayer. The Divine Names in parentheses should not be pronounced.

יְהִי רָצוֹן מִלְּפָנֶיךָ, יהוה אֱלֹהֵינוּ וֵאלֹהֵי אֲבוֹתֵינוּ, אֱלֹהֵי הַמִּשְׁפָּט, שֶׁבִּזְכוּת אֵלוּ הַשֵּׁמוֹת הַיּוֹצְאִים מֵרָאשֵׁי תֵיבוֹת — אַל נָא קָרֵב תְּשׁוּעַת מְצַפֶּיךָ (אנקת״ם); פְּחוּדְךָ סָר, תּוֹצִיאֵם מִמַּאֲסָר (פסת״ם); פְּדֵה סוֹעִים, פְּתַח סוּמִים, יְמִינְךָ מְצַפִּים (פספסי״ם); דְּלֵה יוֹקְשִׁים, וְקַבֵּץ נְפוּצִים, סְמוֹךְ יָהּ מַפַּלְתֵּנוּ (דיונסי״ם) — שֶׁיִּהְיֶה עַתָּה עֵת רָצוֹן לְפָנֶיךָ. וְתִקְרַע בְּרַחֲמֶיךָ הָרַבִּים וַחֲסָדֶיךָ הַגְּדוֹלִים כָּל הַמָּסָכִים אֲשֶׁר הֵם מַבְדִּילִים בֵּינְךָ וּבֵין עַמְּךָ יִשְׂרָאֵל עַד הַיּוֹם הַזֶּה. וְהַעֲבֵר מִלְּפָנֶיךָ כָּל הַמַּסְטִינִים וְהַמְקַטְרִיגִים עַל עַמְּךָ יִשְׂרָאֵל. סְתוֹם פִּי שָׂטָן, וְאַל יַסְטִין עָלֵינוּ, כִּי אֵלֶיךָ תְּלוּיוֹת עֵינֵינוּ. אֲרוֹמִמְךָ אֱלֹהַי הַמֶּלֶךְ, אֱלֹהֵי הַמִּשְׁפָּט, שׁוֹמֵעַ קוֹל תְּרוּעַת עַמּוֹ יִשְׂרָאֵל בְּרַחֲמִים.

בִּזְכוּת אֵלוּ הַשֵּׁמוֹת הַיּוֹצְאִים ... — *In the merit of these Holy Names* ... [Scripture uses many appellations for God. Each of these Divine Names represents an attribute by which God allows man to perceive Him. יה-ו-ה represents the attribute of Divine Kindness. Since this Name is composed of the letters of הָיָה הֹוֶה יִהְיֶה, *He was, He is, He will be*, it is also an indication of God's Eternality. אֱלֹהִים, ELOHIM, represents Divine Justice. This word can also mean *judge* and *power*. Similarly, each Name found in Scripture is but an allusion to a different Divine attribute.

Kabbalah records many Divine Names which are not found explicitly in Scripture but may be derived through various principles. One of the Names is described in the Talmud *(Kiddushin* 71a) and in kabbalistic literature as the Forty-two-letter Name. Another is the Twenty-two letter-Name usually associated with *Bircas Kohanim*. This Name is discussed here. A fuller discussion of this Name appears in ArtScroll's *Bircas Kohanim*, pp. 45-47.]

In his kabbalistic work, *Pardes,* R' Moshe Cordovero explains that the Twenty-two Letter Name comprises four individual Divine Names [אנקת״ם פסת״ם פספסי״ם דיונסי״ם] each capable of effecting the fulfillment of a particular human need. The first Name, אנקת״ם, — a contraction of אַנְקַת תָּמִים, literally *the cry of the perfect ones* — is efficacious in making one's prayer accepted in Heaven; the second Name, פסת״ם, is the Name through which God distributes פְּסַת בַּר, *portions of bread*, to the hungry; through the Name פספסי״ם [related to כְּתֹנֶת פַּסִים, *woolen tunic*, that Jacob made for Joseph *(Genesis* 37:3)] He clothes the naked; and דיונסי״ם indicates that He performs נִסִּים, *miracles*, and wonders. These four Names were invoked by Jacob when he prayed *(Genesis* 28:21) that *God be with me and guard me on this way which I am going; and give me bread to eat and clothes to wear; and that I return in peace ...*

This four-part Name alludes to the *mitzvah* of sounding the *shofar*, according to *Sh'lah* and *Siddur Sha'arei*

The Prayers [116]

Some add the following prayer:

May it be Your will, HASHEM, our God and the God of our ancestors, God of judgment, that in the merit of these Holy Names that form the initials of the sentences — God, please bring near the salvation of those who long for You; Those that fear You, turn about, bring them forth from their confinement; Redeem the storm-tossed, open [the eyes of the] blind, they long for Your right hand; Draw up the oppressed, gather the scattered, support, O YAH, our falling — that the present be a receptive time before You. May You tear up, in Your manifold mercies and Your great kindness, all of the curtains that have separated between You and Your people Israel until this very day. Remove from before You all the accusers and prosecutors of Your people Israel. Seal the mouth of Satan that he may not accuse us, for our eyes are turned toward You. I will exalt You, my God the King, God of judgment; He Who harkens to the sound of the shofar blasts of His people Israel mercifully.

Shamayim, for the first part of the Name [אנקת״ם] has a *gematria*, or numeric equivalent of 591, the same as that of הַשׁוֹפָר, *the shofar*. Additionally, the second part [פסת״ם] equals 580, the same as שֹׁפָר, *shofar*, which is sometimes spelled "defectively," that is, without a ו (e.g., see Exodus 19:16).

An additional allusion is that the *gematria* of פסת״ם פספסי״ם is 910, the equivalent of the words: אֵין שָׂטָן וְאֵין פֶּגַע רָע, *there is neither Satan or evil occurrence*. As was noted previously (p. 63), the initial letters of this verse alludes to the sounding of the *Shofar*, an act which confounds Satan; and its *gematria*, 910, alludes to the month of

תִּשְׁרֵי, *Tishrei*, which has the same *gematria* (*Metzareif Dahava*).

פְּדֵה סוֹעִים — *Redeem the storm-tossed*. The rare root סעה appears only once in Scripture, *Psalms* 55:9. From the context there it means *storm wind*. Here we assume that the word refers to storm-tossed individuals.

וְקַבֵּץ נְפוֹצִים — *Gather the scattered*. The *shofar*, as R' Saadiah Gaon teaches in the ninth symbolic meaning he assigns to the *mitzvah* of sounding the *shofar* (see above p. 61), reminds us of the long awaited day of the ingathering of the exiles from the lands of their dispersion. This is the lesson of the prophet (*Isaiah*

---

1. The famous chassidic leader R' Simchah Bunam of P'shis'cha retold the story of R' Elazar Rokeach of Amsterdam and his journey to the Holy Land:
During the course of the voyage, on the first night of Rosh Hashanah, the ship upon which R' Elazar sailed was met with a storm and sprang a leak. Water began to flood the hold. All the passengers gathered and began bailing as fast as they could. All, that is, except R' Elazar who was deeply absorbed in ecstatic prayer and devotion. But as the night dragged on and it became apparent that the people would be unable to stem the raging water rising in the ship, someone intruded on the rabbi's meditations and informed him of the craft's imminent disaster. 'If so,' replied R' Elazar, 'let us be sure to sound the *shofar* as soon as we see the first ray of sunlight shine over the horizon.' They did as the rabbi bid, and immediately after the *shofar* blasts the sea calmed enough to enable the crew to repair the damage.
R' Simchah Bunam added that R' Elazar's intention in sounding the *shofar* at the first possible opportunity was not in expectation of a miracle. Not at all. Rather when he heard of the perilous situation, he yearned to perform the *mitzvah* at least this one last time. It was in the merit of this intention that the ship and its passengers were saved.

[117] **ROSH HASHANAH** / Its Significance, Laws, and Prayers

The tokea recites the blessings and the congregation responds אָמֵן *to each one. However the response,* בָּרוּךְ הוּא וּבָרוּךְ שְׁמוֹ *is omitted.*
[From the recitation of the blessings until the completion of the final shofar blasts at the end of Mussaf, conversation of any sort is prohibited.]

בָּרוּךְ אַתָּה יהוה אֱלֹהֵינוּ מֶלֶךְ הָעוֹלָם, אֲשֶׁר קִדְּשָׁנוּ בְּמִצְוֹתָיו וְצִוָּנוּ לִשְׁמוֹעַ קוֹל שׁוֹפָר.

בָּרוּךְ אַתָּה יהוה אֱלֹהֵינוּ מֶלֶךְ הָעוֹלָם, שֶׁהֶחֱיָנוּ וְקִיְּמָנוּ וְהִגִּיעָנוּ לַזְּמַן הַזֶּה.

The congregation remains silent as the מַקְרִיא, *caller [the rabbi (or other distinguished congregant knowledgeable in the laws of shofar)] calls the shofar notes for the tokea to blow.*

תְּקִיעָה. שְׁבָרִים תְּרוּעָה. תְּקִיעָה.
תְּקִיעָה. שְׁבָרִים תְּרוּעָה. תְּקִיעָה.
תְּקִיעָה. שְׁבָרִים תְּרוּעָה. תְּקִיעָה.

תְּקִיעָה. שְׁבָרִים. תְּקִיעָה.
תְּקִיעָה. שְׁבָרִים. תְּקִיעָה.
תְּקִיעָה. שְׁבָרִים. תְּקִיעָה.

תְּקִיעָה. תְּרוּעָה. תְּקִיעָה.
תְּקִיעָה. תְּרוּעָה. תְּקִיעָה.
תְּקִיעָה. תְּרוּעָה. תְּקִיעָה-גְדוֹלָה.

27:13): *And it will be on that day, He will blow on a great shofar, and they will come — those who were lost in the land of Assyria, and those who were cast out in the land of Egypt ...*

מַפַּלָתֵינוּ — *Our falling.* In the version used by the Chabad-Lubavitch community this reads מוּפְלָגִים, *those who have become separated (Siddur Baal HaTanya).*[1]

✡ The Blessings Over the Shofar

לִשְׁמוֹעַ קוֹל שׁוֹפָר — *To hear the sound of the shofar.* The blessing does not read

---

1. In the version recorded in *Siddur Baal HaTanya* the remainder of the prayer appears in a shorter form: שֶׁתִּקְרַע הַמָּסָכִים וְהַמְקַטְרִיגִים אֲשֶׁר הֵם מַבְדִּילִים בֵּינְךָ וּבֵין עַמְּךָ יִשְׂרָאֵל. אֲרוֹמִמְךָ אֱלֹהָי, הַמֶּלֶךְ הַמִּשְׁפָּט, שׁוֹמֵעַ קוֹל, *that You tear up the curtains and the prosecutors that have separated between You and Your people Israel, I will exalt You my God, King of judgment; He Who hearkens to the sound ...*

The Prayers [118]

The tokea recites the blessings and the congregation responds Amen to each one. However the response, 'Blessed is He and Blessed is His Name' is omitted. [From the recitation of the blessings until the completion of the final shofar blasts at the end of Mussaf, conversation of any sort is prohibited.]

Blessed are You, HASHEM, our God, King of the universe, Who has sanctified us with His commandments and has commanded us to hear the sound of the shofar.

Blessed are You, HASHEM, our God, King of the universe, Who has kept us alive, sustained us, and brought us to this season.

The congregation remains silent as the rabbi (or other distinguished congregant knowledgeable in the laws of shofar) calls the shofar notes for the tokea to blow.

TEKIAH. SHEVARIM TERUAH. TEKIAH.
TEKIAH. SHEVARIM TERUAH. TEKIAH.
TEKIAH. SHEVARIM TERUAH. TEKIAH.

TEKIAH. SHEVARIM. TEKIAH.
TEKIAH. SHEVARIM. TEKIAH.
TEKIAH. SHEVARIM. TEKIAH.

TEKIAH. TERUAH. TEKIAH.
TEKIAH. TERUAH. TEKIAH.
TEKIAH. TERUAH. TEKIAH-GEDOLAH.

'to sound the shofar,' but 'to hear the sound.' *Rosh* (citing *Behag*) explains that the *mitzvah* is not fulfilled with the *sounding* of the *shofar* but with *hearing* it. Thus the ruling that one who blows the *shofar*, but does not hear it — e.g., he holds the *shofar* in such a way that the bell end is enclosed in a container, and therefore he does not hear the *shofar* but its echo reverbrating from the container — has not fulfilled his obligation *(Orach Chaim 587)*. Nevertheless, if the wording לִתְקוֹעַ בְּשׁוֹפָר, *to blow on the shofar*, was used, the blessing is valid *(Mishnah Berurah 585:4)*.

שֶׁהֶחֱיָנוּ ... — *Who has kept us alive* ... This Blessing is discussed above, p. 102.

תְּקִיעָה שְׁבָרִים תְּרוּעָה ... — *Tekiah, Shevarim, Teruah* ... The reasons for and implications of the different series of notes is discussed in the section on Insights, pp. 65-67.

תְּקִיעָה־גְדוֹלָה — *Tekiah-gedolah* [lit. *a long tekiah*]. The purpose of the extended *tekiah* at the completion of the series of thirty *shofar* blasts is to indicate that this section of the *mitzvah* has been completed, and the congregation may resume its prayer service. This is analogous to the extended *shofar* blast (see *Exodus* 19:13) that marked the departure of the *Shechinah* (Divine Presence) from Mount Sinai after the Acceptance of the Torah *(Maharil)*.

After the series of thirty blasts is completed, some say:

יְהִי רָצוֹן מִלְּפָנֶיךָ, יהוה אֱלֹהֵינוּ וֵאלֹהֵי אֲבוֹתֵינוּ, שֶׁיַּעֲלוּ אֵלּוּ הַמַּלְאָכִים הַיּוֹצְאִים מִן הַשּׁוֹפָר, וּמִן הַתְּקִיעָה, וּמִן הַשְּׁבָרִים, וּמִן הַתְּרוּעָה, וּמִן תְּקִיעָה שְׁבָרִים תְּרוּעָה תְּקִיעָה, וּמִן תְּקִיעָה שְׁבָרִים תְּקִיעָה, וּמִן תְּקִיעָה תְּרוּעָה תְּקִיעָה, לִפְנֵי כִסֵּא כְבוֹדֶךָ וְיַמְלִיצוּ טוֹב בַּעֲדֵנוּ, לְכַפֵּר עַל כָּל חַטֹּאתֵינוּ.

The chazzan and congregation recite these four verses responsively:

אַשְׁרֵי הָעָם יוֹדְעֵי תְרוּעָה, יהוה בְּאוֹר פָּנֶיךָ יְהַלֵּכוּן. בְּשִׁמְךָ יְגִילוּן כָּל הַיּוֹם, וּבְצִדְקָתְךָ יָרוּמוּ. כִּי תִפְאֶרֶת עֻזָּמוֹ אָתָּה, וּבִרְצוֹנְךָ תָּרוּם קַרְנֵנוּ. אַשְׁרֵי יוֹשְׁבֵי בֵיתֶךָ, עוֹד יְהַלְלוּךָ סֶּלָה.

תהלים
פט:טז-יח

שם פד:ה

וְיַמְלִיצוּ טוֹב בַּעֲדֵנוּ — *And invoke goodness on our behalf.* The efficacy of the *shofar* in eliciting Divine mercy and compassion is illustrated by the following parable (cited in *Toras Avos*):

A king's children were once kidnapped. Over a period of time they became friendly with their abductors and slowly, unwittingly, began to imitate their ways and their speech. As more time went by they were unaware of the subtle changes that took place in their character and mannerisms. Nevertheless, this new life-style soon disgusted them and they longed to return to their royal background. When the opportunity presented itself, the princes fled from their captors and made their way to the king's palace. But how surprised and distraught they were when the king ignored their claims that they were his long-lost sons and paid them no heed. At first they did not realize that the coarse speech and boorish manner they had acquired during their years of captivity were proof to the king that these were impostors who stood before him. But after hearing the conversation and observing the actions of the nobility and the court officers, they understood how different they had become while they were absent from the king's palace. It then dawned on them that they did not even 'speak the same language' as the king. Finally they burst into tears, and the wordless cries that they emitted evoked the king's compassion, for he recognized the cries as those of his sons.

אַשְׁרֵי ... תָּרוּם קַרְנֵנוּ — *Praises ... our shofar will be exalted.* The inclusion of these three verses is first mentioned by R' David Abudraham and is cited in *Tur* 591 and *Rama* 590:9.

[Allusions to the three blessings of *Malchuyos, Zichronos, Shofaros* (see p. 67) may be found in these verses respectively:

□ אַשְׁרֵי הָעָם, *Praises to the people*, or *nation*, refers to *Malchuyos*, Kingship, for, as R' Bachya ben Asher points out in *Kad HaKemach*, אֵין מֶלֶךְ בְּלֹא עָם, there can be no king without a nation.

□ בְּשִׁמְךָ, *In Your Name*, alludes to

The Prayers [120]

After the series of thirty blasts is completed, some say:

May it be Your will, HASHEM, our God and the God of our ancestors, that those angels that are evoked by the shofar, by the tekiah, by the shevarim, by the teruah, by the tekiah shevarim teruah tekiah, by the tekiah shevrim tekiah, and by the tekiah teruah tekiah, ascend before the Throne of Your glory and invoke goodness on our behalf, to pardon all our sins.

The chazzan and congregation recite these four verses responsively:

Praises to the people who know the teruah;
HASHEM, in the light of Your countenance they walk.

In Your Name they rejoice all day long,
and through Your righteousness they are exalted.

For the splendor of their power are You,
and through Your will our shofar will be exalted.

Praises to those who dwell in Your house, may
they always praise You, selah!

Zichronos, Remembrances, based on a Talmudic passage in *Pesachim* 50a. God refers to His Name as both שְׁמִי and זִכְרִי, *My Name* and *My Remembrance* (*Exodus* 3:15). What is meant by these two separate references? R' Avina explains that God meant to imply that His true Name — the Four-Letter י־ה־ו־ה — should not be pronounced as it is written. Thus, He has a "Name," and a "Remembrance," meaning the pronunciation *Adonai*, which Israel uses when it reads the Name.

☐ Finally, the third verse which ends, תָּרוּם קַרְנֵנוּ, *our shofaros will be exalted*, alludes to the blessing of *Shofaros*.]

יוֹדְעֵי תְרוּעָה — Who know the teruah [lit. *the blowing*]. The Midrash (*Vayikra Rabbah* 29:3) raises the question: Do the other nations of the world not know how to blow horns? They have many horns, trumpets and *shofaros!* Rather the verse must be understood: *Praises to the people who know* [how to appease their Creator with] *the teruah.* For when they sound the *shofar*, He [anthropomorphically speaking] rises from the Throne of Justice, goes to the Throne of Mercy, and is filled with compassion for them.[1]

Another interpretation of this verse is based upon the symbolic meaning of the

---

1. *Tiferes Uziel* used a parable to explain why only Israel is privy to the secret of the *teruah*. A king and his son, who had married and had moved to a distant land, carried on a correspondence which contained many items of a personal nature. In order to prevent the couriers from intercepting their messages, the two devised a coded language which they revealed to no one else. Anybody could now read the letters, but would not understand their hidden meanings. On Rosh Hashanah, God — the King — does not want the messages from His son — Israel — to be intercepted by the Accuser or any of his henchmen. He therefore taught Israel a secret language — the sounds of the *shofar* — to use in sending them their personal message of repentance.

The congregation completes the recital of אַשְׁרֵי and the regular prayer order is continued. During the Amidah, the shofar is sounded three times. In some communities this is done both during the silent Amidah and the chazzan's repetition; in others, only during the chazzan's repetition. After each series the congregation, followed by the chazzan, recites:

הַיּוֹם הֲרַת עוֹלָם, הַיּוֹם יַעֲמִיד בַּמִּשְׁפָּט כָּל יְצוּרֵי עוֹלָמִים, אִם כְּבָנִים אִם כַּעֲבָדִים. אִם כְּבָנִים, רַחֲמֵנוּ כְּרַחֵם אָב עַל בָּנִים; וְאִם כַּעֲבָדִים עֵינֵינוּ לְךָ תְלוּיוֹת, עַד שֶׁתְּחָנֵּנוּ וְתוֹצִיא כָאוֹר מִשְׁפָּטֵנוּ, אָיוֹם קָדוֹשׁ.

The final word of the following prayer varies with the blessing just completed.

אֲרֶשֶׁת שְׂפָתֵינוּ יֶעֱרַב לְפָנֶיךָ, אֵל רָם וְנִשָּׂא, מֵבִין וּמַאֲזִין, מַבִּיט וּמַקְשִׁיב לְקוֹל תְּקִיעָתֵנוּ. וּתְקַבֵּל בְּרַחֲמִים וּבְרָצוֹן סֵדֶר

מַלְכִיּוֹתֵינוּ. (after the first series)

זִכְרוֹנוֹתֵינוּ. (after the second series)

שׁוֹפְרוֹתֵינוּ. (after the third series)

fragmental *teruah* note. As pointed out above (p. 64), the *teruah* represents a broken heart. But, *Shem MiShmuel* points out that there are two causes for a broken heart. A person may fall into a state of depression, look at the world through lenses of hopelessness and be heartbroken as a result. This is not the broken heart sought by God (see *Psalms* 51:19), nor the heart that walks in the light of God's countenance. Praises are befitting the heart which is broken through one's intelligent realization of his own worthlessness in comparison to his Creator. A broken, contrite heart, humbled not by melancholia but by knowledge of God and His ways, is the allusion of the *teruah*. Thus, the verse does not read תּוֹקְעֵי תְרוּעָה, *those who blow the teruah*, but יוֹדְעֵי תְרוּעָה, *those whose "know" the teruah.*

תָּרוּם קַרְנֵנוּ — *Our shofar will be exalted.* [The word קֶרֶן, literally *horn*, is used figuratively in Scripture to indicate such concepts as might, power, pride, majesty, etc. Although in the context of psalm 89 it refers to the kings of Israel (see *Radak*), its use in conjunction with the sounding of the *shofar* points to a more literal translation.]

הַיּוֹם הֲרַת עוֹלָם — *Today is the birth[day] of the world.* The phrase is couched in the present tense, for on Rosh Hashanah of each year the Creation is renewed in its entirety. This renewal is also the basis of the phrase: זֶה הַיּוֹם תְּחִלַּת מַעֲשֶׂיךָ, *This day was the beginning of Your works*, that appears in the *Zichronos* blessing (*Yaaros Devash*).

Although the root הרה usually refers to conception, it sometimes is used to

The Prayers [122]

The congregation completes the recital of אַשְׁרֵי and the regular prayer order is continued. During the Amidah, the shofar is sounded three times. In some communities this is done both during the silent Amidah and the chazzan's repetition; in others, only during the chazzan's repetition. After each series the congregation, followed by the chazzan, recites:

Today is the birth[day] of the world. Today all creatures of the world stand in judgment — whether as children [of God] or as servants. If as children, be merciful with us as the mercy of a father for children. If as servants, our eyes [look toward and] depend upon You, until You be gracious to us and release our verdict [clear and pure] as light, O Awesome and Holy One.

The final word of the following prayer varies with the blessing just completed.

May the utterance of our lips be pleasing before You, O Most High and Exalted God; He Who understands and harkens, peers at and listens to the sound of our shofar blasts. And accept, with mercy and with favor, the order of our

(after the first series) Malchuyos.
(after the second series) Zichronos.
(after the third series) Shofaros.

mean birth. This is its meaning here. Alternatively, according to Rabbeinu Tam's interpretation of the dispute regarding the date of Creation (see p. 43), the Creation took place on two levels: on the plane of thought, in Tishrei; in the realm of deed, in Nissan. Thus Rosh Hashanah is literally the day on which the word was conceived.

אִם כְּבָנִים אִם כַּעֲבָדִים — Whether as children [of God] or as servants. Children serve their parents out of a feeling of love. They only desire to make their parents comfortable and proud of them. Servants, on the other hand, serve out of fear; fear that their master will find them lacking and punish them. This, says R' Avraham of Slonim, is the meaning of the stich: *Today all creatures of the world stand in judgment* — they are judged as to whether their service of God was out of love or out of fear — *whether as children or as servants.*

אֲרֶשֶׁת שְׂפָתֵינוּ — *The utterance of our lips.* The translation of the rare word אֲרֶשֶׁת, *utterance,* follows most major commentaries to *Psalms* 21:3, the only place in Scripture where this word appears. There the phrase reads אֲרֶשֶׁת שְׂפָתָיו, *the utterance of his lips.*

According to *Midrash Tehillim,* however, אֲרֶשֶׁת is related to רְשׁוּת, *permission* or *authority,* and refers to the authority granted God's chosen to issue requests which He will fulfill. Thus, אֲרֶשֶׁת שְׂפָתָיו means *the authority invested in his lips.* [Perhaps this interpretation is also applicable to our prayer, i.e., 'May the words that You have granted us permission to speak before you be pleasing unto You ...']

[123] **ROSH HASHANAH** / Its Significance, Laws, and Prayers

קידושא רבא

On the Sabbath begin here:

וְשָׁמְרוּ בְנֵי יִשְׂרָאֵל אֶת הַשַּׁבָּת, לַעֲשׂוֹת אֶת הַשַּׁבָּת לְדֹרֹתָם בְּרִית עוֹלָם. בֵּינִי וּבֵין בְּנֵי יִשְׂרָאֵל אוֹת הִוא לְעֹלָם, כִּי שֵׁשֶׁת יָמִים עָשָׂה יהוה אֶת־הַשָּׁמַיִם וְאֶת הָאָרֶץ, וּבַיּוֹם הַשְּׁבִיעִי שָׁבַת וַיִּנָּפַשׁ.

זָכוֹר אֶת יוֹם הַשַּׁבָּת לְקַדְּשׁוֹ. שֵׁשֶׁת יָמִים תַּעֲבֹד וְעָשִׂיתָ כָּל מְלַאכְתֶּךָ. וְיוֹם הַשְּׁבִיעִי שַׁבָּת לַיהוה אֱלֹהֶיךָ, לֹא תַעֲשֶׂה כָל מְלָאכָה — אַתָּה וּבִנְךָ וּבִתֶּךָ, עַבְדְּךָ וַאֲמָתְךָ וּבְהֶמְתֶּךָ וְגֵרְךָ אֲשֶׁר בִּשְׁעָרֶיךָ. כִּי שֵׁשֶׁת יָמִים עָשָׂה יהוה אֶת הַשָּׁמַיִם וְאֶת הָאָרֶץ, אֶת הַיָּם וְאֶת כָּל אֲשֶׁר בָּם, וַיָּנַח בַּיּוֹם הַשְּׁבִיעִי; עַל כֵּן בֵּרַךְ יהוה אֶת יוֹם הַשַּׁבָּת וַיְקַדְּשֵׁהוּ.

שמות
לא: טז-יז

שם כ:ח-יא

On all other days begin here:

וַיְדַבֵּר מֹשֶׁה אֶת מֹעֲדֵי יהוה אֶל בְּנֵי יִשְׂרָאֵל.

ויקרא
כג:מד

תִּקְעוּ בַחֹדֶשׁ שׁוֹפָר בַּכֵּסֶה לְיוֹם חַגֵּנוּ. כִּי חֹק לְיִשְׂרָאֵל הוּא, מִשְׁפָּט לֵאלֹהֵי יַעֲקֹב.

תהלים
פא:ד-ה

סַבְרִי מָרָנָן וְרַבָּנָן וְרַבּוֹתַי:

בָּרוּךְ אַתָּה יהוה אֱלֹהֵינוּ מֶלֶךְ הָעוֹלָם, בּוֹרֵא פְּרִי הַגָּפֶן.

⋙ **Kiddusha Rabba**

The daytime *Kiddush* is purely Rabbinic in origin. Because it is less important than the evening *Kiddush*, it is euphemistically called קִידוּשָׁא רַבָּא, *the Great Kiddush*. This is similar to the expression סַגִי נְהוֹר, *much light*, used to describe a sightless person (*Ran* to *Pesachim* 106b). Originally this Kid-dush consisted of nothing more than the blessing over wine (*Pesachim* 106b), but over the centuries Scriptural verses were added for both the Sabbath and Yom Tov.

וְשָׁמְרוּ ... זָכוֹר — *And the Children of Israel observed ... Always remember ...* These two Biblical passages (*Exodus* 31:16-17; 20:8-11) form the *Kiddusha*

The Prayers [124]

ᴥ Kiddusha Rabba

On the Sabbath begin here:

And the Children of Israel observed the Sabbath, to make the Sabbath for their generations an eternal covenant. Between Me and the Children of Israel it is a sign forever, for in six days did HASHEM make the heaven and the earth, and on the seventh day He rested and was refreshed.

Always remember the Sabbath to hallow it. For six days you may labor and do all your work. But the seventh day is the Sabbath for HASHEM, your God; you may do no work — you, your son and your daughter, your slave and your maidservant, your animal, and the stranger who is in your gates. For in six days did HASHEM make the heaven and the earth, the sea and all that is in them and He rested on the seventh day; therefore HASHEM blessed the Sabbath day and sanctified it.

On all other days begin here:

And Moses spoke of HASHEM's appointed times to the Children of Israel.

Blow the shofar at the moon's renewal, at the time appointed for our festive day. Because it is a decree for Israel, a judgment for the God of Jacob.

By your leave, my masters and teachers:

Blessed are you, HASHEM, our God, King of the universe, Who creates the fruit of the vine.

Rabba of the Sabbath. A full commentary appears in the ArtScroll *Zemiroth*. In many communities only the fragment beginning עַל כֵּן, *Therefore* ... is recited.

וּבַיּוֹם הַשְּׁבִיעִי שָׁבַת — *And on the seventh day He rested.* Because God's work of creation had been completed, He found the contentment symbolized by 'rest,' for when one's work is successfully completed, he is content *(Sforno)*.

וַיִּנָּפַשׁ — *And was refreshed.* One who rests is able to catch his breath and refresh his soul [וַיִּנָּפַשׁ from נֶפֶשׁ, *soul*]. Although such an expression can hardly apply to God Who knows no 'work,' 'fatigue,' or 'refreshment' in the human sense, Scripture uses the anthropomorphic expression to make the concept comprehensible to human terms *(Rashi)*.

וַיְדַבֵּר מֹשֶׁה ... — *And Moses spoke ...* This is the closing verse of the section in *Leviticus* that discusses all of the festivals. According to *Siddur Sha'arei*

Shamayim and *Matteh Efraim*, this verse — which is recited as the *Kiddusha Rabba* of every *Yom Tov* — is the only verse recited on Rosh Hashanah and it is immediately followed by the blessing over wine. Nevertheless, many are accustomed to recite the additional verses (*Psalms* 81:4-5) that allude to the sanctity of the day. [The commentary below on these two verses is condensed from ArtScroll *Tehillim*. But see p. 56 for other interpretations.]

תִּקְעוּ בַחֹדֶשׁ שׁוֹפָר — *Blow the shofar at the moon's renewal*. Radak explains that the first day of the month is called חֹדֶשׁ [related to חָדָשׁ, *new*] because the moon which waned and disappeared at the end of the previous month then reappears and begins a new cycle. Rosh Hashanah, which occurs on the first day of *Tishrei*, also coincides with the renewal of the moon. It is the only one of all the Jewish festivals which occurs at this time of the month.

Midrash Tehillim adds that Rosh Hashanah is a time for חִדּוּשׁ, *renewal*, of one's deeds and שׁוֹפָר [cognate with שִׁיפּוּר, *beauty*], *improvement*, of one's deeds.

בַּכֶּסֶה לְיוֹם חַגֵּנוּ — *At the time appointed for our festive day*. The translation of כֶּסֶה, *the time appointed*, follows Rashi, Radak and Ibn Ezra. Others relate כֶּסֶה to כָּסָה, *covered*. All other Jewish holidays occur later in the month, when the major part of the moon is visible. Only Rosh Hashanah occurs at the very beginning of the month, when the moon is still covered (*Rosh Hashanah* 8a).

Furthermore, God judges Israel on this day and mercifully covers and forgives their sins (*Midrash Tehillim*).

Sforno translates כֶּסֶה as cognate with כִּסֵּא, *throne*. Rosh Hashanah is *our festive day* despite the fact that the Almighty then sits on His *throne* of strict Justice.

כִּי חֹק לְיִשְׂרָאֵל הוּא — *Because it is a decree for Israel*. The *shofar* is sounded on Rosh Hashanah not because of mere custom, but because God has commanded this as a decree for Israel on this Day of Judgment (*Rashi*).

The Talmud (*Beitzah* 16a) translates חֹק as *a fixed ration*. On Rosh Hashanah, the Heavenly Tribunal fixes each man's sustenance for the coming year. However, if one spends extra to honor the Sabbath and festivals and to teach his children Torah, then God returns the money to him generously. If he spends little, then God decreases his allotment (see above p. 104).

מִשְׁפָּט לֵאלֹהֵי יַעֲקֹב — *A judgment for the God of Jacob*. The Talmud (*Yer. Rosh Hashanah* 1:3) stresses that when the Jewish people display confidence in God's mercy, Rosh Hashanah is transformed from a day of judgment to one of forgiveness.